MYSTERY GIRL ™

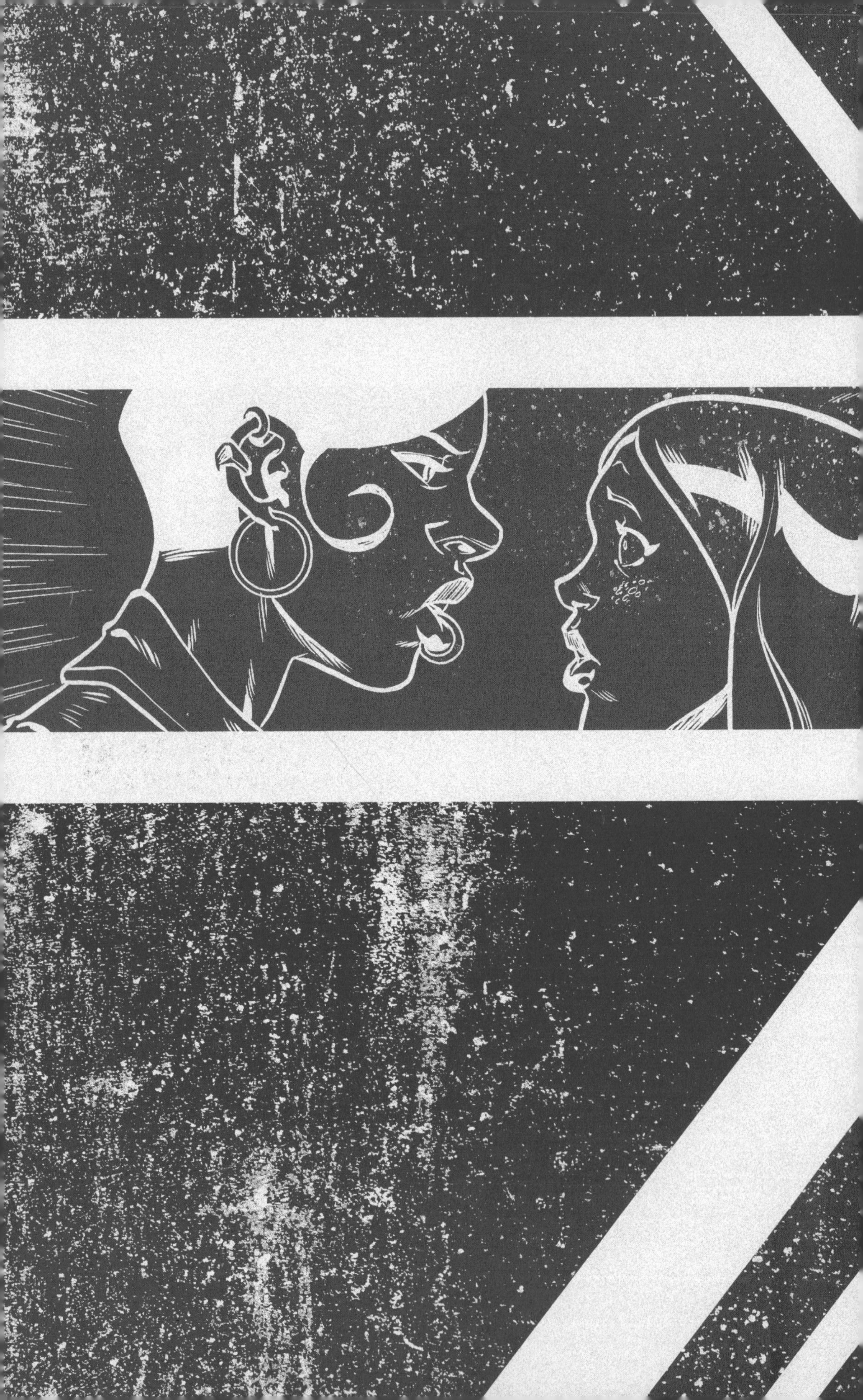

MYSTERY GIRL

WITHDRAWN

SCRIPT BY
PAUL TOBIN

ART AND COVER BY
**ALBERTO J.
ALBURQUERQUE**

COLORS BY
MARISSA LOUISE

LETTERS BY
MARSHALL DILLON

DARK HORSE BOOKS

PRESIDENT AND PUBLISHER
MIKE RICHARDSON

EDITORS
**SHANTEL LaROCQUE
AND BRENDAN WRIGHT**

ASSISTANT EDITORS
**KATII O'BRIEN
AND IAN TUCKER**

COLLECTION DESIGNER
JIMMY PRESLER

DIGITAL ART TECHNICIAN
CHRISTINA McKENZIE

DarkHorse.com
International Licensing: (503) 905-2377
To find a comics shop in your area, call
the Comic Shop Locator Service toll-free
at 1-888-266-4226.

First edition: July 2016
ISBN 978-1-61655-959-5

10 9 8 7 6 5 4 3 2 1
Printed in China

Published by Dark Horse Books
A division of Dark Horse Comics, Inc.
10956 SE Main Street
Milwaukie, OR 97222

MYSTERY GIRL VOLUME 1

This volume collects *Mystery Girl* #1–#4, previously published by Dark
Horse Comics.

Neil Hankerson Executive Vice President • **Tom Weddle** Chief Financial Officer • **Randy Stradley** Vice President of Publishing • **Michael Martens** Vice
President of Book Trade Sales • **Matt Parkinson** Vice President of Marketing • **David Scroggy** Vice President of Product Development • **Dale LaFountain**
Vice President of Information Technology • **Cara Niece** Vice President of Production and Scheduling • **Nick McWhorter** Vice President of Media Licensing • **Ken
Lizzi** General Counsel • **Dave Marshall** Editor in Chief • **Davey Estrada** Editorial Director • **Scott Allie** Executive Senior Editor • **Chris Warner** Senior
Books Editor • **Cary Grazzini** Director of Print and Development • **Lia Ribacchi** Art Director • **Mark Bernardi** Director of Digital Publishing • **Michael
Gombos** Director of International Publishing and Licensing

Library of Congress Cataloging-in-Publication Data

Names: Tobin, Paul, 1965- author. | Alburquerque, Alberto J., illustrator. | Louise, Marissa, illustrator. | Dillon, Marshall, illustrator.
Title: Mystery Girl. Volume 1 / script by Paul Tobin ; art and cover by Alberto J. Alburquerque ; colors by Marissa Louise ; letters by Marshall Dillon.
Description: First edition. | Milwaukie, OR : Dark Horse Books, 2016. | "This volume collects Mystery Girl #1/#4, previously published by Dark Horse Comics."
Identifiers: LCCN 2016001056 | ISBN 9781616559595 (paperback)
Subjects: LCSH: Graphic novels. | BISAC: COMICS & GRAPHIC NOVELS / Crime & Mystery. | GSAFD: Mystery comic books, strips, etc.
Classification: LCC PN6727.T6 M96 2016 | DDC 741.5/973–dc23
LC record available at http://lccn.loc.gov/2016001056

CHAPTER 1

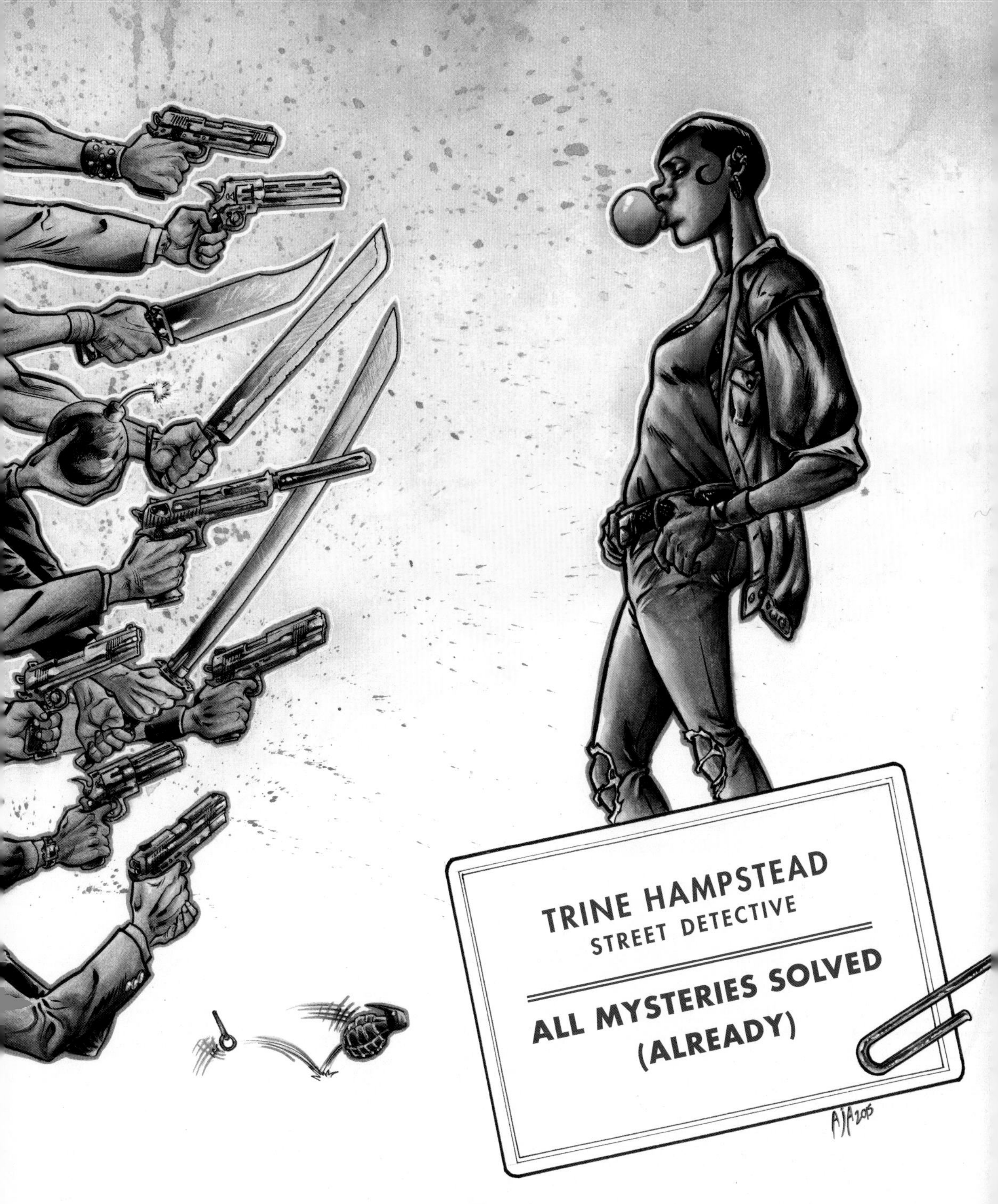
TRINE HAMPSTEAD
STREET DETECTIVE
ALL MYSTERIES SOLVED
(ALREADY)

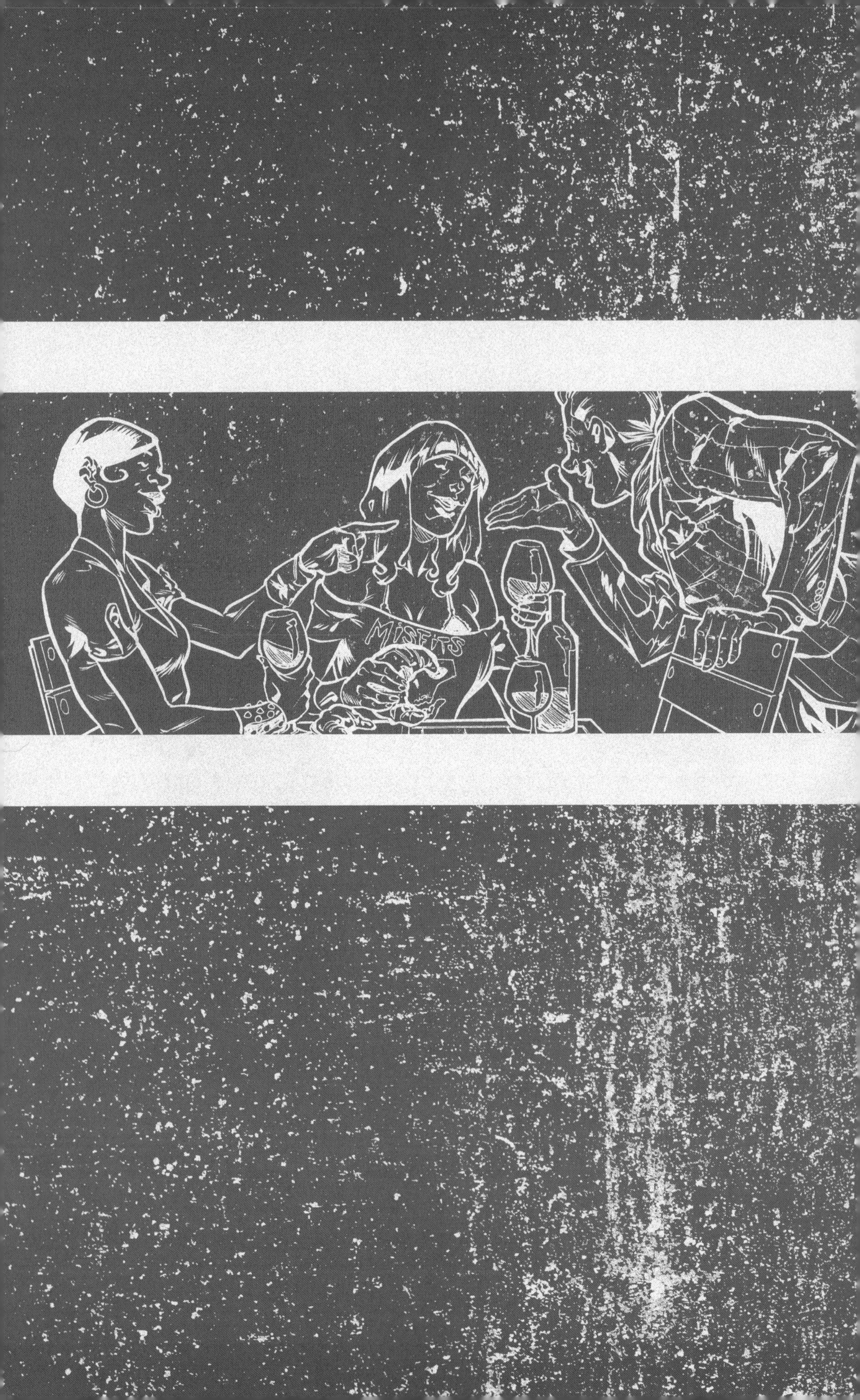
MISFITS

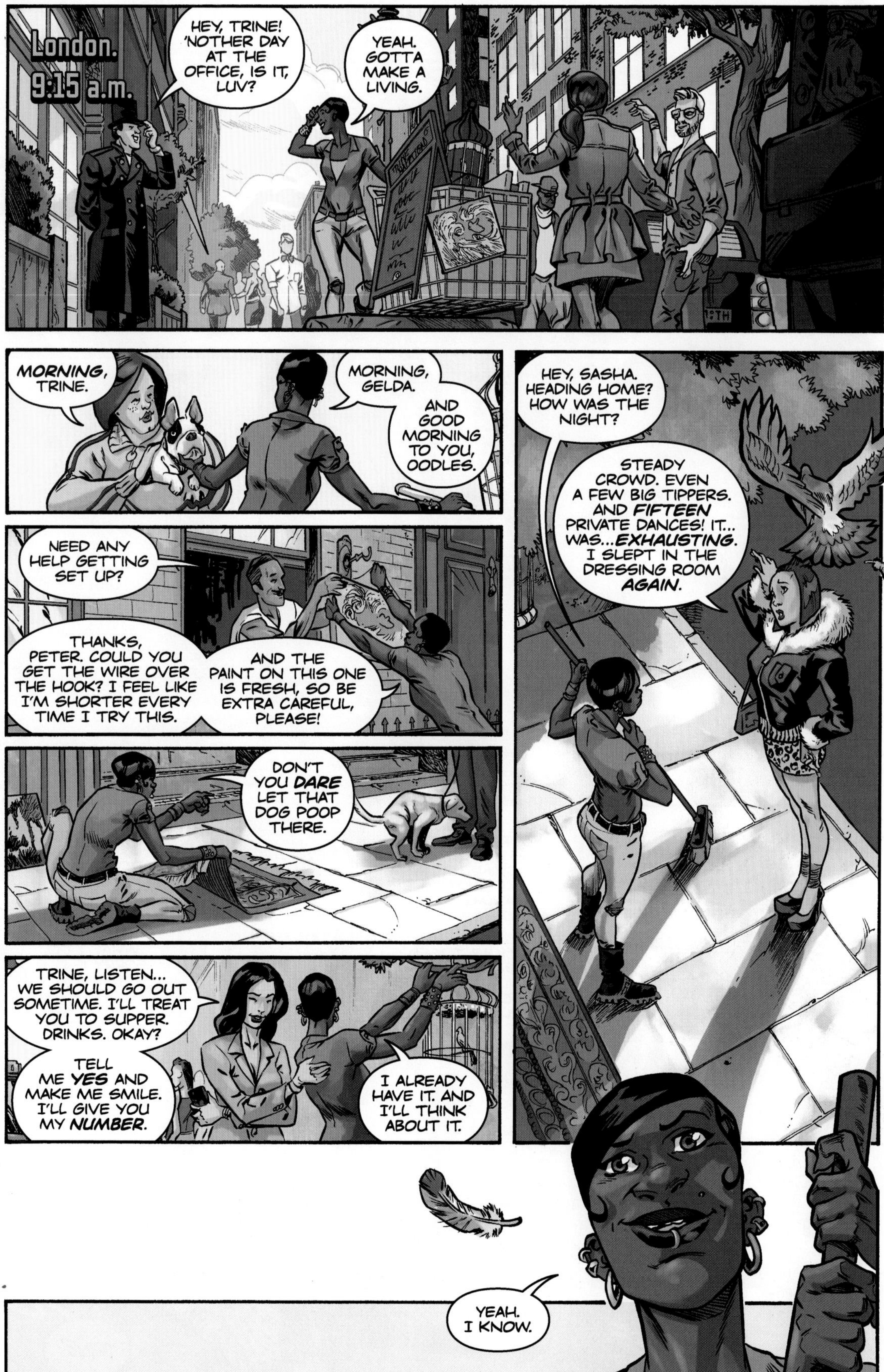
London.
9:15 a.m.
HEY, TRINE! 'NOTHER DAY AT THE OFFICE, IS IT, LUV?
YEAH. GOTTA MAKE A LIVING.
MORNING, TRINE.
MORNING, GELDA.
AND GOOD MORNING TO YOU, OODLES.
NEED ANY HELP GETTING SET UP?
THANKS, PETER. COULD YOU GET THE WIRE OVER THE HOOK? I FEEL LIKE I'M SHORTER EVERY TIME I TRY THIS.
AND THE PAINT ON THIS ONE IS FRESH, SO BE EXTRA CAREFUL, PLEASE!
DON'T YOU DARE LET THAT DOG POOP THERE.
TRINE, LISTEN... WE SHOULD GO OUT SOMETIME. I'LL TREAT YOU TO SUPPER. DRINKS. OKAY?
TELL ME YES AND MAKE ME SMILE. I'LL GIVE YOU MY NUMBER.
I ALREADY HAVE IT. AND I'LL THINK ABOUT IT.
HEY, SASHA. HEADING HOME? HOW WAS THE NIGHT?
STEADY CROWD. EVEN A FEW BIG TIPPERS. AND FIFTEEN PRIVATE DANCES! IT... WAS...EXHAUSTING. I SLEPT IN THE DRESSING ROOM AGAIN.
YEAH. I KNOW.

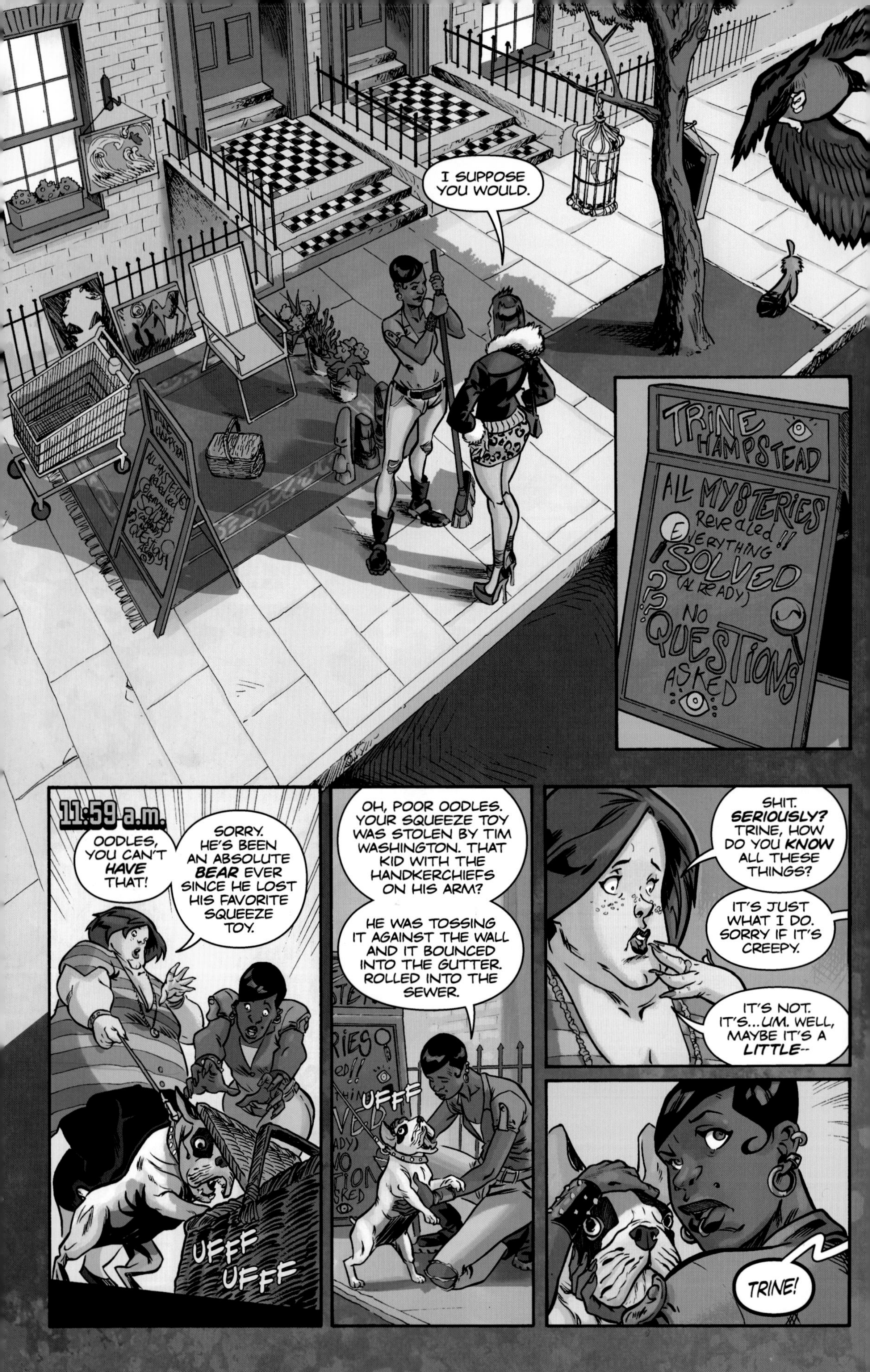
I SUPPOSE YOU WOULD.
TRINE HAMPSTEAD
ALL MYSTERIES Revealed!! EVERYTHING SOLVED (ALREADY) NO QUESTIONS ASKED
11:59 a.m.
OODLES, YOU CAN'T HAVE THAT!
SORRY. HE'S BEEN AN ABSOLUTE BEAR EVER SINCE HE LOST HIS FAVORITE SQUEEZE TOY.
UFFF UFFF
OH, POOR OODLES. YOUR SQUEEZE TOY WAS STOLEN BY TIM WASHINGTON. THAT KID WITH THE HANDKERCHIEFS ON HIS ARM?
HE WAS TOSSING IT AGAINST THE WALL AND IT BOUNCED INTO THE GUTTER. ROLLED INTO THE SEWER.
UFFF
SHIT. SERIOUSLY? TRINE, HOW DO YOU KNOW ALL THESE THINGS?
IT'S JUST WHAT I DO. SORRY IF IT'S CREEPY.
IT'S NOT. IT'S...UM. WELL, MAYBE IT'S A LITTLE--
TRINE!

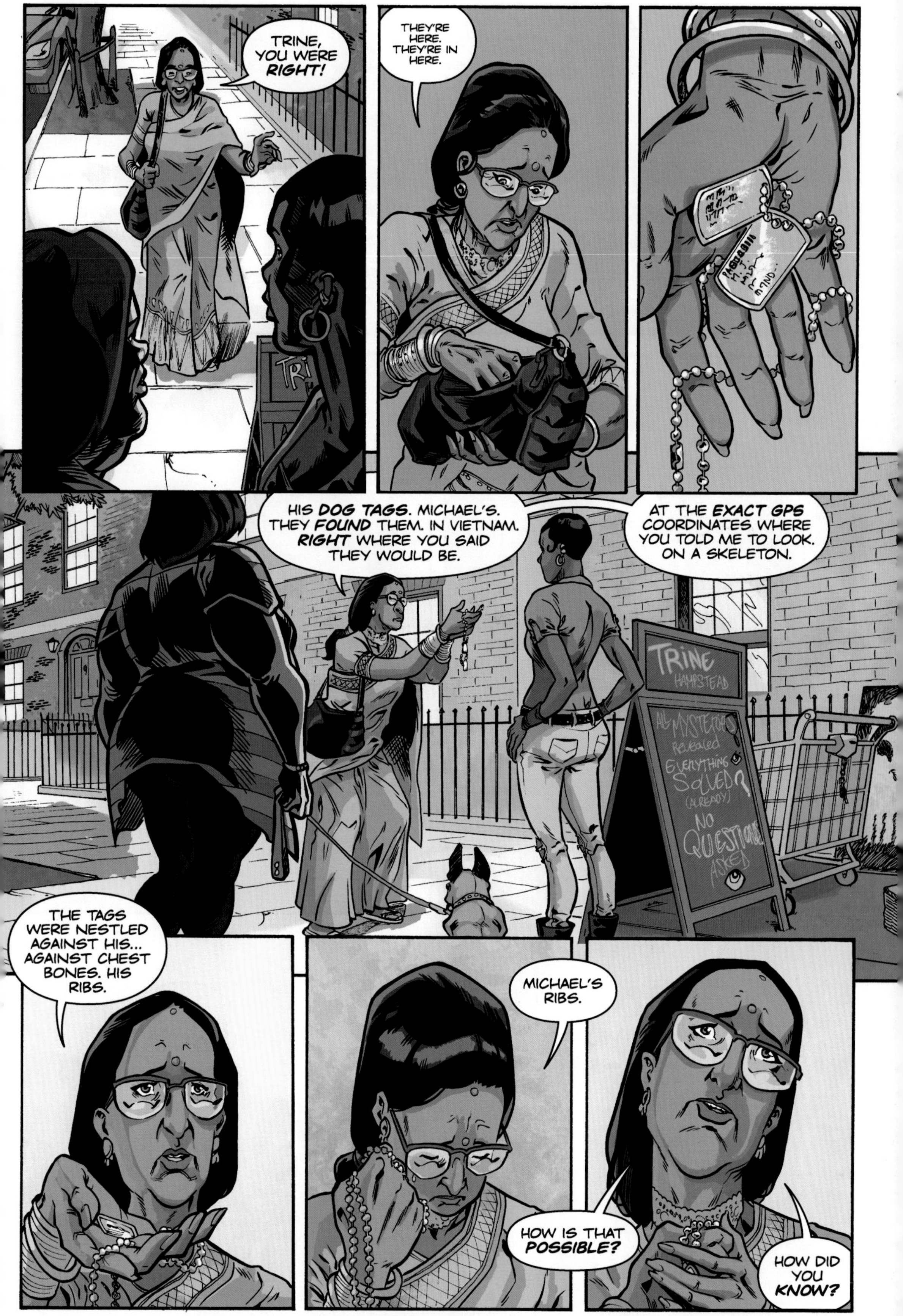
TRINE, YOU WERE RIGHT!
THEY'RE HERE. THEY'RE IN HERE.
HIS DOG TAGS. MICHAEL'S. THEY FOUND THEM. IN VIETNAM. RIGHT WHERE YOU SAID THEY WOULD BE.
AT THE EXACT GPS COORDINATES WHERE YOU TOLD ME TO LOOK. ON A SKELETON.
TRINE
HAMPSTEAD
Revealed
EVERYTHING
SOLVED?
(ALREADY)
NO
ASKED
THE TAGS WERE NESTLED AGAINST HIS... AGAINST CHEST BONES. HIS RIBS.
MICHAEL'S RIBS.
HOW IS THAT POSSIBLE?
HOW DID YOU KNOW?

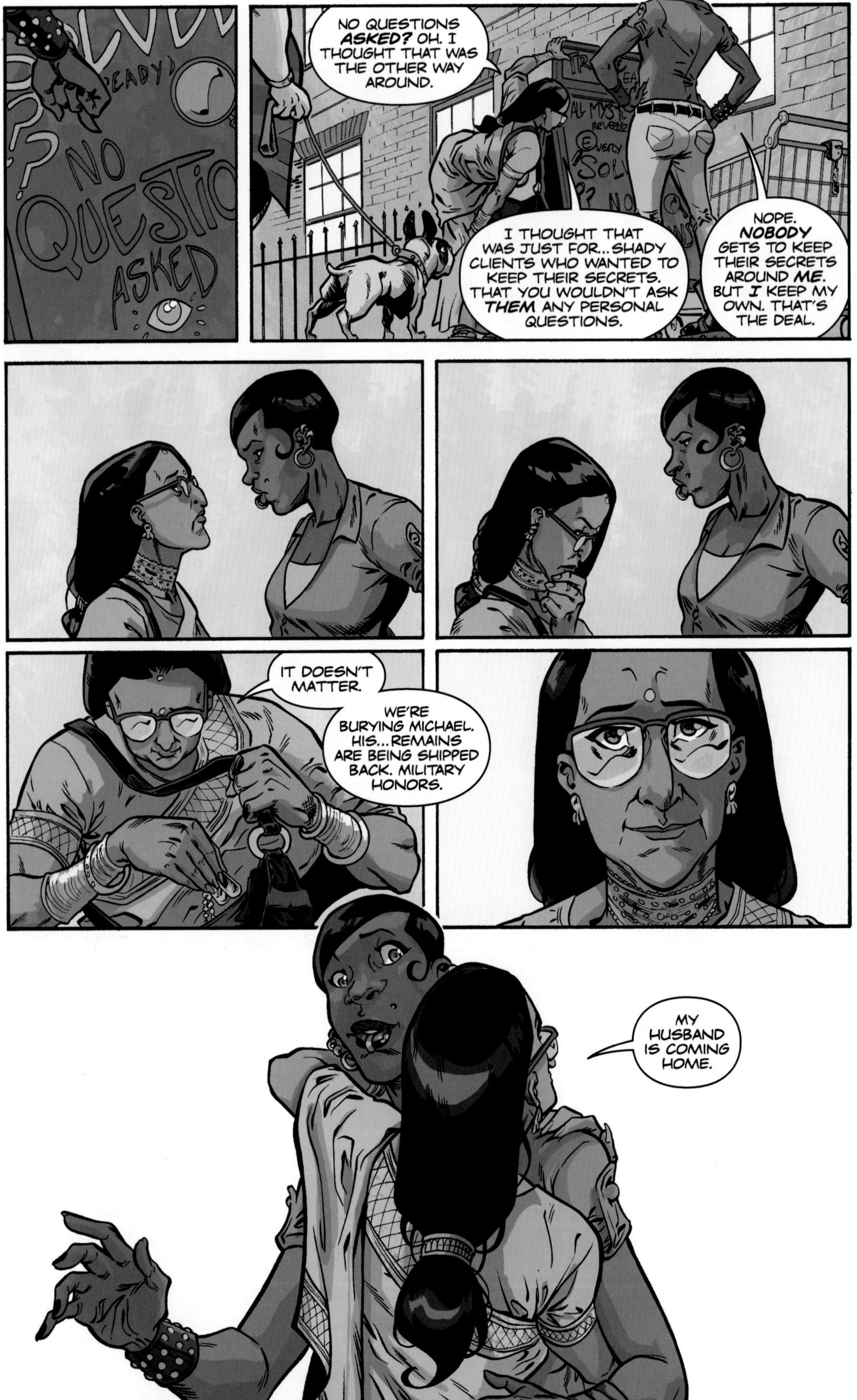
NO QUESTIONS ASKED? OH. I THOUGHT THAT WAS THE OTHER WAY AROUND.
I THOUGHT THAT WAS JUST FOR...SHADY CLIENTS WHO WANTED TO KEEP THEIR SECRETS. THAT YOU WOULDN'T ASK THEM ANY PERSONAL QUESTIONS.
NOPE. NOBODY GETS TO KEEP THEIR SECRETS AROUND ME. BUT I KEEP MY OWN. THAT'S THE DEAL.
IT DOESN'T MATTER.
WE'RE BURYING MICHAEL. HIS...REMAINS ARE BEING SHIPPED BACK. MILITARY HONORS.
MY HUSBAND IS COMING HOME.

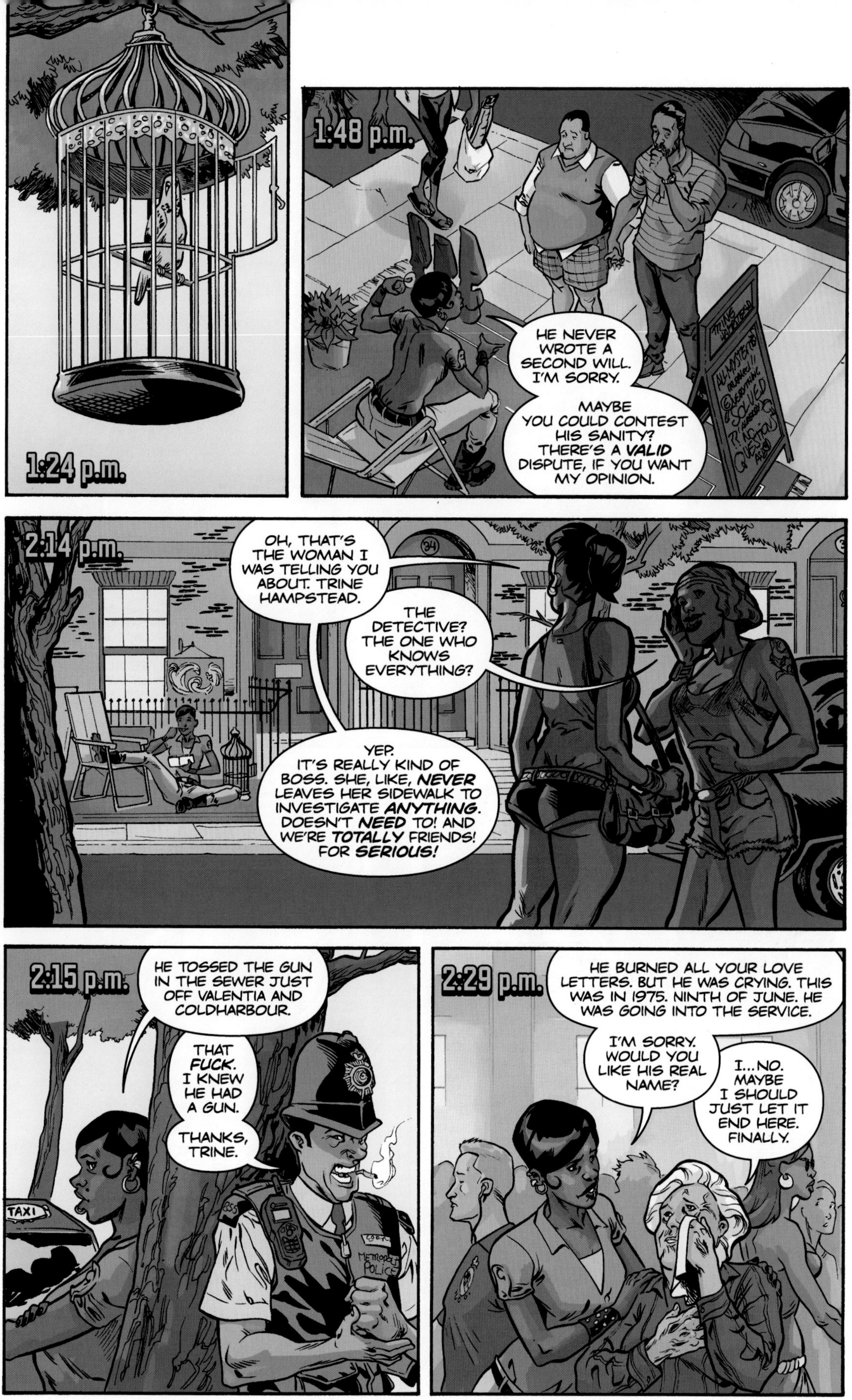
1:24 p.m.
1:48 p.m.
HE NEVER WROTE A SECOND WILL. I'M SORRY.
MAYBE YOU COULD CONTEST HIS SANITY? THERE'S A **VALID** DISPUTE, IF YOU WANT MY OPINION.
2:14 p.m.
OH, THAT'S THE WOMAN I WAS TELLING YOU ABOUT. TRINE HAMPSTEAD.
THE DETECTIVE? THE ONE WHO KNOWS EVERYTHING?
YEP. IT'S REALLY KIND OF BOSS. SHE, LIKE, **NEVER** LEAVES HER SIDEWALK TO INVESTIGATE **ANYTHING**. DOESN'T **NEED** TO! AND WE'RE **TOTALLY** FRIENDS! FOR **SERIOUS!**
2:15 p.m.
HE TOSSED THE GUN IN THE SEWER JUST OFF VALENTIA AND COLDHARBOUR.
THAT **FUCK**. I KNEW HE HAD A GUN.
THANKS, TRINE.
TAXI
2:29 p.m.
HE BURNED ALL YOUR LOVE LETTERS. BUT HE WAS CRYING. THIS WAS IN 1975. NINTH OF JUNE. HE WAS GOING INTO THE SERVICE.
I'M SORRY. WOULD YOU LIKE HIS REAL NAME?
I...NO. MAYBE I SHOULD JUST LET IT END HERE. FINALLY.

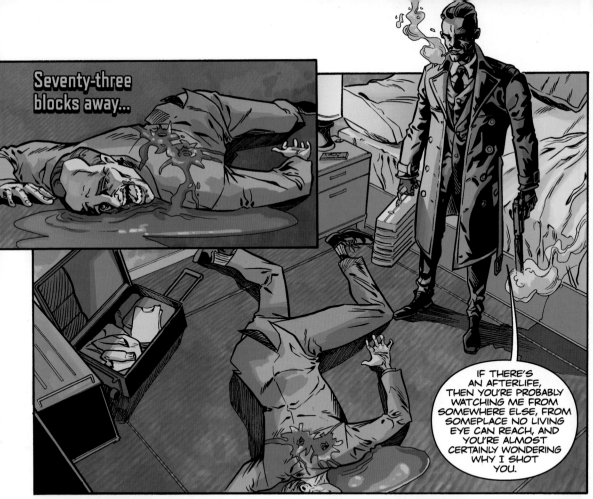

Seventy-three blocks away...

IF THERE'S AN AFTERLIFE, THEN YOU'RE PROBABLY WATCHING ME FROM SOMEWHERE ELSE, FROM SOMEPLACE NO LIVING EYE CAN REACH, AND YOU'RE ALMOST CERTAINLY WONDERING WHY I SHOT YOU.

IT'S SIMPLE. IT WAS TIME FOR YOU TO BE SHOT.

OH, THERE'S THE MATTER OF THIS BRIEFCASE, AND THE WEIMAR-STEINBERG JOURNALS, AND THE MONEY I WAS PAID TO ACQUIRE THEM...

...AND THERE'S PROBABLY SOME MOTHER ISSUES THAT I *REALLY* SHOULD TALK TO SOMEONE ABOUT, BUT SERIOUSLY, I COULD HAVE DEALT WITH ALL OF THIS *WITHOUT* SHOOTING YOU.

BUT HERE'S THE THING...

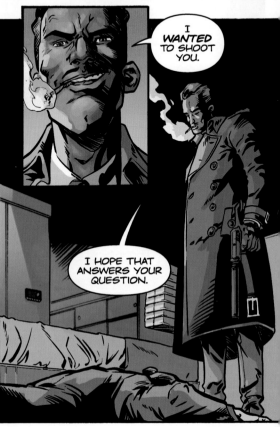

I *WANTED* TO SHOOT YOU.

I HOPE THAT ANSWERS YOUR QUESTION.

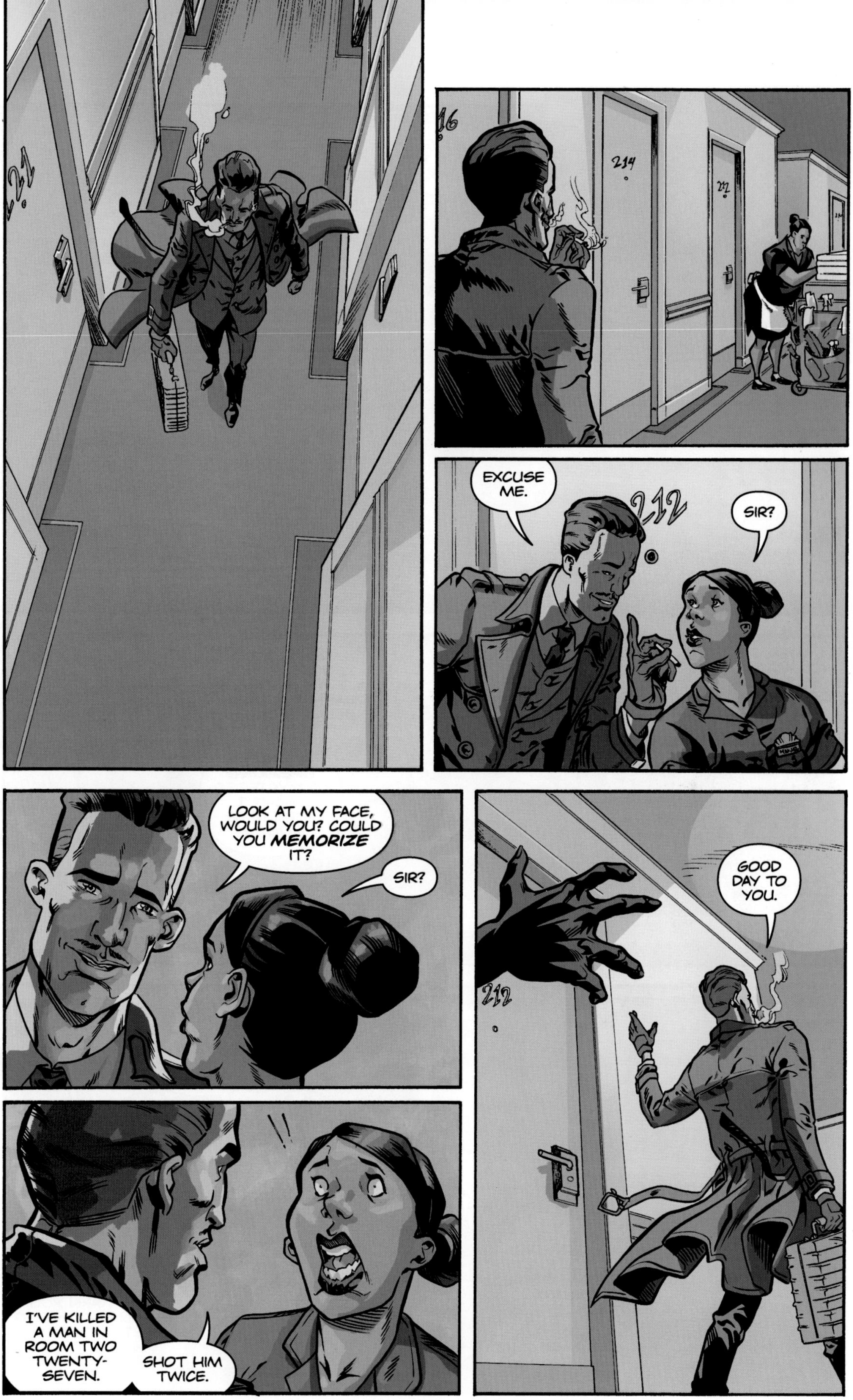
221
216
214
212
EXCUSE ME.
212
SIR?
LOOK AT MY FACE, WOULD YOU? COULD YOU MEMORIZE IT?
SIR?
I'VE KILLED A MAN IN ROOM TWO TWENTY-SEVEN.
SHOT HIM TWICE.
!
212
GOOD DAY TO YOU.

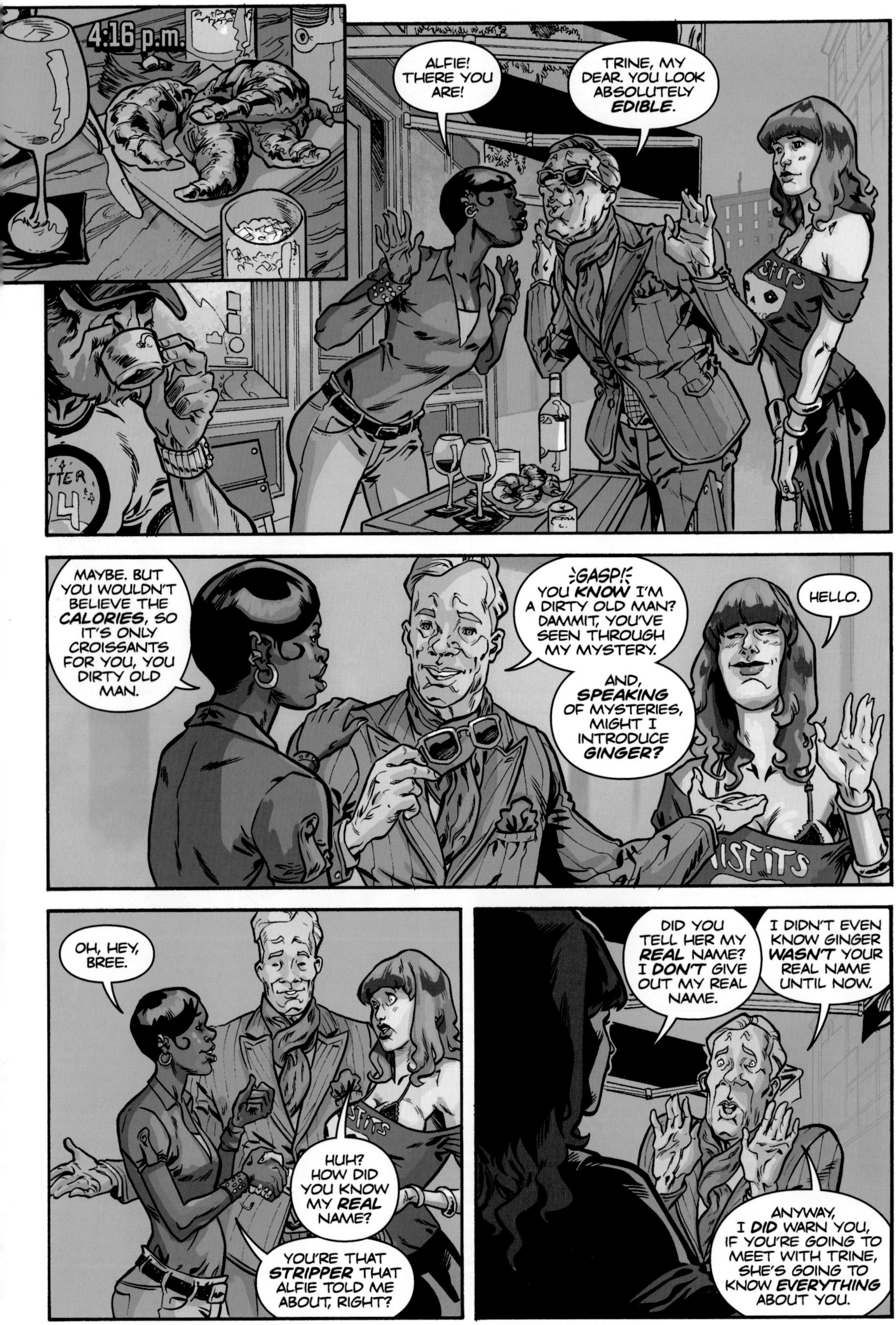
4:16 p.m.
ALFIE! THERE YOU ARE!
TRINE, MY DEAR. YOU LOOK ABSOLUTELY EDIBLE.
MAYBE. BUT YOU WOULDN'T BELIEVE THE CALORIES, SO IT'S ONLY CROISSANTS FOR YOU, YOU DIRTY OLD MAN.
GASP! YOU KNOW I'M A DIRTY OLD MAN? DAMMIT, YOU'VE SEEN THROUGH MY MYSTERY.
AND, SPEAKING OF MYSTERIES, MIGHT I INTRODUCE GINGER?
HELLO.
OH, HEY, BREE.
HUH? HOW DID YOU KNOW MY REAL NAME?
YOU'RE THAT STRIPPER THAT ALFIE TOLD ME ABOUT, RIGHT?
DID YOU TELL HER MY REAL NAME? I DON'T GIVE OUT MY REAL NAME.
I DIDN'T EVEN KNOW GINGER WASN'T YOUR REAL NAME UNTIL NOW.
ANYWAY, I DID WARN YOU, IF YOU'RE GOING TO MEET WITH TRINE, SHE'S GOING TO KNOW EVERYTHING ABOUT YOU.

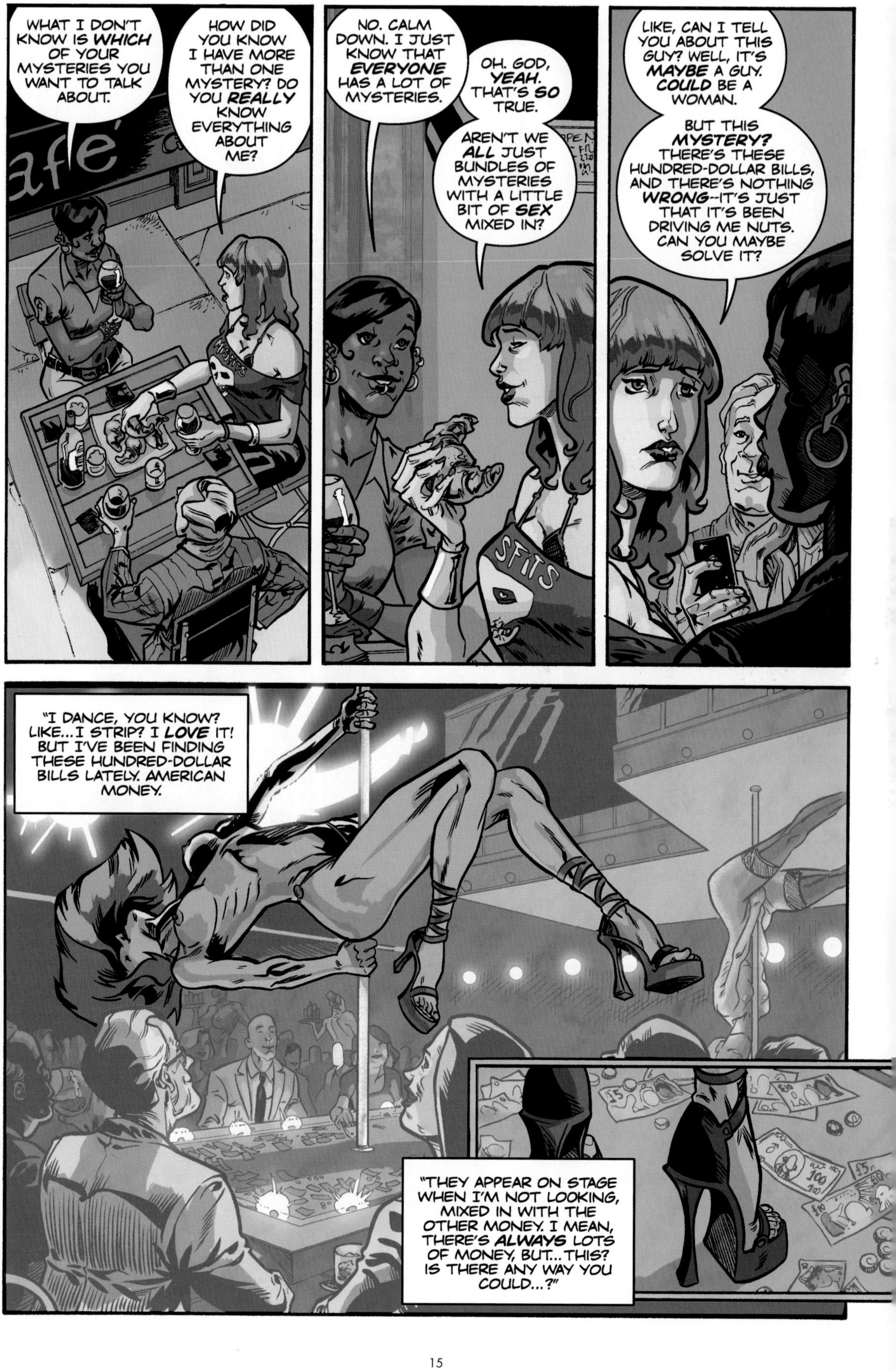
WHAT I DON'T KNOW IS WHICH OF YOUR MYSTERIES YOU WANT TO TALK ABOUT.
HOW DID YOU KNOW I HAVE MORE THAN ONE MYSTERY? DO YOU REALLY KNOW EVERYTHING ABOUT ME?
afe'
NO. CALM DOWN. I JUST KNOW THAT EVERYONE HAS A LOT OF MYSTERIES.
OH. GOD, YEAH. THAT'S SO TRUE.
AREN'T WE ALL JUST BUNDLES OF MYSTERIES WITH A LITTLE BIT OF SEX MIXED IN?
LIKE, CAN I TELL YOU ABOUT THIS GUY? WELL, IT'S MAYBE A GUY. COULD BE A WOMAN.
BUT THIS MYSTERY? THERE'S THESE HUNDRED-DOLLAR BILLS, AND THERE'S NOTHING WRONG--IT'S JUST THAT IT'S BEEN DRIVING ME NUTS. CAN YOU MAYBE SOLVE IT?
"I DANCE, YOU KNOW? LIKE... I STRIP? I LOVE IT! BUT I'VE BEEN FINDING THESE HUNDRED-DOLLAR BILLS LATELY. AMERICAN MONEY.
"THEY APPEAR ON STAGE WHEN I'M NOT LOOKING, MIXED IN WITH THE OTHER MONEY. I MEAN, THERE'S ALWAYS LOTS OF MONEY, BUT... THIS? IS THERE ANY WAY YOU COULD...?"

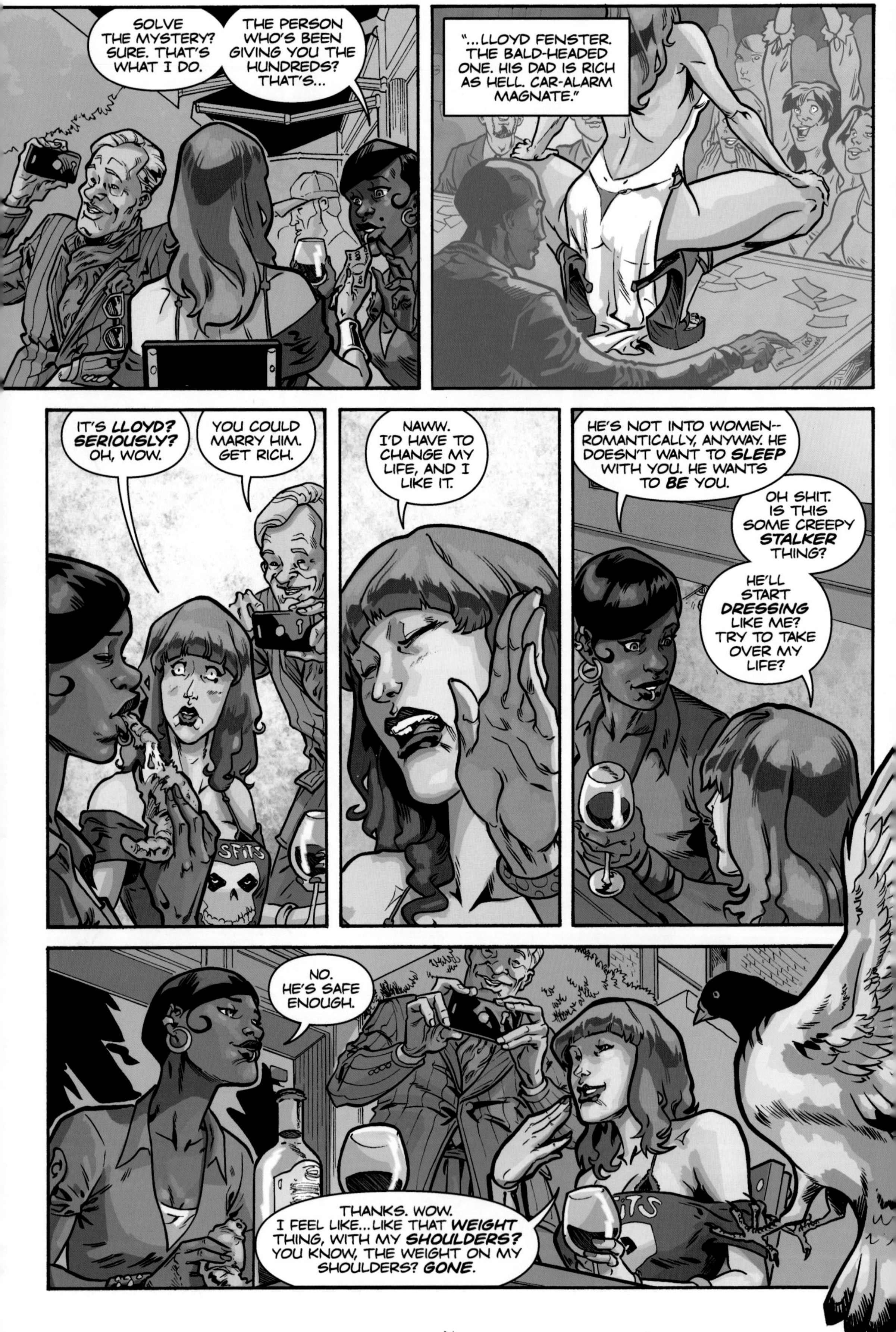
SOLVE THE MYSTERY? SURE. THAT'S WHAT I DO.
THE PERSON WHO'S BEEN GIVING YOU THE HUNDREDS? THAT'S...
"...LLOYD FENSTER. THE BALD-HEADED ONE. HIS DAD IS RICH AS HELL. CAR-ALARM MAGNATE."
IT'S LLOYD? SERIOUSLY? OH, WOW.
YOU COULD MARRY HIM. GET RICH.
NAWW. I'D HAVE TO CHANGE MY LIFE, AND I LIKE IT.
HE'S NOT INTO WOMEN-- ROMANTICALLY, ANYWAY. HE DOESN'T WANT TO SLEEP WITH YOU. HE WANTS TO BE YOU.
OH SHIT. IS THIS SOME CREEPY STALKER THING?
HE'LL START DRESSING LIKE ME? TRY TO TAKE OVER MY LIFE?
NO. HE'S SAFE ENOUGH.
THANKS. WOW. I FEEL LIKE...LIKE THAT WEIGHT THING, WITH MY SHOULDERS? YOU KNOW, THE WEIGHT ON MY SHOULDERS? GONE.

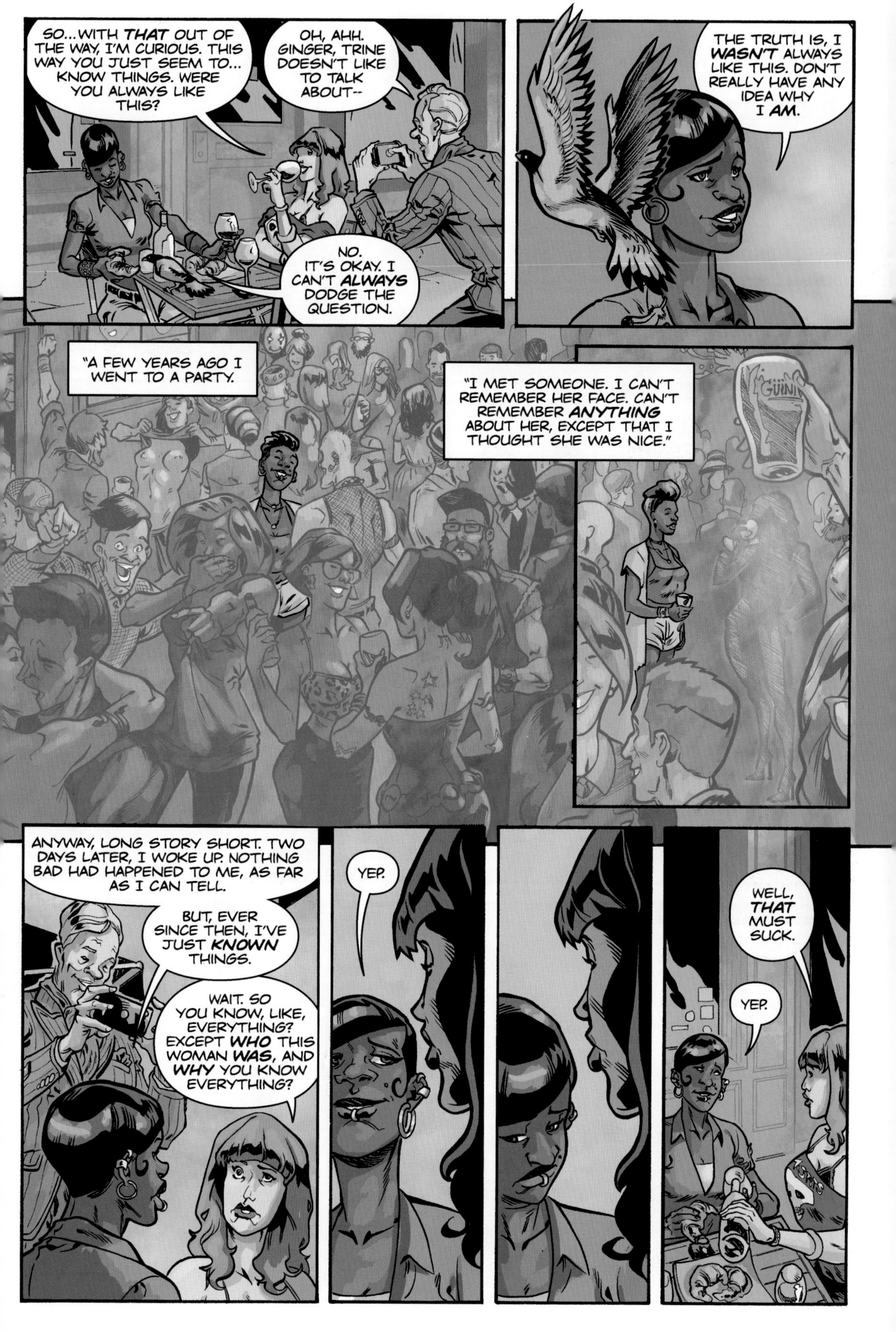
SO...WITH THAT OUT OF THE WAY, I'M CURIOUS. THIS WAY YOU JUST SEEM TO... KNOW THINGS. WERE YOU ALWAYS LIKE THIS?
OH, AHH. GINGER, TRINE DOESN'T LIKE TO TALK ABOUT--
NO. IT'S OKAY. I CAN'T ALWAYS DODGE THE QUESTION.
THE TRUTH IS, I WASN'T ALWAYS LIKE THIS. DON'T REALLY HAVE ANY IDEA WHY I AM.
"A FEW YEARS AGO I WENT TO A PARTY.
"I MET SOMEONE. I CAN'T REMEMBER HER FACE. CAN'T REMEMBER ANYTHING ABOUT HER, EXCEPT THAT I THOUGHT SHE WAS NICE."
ANYWAY, LONG STORY SHORT. TWO DAYS LATER, I WOKE UP. NOTHING BAD HAD HAPPENED TO ME, AS FAR AS I CAN TELL.
BUT, EVER SINCE THEN, I'VE JUST KNOWN THINGS.
WAIT. SO YOU KNOW, LIKE, EVERYTHING? EXCEPT WHO THIS WOMAN WAS, AND WHY YOU KNOW EVERYTHING?
YEP.
WELL, THAT MUST SUCK.
YEP.

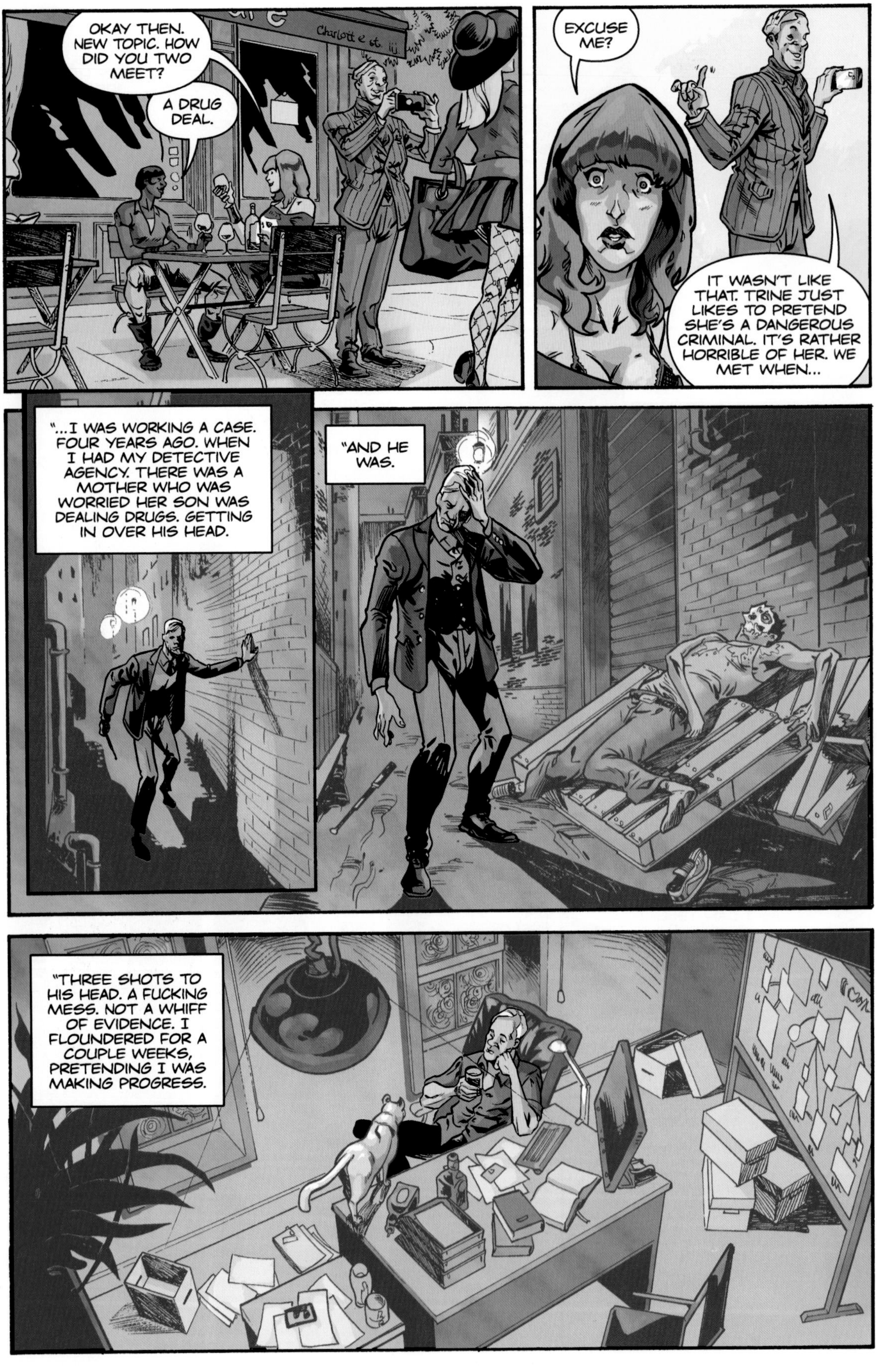
OKAY THEN. NEW TOPIC. HOW DID YOU TWO MEET?
A DRUG DEAL.
Charlott e st.
EXCUSE ME?
IT WASN'T LIKE THAT. TRINE JUST LIKES TO PRETEND SHE'S A DANGEROUS CRIMINAL. IT'S RATHER HORRIBLE OF HER. WE MET WHEN...
"...I WAS WORKING A CASE. FOUR YEARS AGO. WHEN I HAD MY DETECTIVE AGENCY. THERE WAS A MOTHER WHO WAS WORRIED HER SON WAS DEALING DRUGS. GETTING IN OVER HIS HEAD.
"AND HE WAS.
"THREE SHOTS TO HIS HEAD. A FUCKING MESS. NOT A WHIFF OF EVIDENCE. I FLOUNDERED FOR A COUPLE WEEKS, PRETENDING I WAS MAKING PROGRESS.

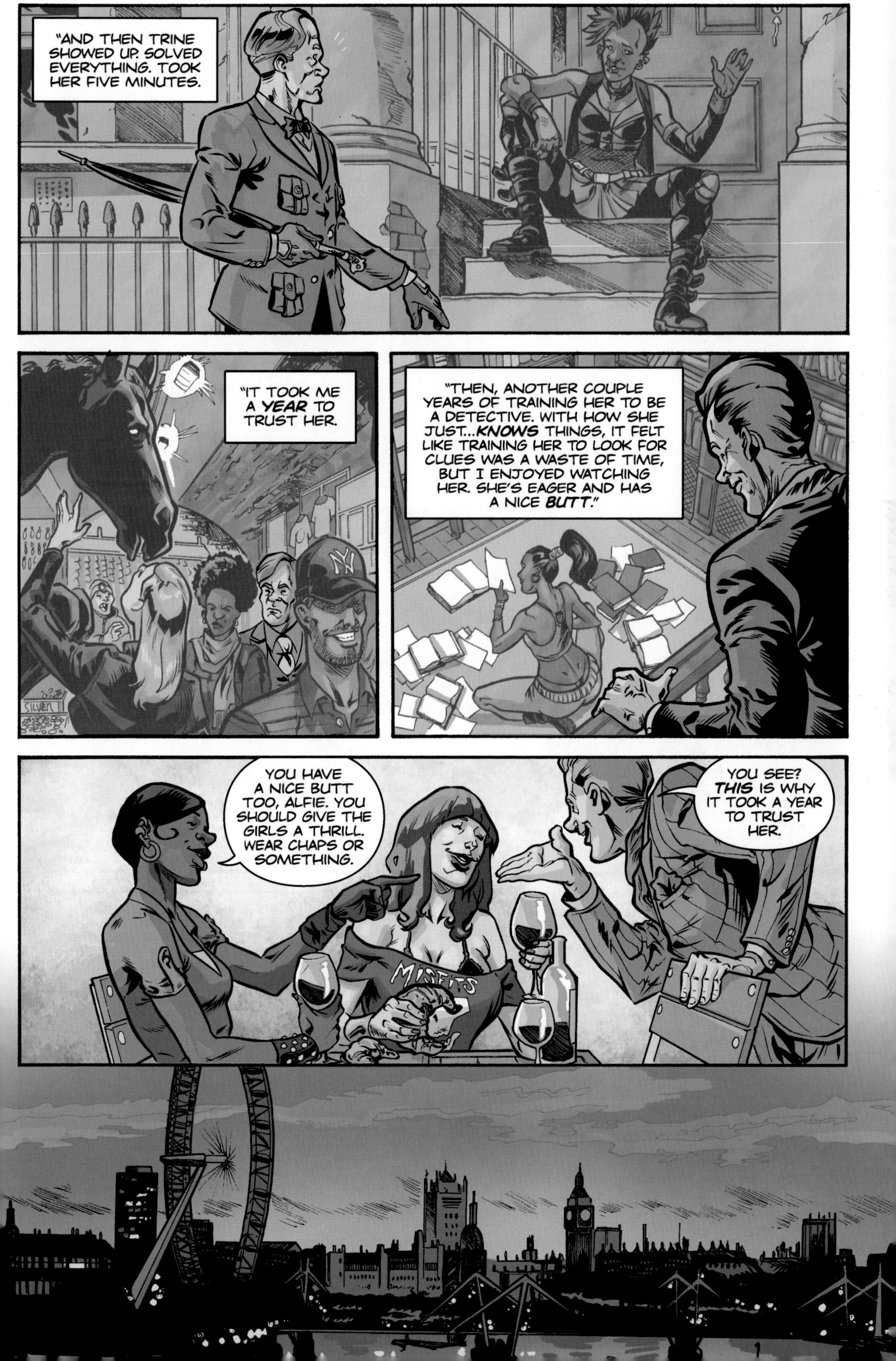
"AND THEN TRINE SHOWED UP. SOLVED EVERYTHING. TOOK HER FIVE MINUTES.
"IT TOOK ME A *YEAR* TO TRUST HER.
"THEN, ANOTHER COUPLE YEARS OF TRAINING HER TO BE A DETECTIVE. WITH HOW SHE JUST...*KNOWS* THINGS, IT FELT LIKE TRAINING HER TO LOOK FOR CLUES WAS A WASTE OF TIME, BUT I ENJOYED WATCHING HER. SHE'S EAGER AND HAS A NICE *BUTT*."
YOU HAVE A NICE BUTT TOO, ALFIE. YOU SHOULD GIVE THE GIRLS A THRILL. WEAR CHAPS OR SOMETHING.
YOU SEE? *THIS* IS WHY IT TOOK A YEAR TO TRUST HER.
MISFITS

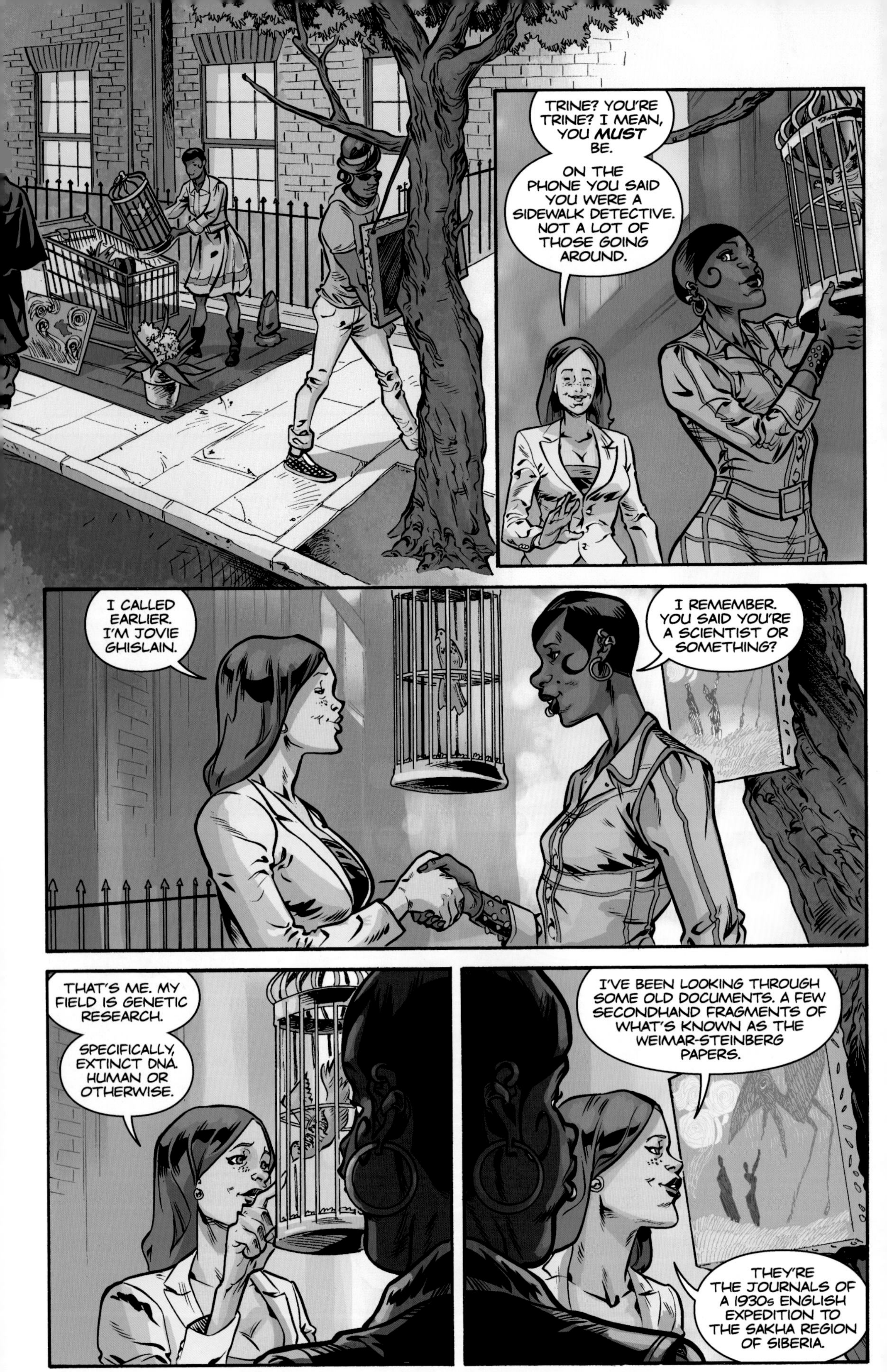
TRINE? YOU'RE TRINE? I MEAN, YOU *MUST* BE.
ON THE PHONE YOU SAID YOU WERE A SIDEWALK DETECTIVE. NOT A LOT OF THOSE GOING AROUND.
I CALLED EARLIER. I'M JOVIE GHISLAIN.
I REMEMBER. YOU SAID YOU'RE A SCIENTIST OR SOMETHING?
THAT'S ME. MY FIELD IS GENETIC RESEARCH.
SPECIFICALLY, EXTINCT DNA. HUMAN OR OTHERWISE.
I'VE BEEN LOOKING THROUGH SOME OLD DOCUMENTS. A FEW SECONDHAND FRAGMENTS OF WHAT'S KNOWN AS THE WEIMAR-STEINBERG PAPERS.
THEY'RE THE JOURNALS OF A 1930s ENGLISH EXPEDITION TO THE SAKHA REGION OF SIBERIA.

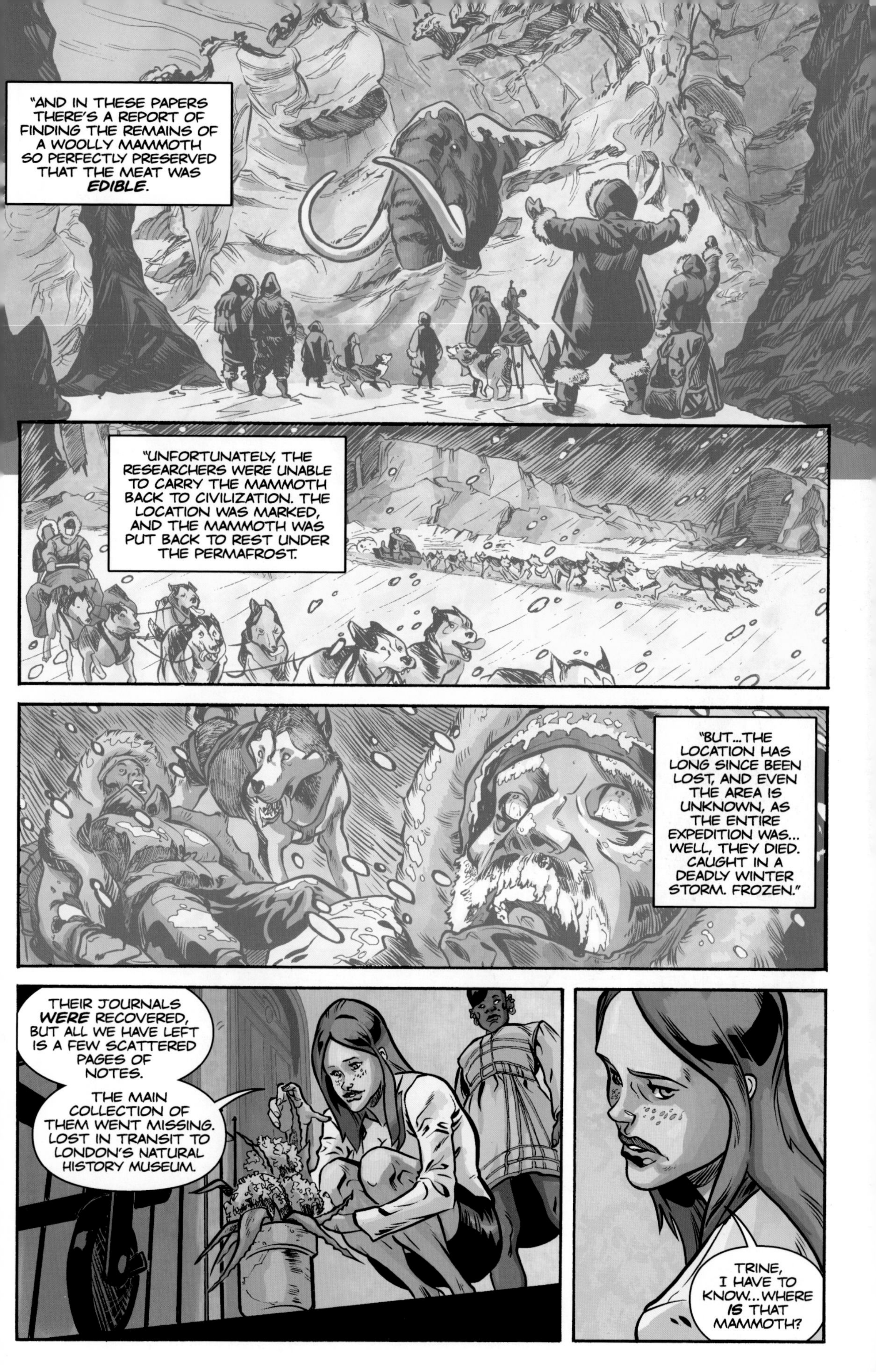
"AND IN THESE PAPERS THERE'S A REPORT OF FINDING THE REMAINS OF A WOOLLY MAMMOTH SO PERFECTLY PRESERVED THAT THE MEAT WAS *EDIBLE*.
"UNFORTUNATELY, THE RESEARCHERS WERE UNABLE TO CARRY THE MAMMOTH BACK TO CIVILIZATION. THE LOCATION WAS MARKED, AND THE MAMMOTH WAS PUT BACK TO REST UNDER THE PERMAFROST.
"BUT...THE LOCATION HAS LONG SINCE BEEN LOST, AND EVEN THE AREA IS UNKNOWN, AS THE ENTIRE EXPEDITION WAS... WELL, THEY DIED. CAUGHT IN A DEADLY WINTER STORM. FROZEN."
THEIR JOURNALS *WERE* RECOVERED, BUT ALL WE HAVE LEFT IS A FEW SCATTERED PAGES OF NOTES.
THE MAIN COLLECTION OF THEM WENT MISSING. LOST IN TRANSIT TO LONDON'S NATURAL HISTORY MUSEUM.
TRINE, I HAVE TO KNOW...WHERE *IS* THAT MAMMOTH?

AND...YOU THINK *I* WOULD KNOW ABOUT SOME MAMMOTH BURIED IN SIBERIA FOR WHO *KNOWS* HOW MANY YEARS?

WELL, I...THAT IS...

I HAVE SOME FRIENDS THAT SAID YOU HAVE SOME... THEY SAID *WEIRDNESS*. THAT IF YOU *HEAR* ABOUT A MYSTERY, YOU JUST... *KNOW* THE ANSWER.

I'M SORRY--THIS WAS STUPID. I SHOULD HAVE--

I KNOW WHERE IT'S AT.

OH GOD. REALLY? YOU *DO?*

I *KNEW* IT!

WHERE? WHERE *IS* IT? TELL ME!

NO.

W-WHAT?

NO. I WON'T TELL YOU.

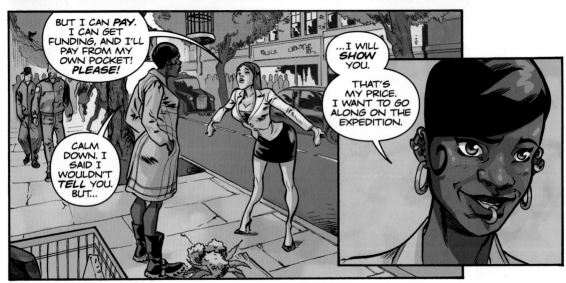

BUT I CAN *PAY*. I CAN GET FUNDING, AND I'LL PAY FROM MY OWN POCKET! *PLEASE!*

CALM DOWN. I SAID I WOULDN'T *TELL* YOU. BUT...

...I WILL *SHOW* YOU.

THAT'S MY PRICE. I WANT TO GO ALONG ON THE EXPEDITION.

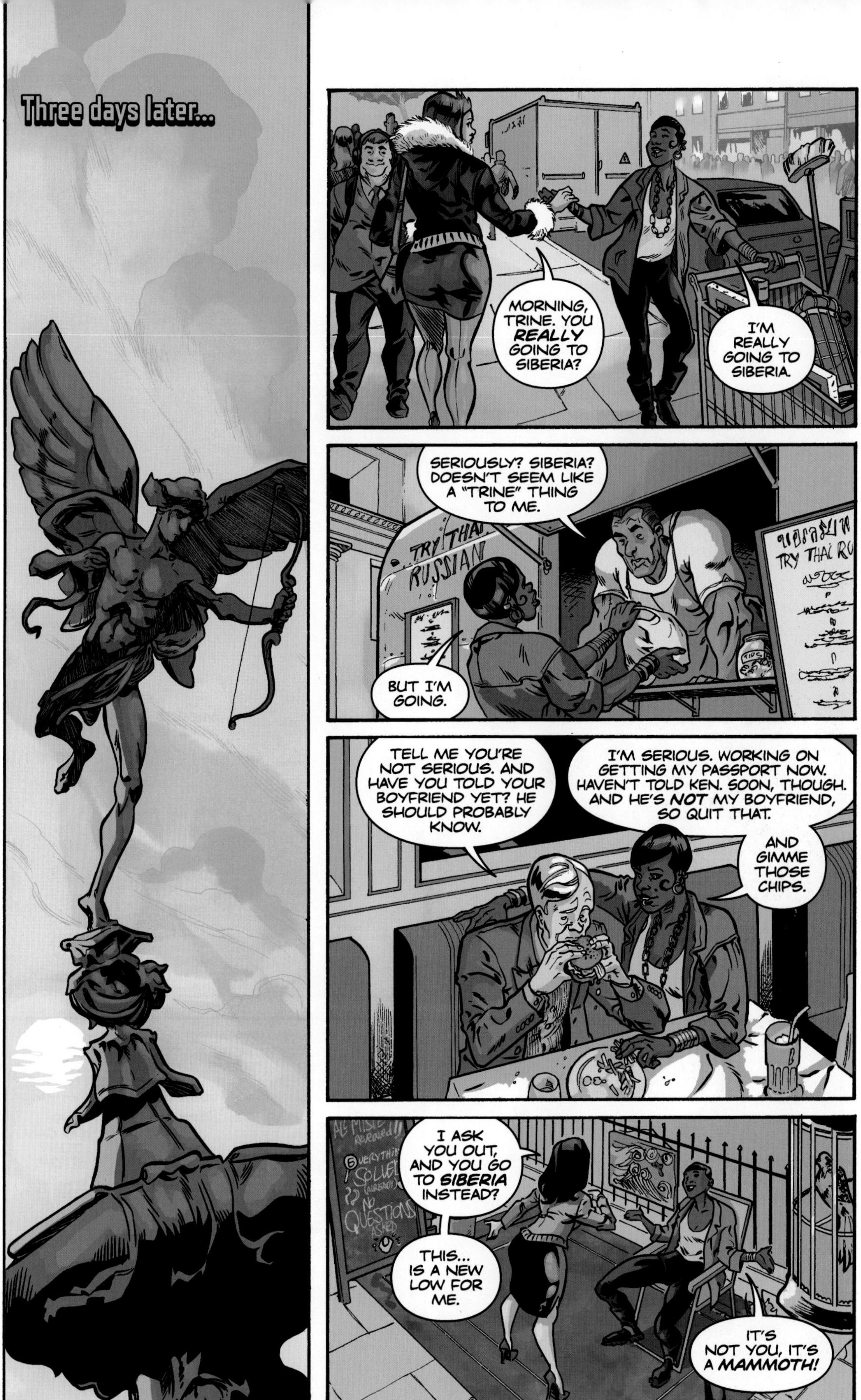
Three days later...
MORNING, TRINE. YOU REALLY GOING TO SIBERIA?
I'M REALLY GOING TO SIBERIA.
SERIOUSLY? SIBERIA? DOESN'T SEEM LIKE A "TRINE" THING TO ME.
BUT I'M GOING.
TRY THAI
RUSSIAN
TELL ME YOU'RE NOT SERIOUS. AND HAVE YOU TOLD YOUR BOYFRIEND YET? HE SHOULD PROBABLY KNOW.
I'M SERIOUS. WORKING ON GETTING MY PASSPORT NOW. HAVEN'T TOLD KEN. SOON, THOUGH. AND HE'S NOT MY BOYFRIEND, SO QUIT THAT.
AND GIMME THOSE CHIPS.
I ASK YOU OUT, AND YOU GO TO SIBERIA INSTEAD?
THIS... IS A NEW LOW FOR ME.
IT'S NOT YOU, IT'S A MAMMOTH!

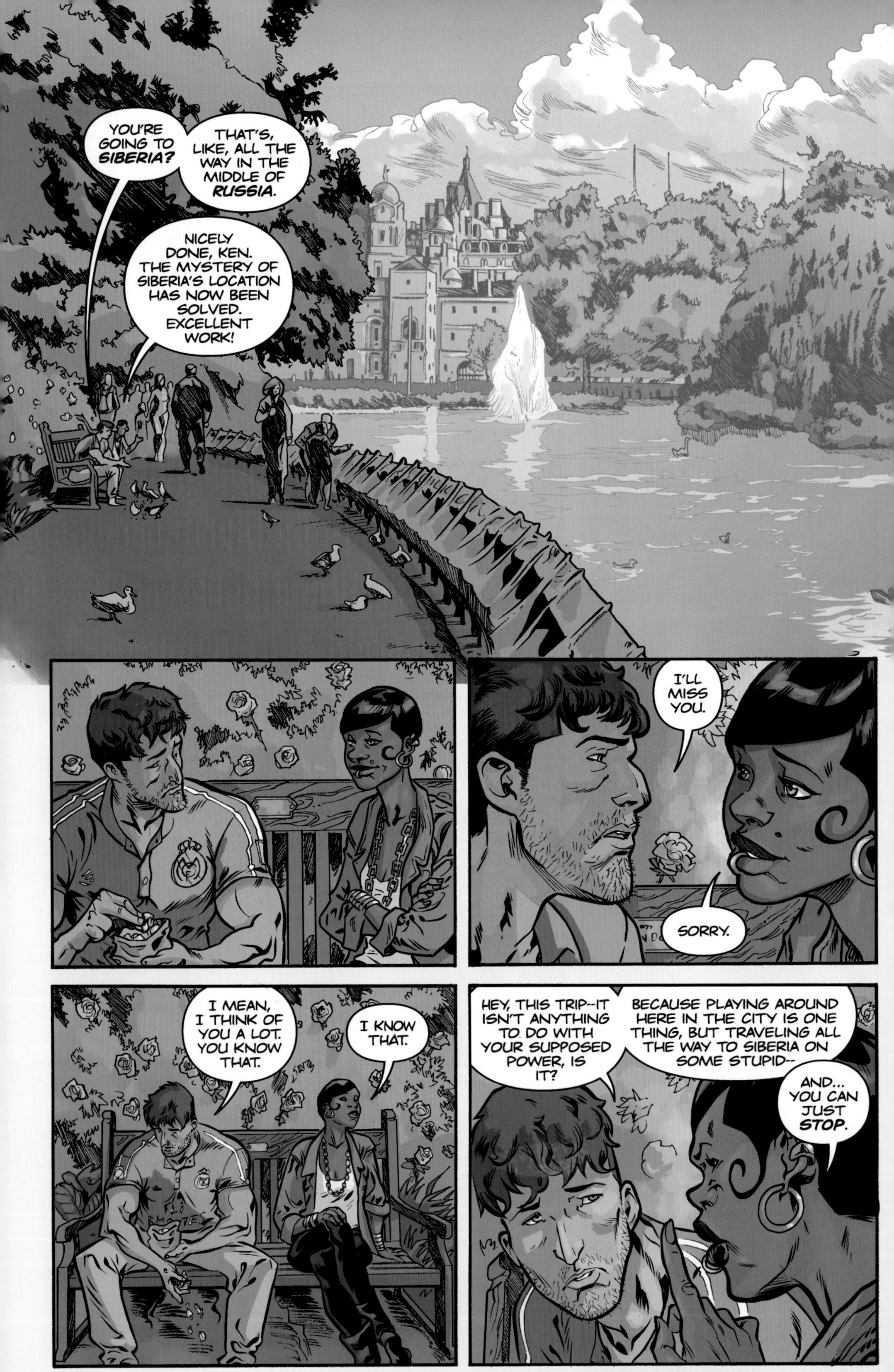
YOU'RE GOING TO SIBERIA?
THAT'S, LIKE, ALL THE WAY IN THE MIDDLE OF RUSSIA.
NICELY DONE, KEN. THE MYSTERY OF SIBERIA'S LOCATION HAS NOW BEEN SOLVED. EXCELLENT WORK!
I'LL MISS YOU.
SORRY.
I MEAN, I THINK OF YOU A LOT. YOU KNOW THAT.
I KNOW THAT.
HEY, THIS TRIP--IT ISN'T ANYTHING TO DO WITH YOUR SUPPOSED POWER, IS IT?
BECAUSE PLAYING AROUND HERE IN THE CITY IS ONE THING, BUT TRAVELING ALL THE WAY TO SIBERIA ON SOME STUPID--
AND... YOU CAN JUST STOP.

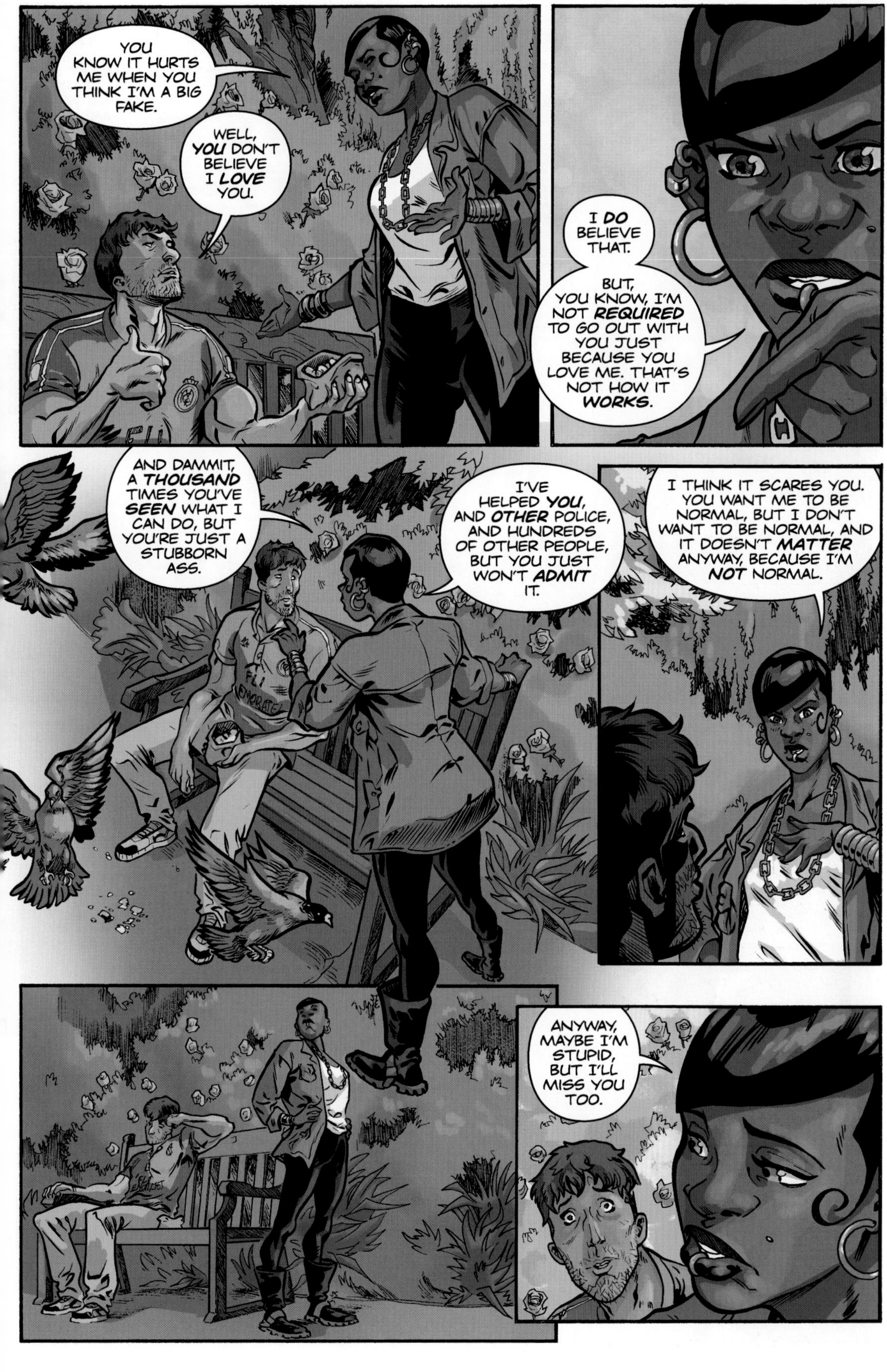
YOU KNOW IT HURTS ME WHEN YOU THINK I'M A BIG FAKE.
WELL, YOU DON'T BELIEVE I LOVE YOU.
I DO BELIEVE THAT.
BUT, YOU KNOW, I'M NOT REQUIRED TO GO OUT WITH YOU JUST BECAUSE YOU LOVE ME. THAT'S NOT HOW IT WORKS.
AND DAMMIT, A THOUSAND TIMES YOU'VE SEEN WHAT I CAN DO, BUT YOU'RE JUST A STUBBORN ASS.
I'VE HELPED YOU, AND OTHER POLICE, AND HUNDREDS OF OTHER PEOPLE, BUT YOU JUST WON'T ADMIT IT.
I THINK IT SCARES YOU. YOU WANT ME TO BE NORMAL, BUT I DON'T WANT TO BE NORMAL, AND IT DOESN'T MATTER ANYWAY, BECAUSE I'M NOT NORMAL.
ANYWAY, MAYBE I'M STUPID, BUT I'LL MISS YOU TOO.

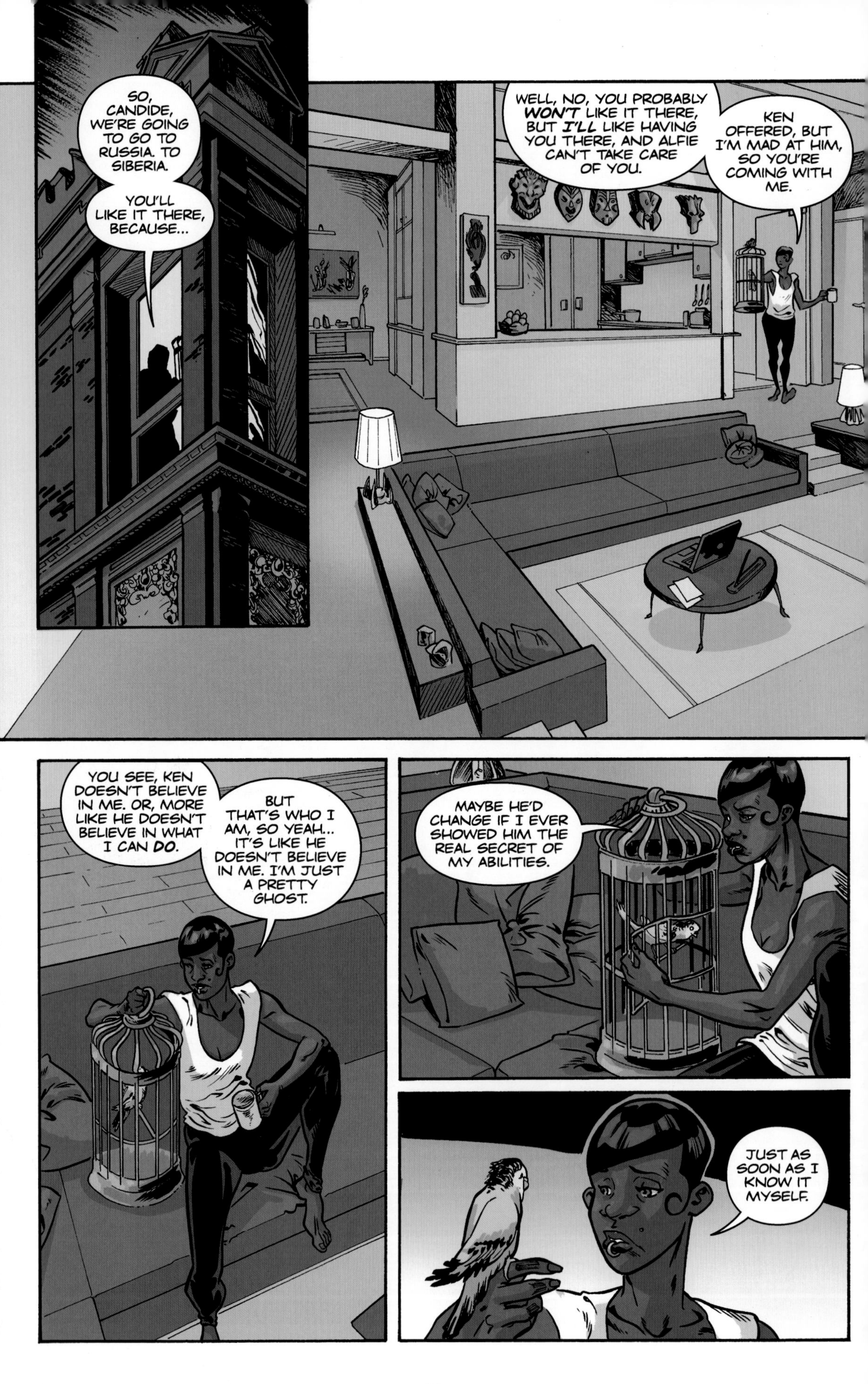

SO, CANDIDE, WE'RE GOING TO GO TO RUSSIA. TO SIBERIA.
YOU'LL LIKE IT THERE, BECAUSE...
WELL, NO, YOU PROBABLY **WON'T** LIKE IT THERE, BUT **I'LL** LIKE HAVING YOU THERE, AND ALFIE CAN'T TAKE CARE OF YOU.
KEN OFFERED, BUT I'M MAD AT HIM, SO YOU'RE COMING WITH ME.
YOU SEE, KEN DOESN'T BELIEVE IN ME. OR, MORE LIKE HE DOESN'T BELIEVE IN WHAT I CAN **DO**.
BUT THAT'S WHO I AM, SO YEAH... IT'S LIKE HE DOESN'T BELIEVE IN ME. I'M JUST A PRETTY GHOST.
MAYBE HE'D CHANGE IF I EVER SHOWED HIM THE REAL SECRET OF MY ABILITIES.
JUST AS SOON AS I KNOW IT MYSELF.

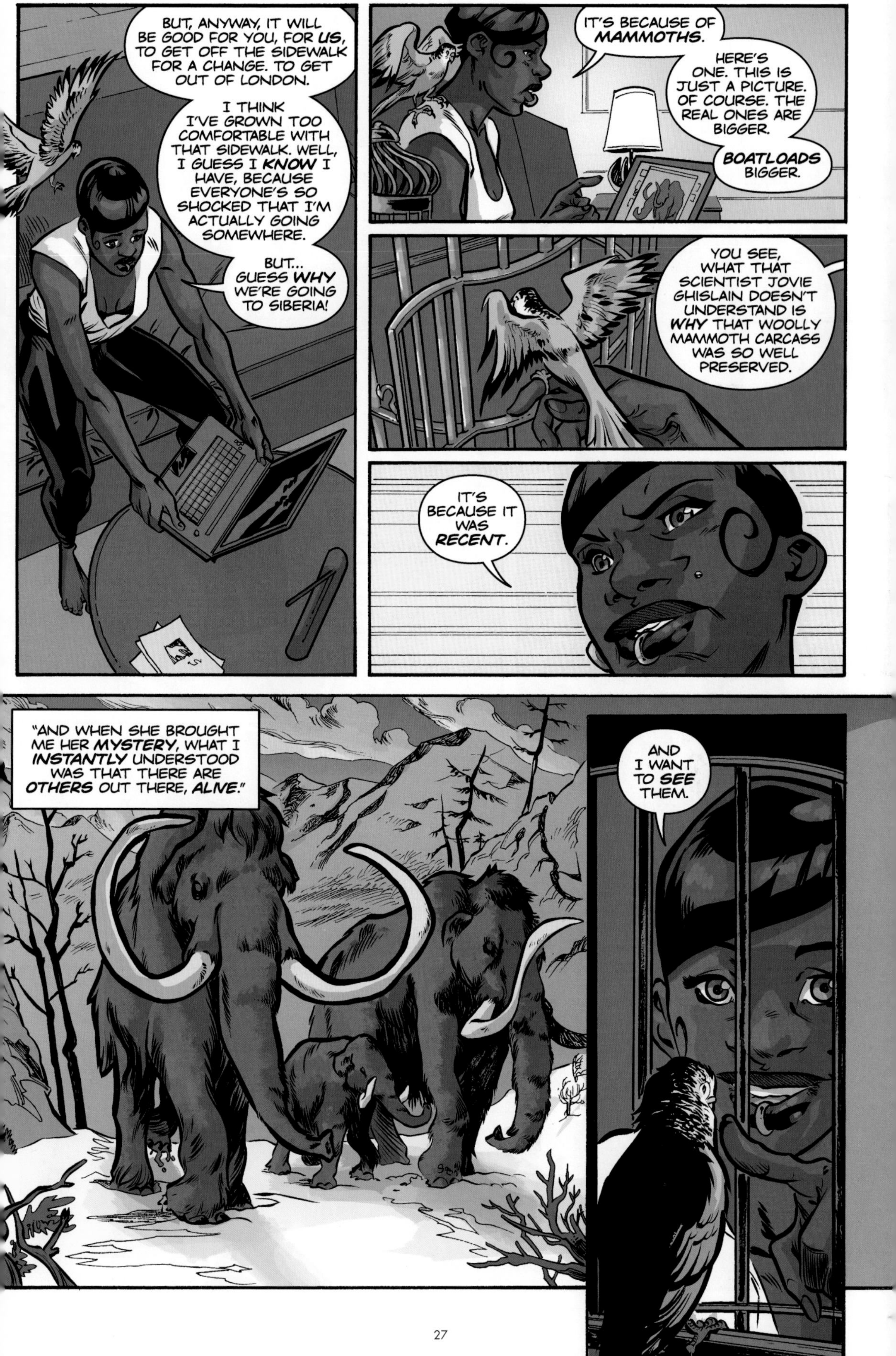
BUT, ANYWAY, IT WILL BE GOOD FOR YOU, FOR US, TO GET OFF THE SIDEWALK FOR A CHANGE. TO GET OUT OF LONDON.
I THINK I'VE GROWN TOO COMFORTABLE WITH THAT SIDEWALK. WELL, I GUESS I KNOW I HAVE, BECAUSE EVERYONE'S SO SHOCKED THAT I'M ACTUALLY GOING SOMEWHERE.
BUT... GUESS WHY WE'RE GOING TO SIBERIA!
IT'S BECAUSE OF MAMMOTHS.
HERE'S ONE. THIS IS JUST A PICTURE. OF COURSE. THE REAL ONES ARE BIGGER.
BOATLOADS BIGGER.
YOU SEE, WHAT THAT SCIENTIST JOVIE GHISLAIN DOESN'T UNDERSTAND IS WHY THAT WOOLLY MAMMOTH CARCASS WAS SO WELL PRESERVED.
IT'S BECAUSE IT WAS RECENT.
"AND WHEN SHE BROUGHT ME HER MYSTERY, WHAT I INSTANTLY UNDERSTOOD WAS THAT THERE ARE OTHERS OUT THERE, ALIVE."
AND I WANT TO SEE THEM.

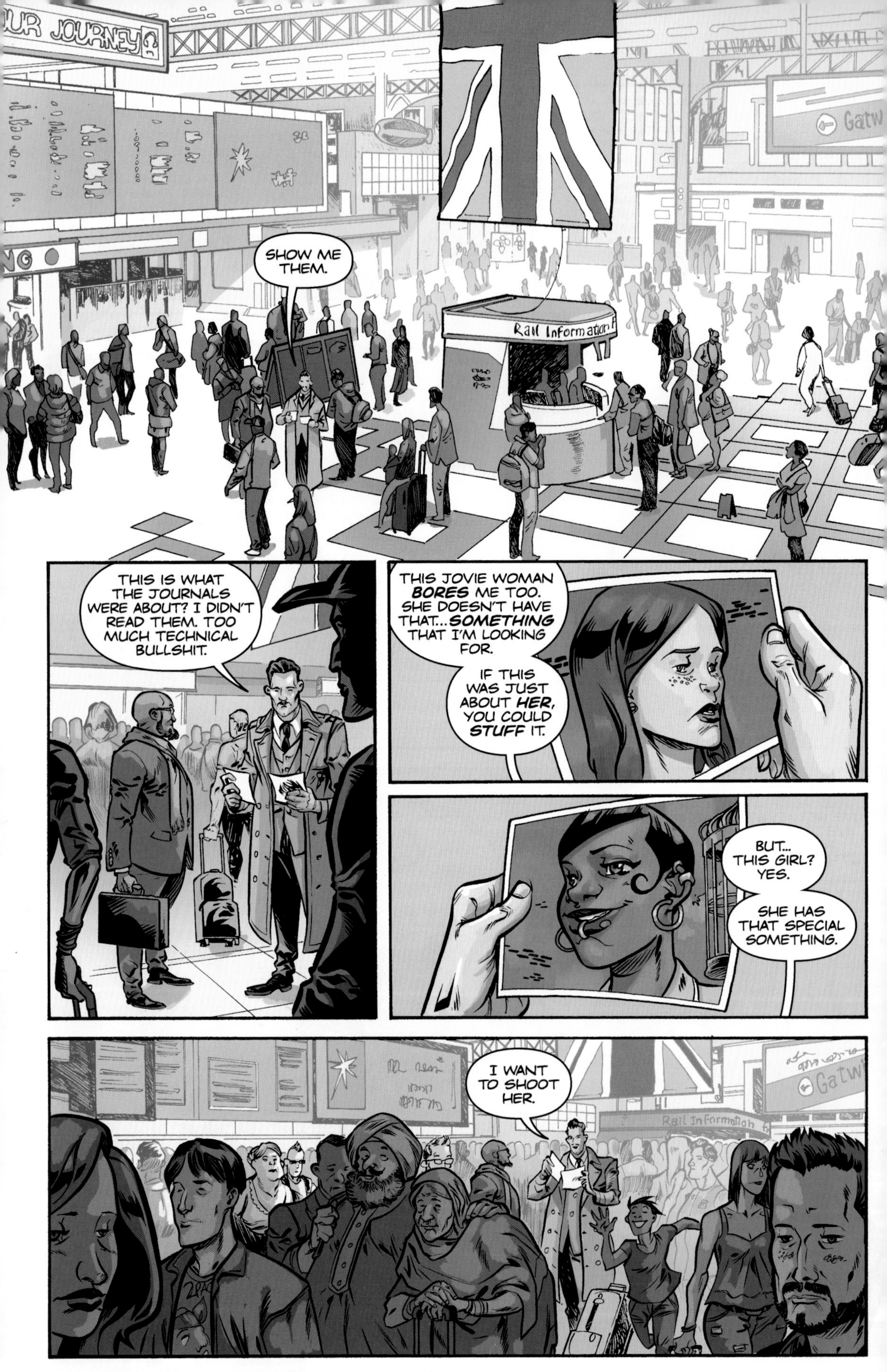
OUR JOURNEY
SHOW ME THEM.
Rail Information
Gatw
THIS IS WHAT THE JOURNALS WERE ABOUT? I DIDN'T READ THEM. TOO MUCH TECHNICAL BULLSHIT.
THIS JOVIE WOMAN BORES ME TOO. SHE DOESN'T HAVE THAT... SOMETHING THAT I'M LOOKING FOR.
IF THIS WAS JUST ABOUT HER, YOU COULD STUFF IT.
BUT... THIS GIRL? YES.
SHE HAS THAT SPECIAL SOMETHING.
I WANT TO SHOOT HER.
Rail Information
Gatw

CHAPTER 2

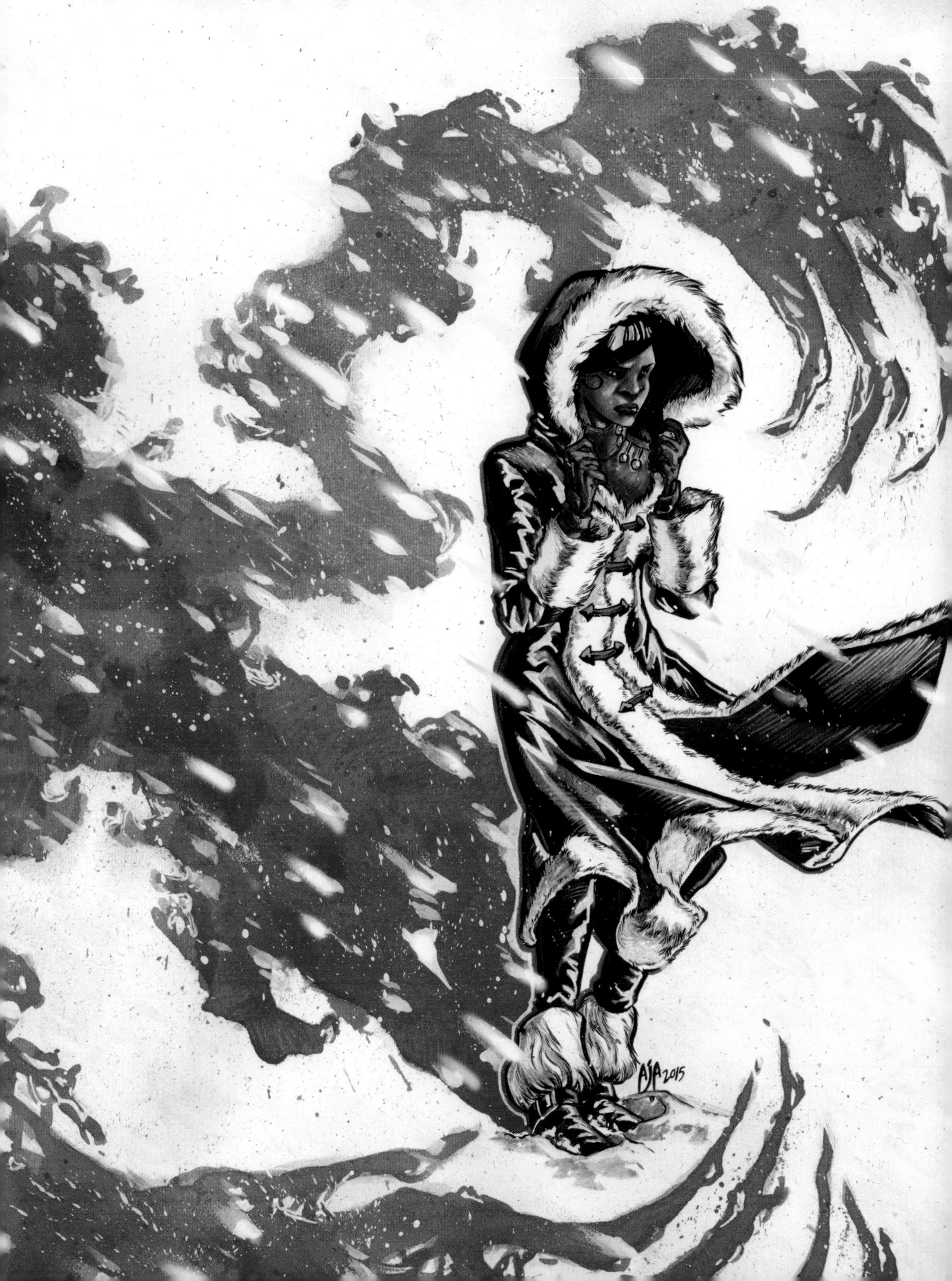
AJA 2015

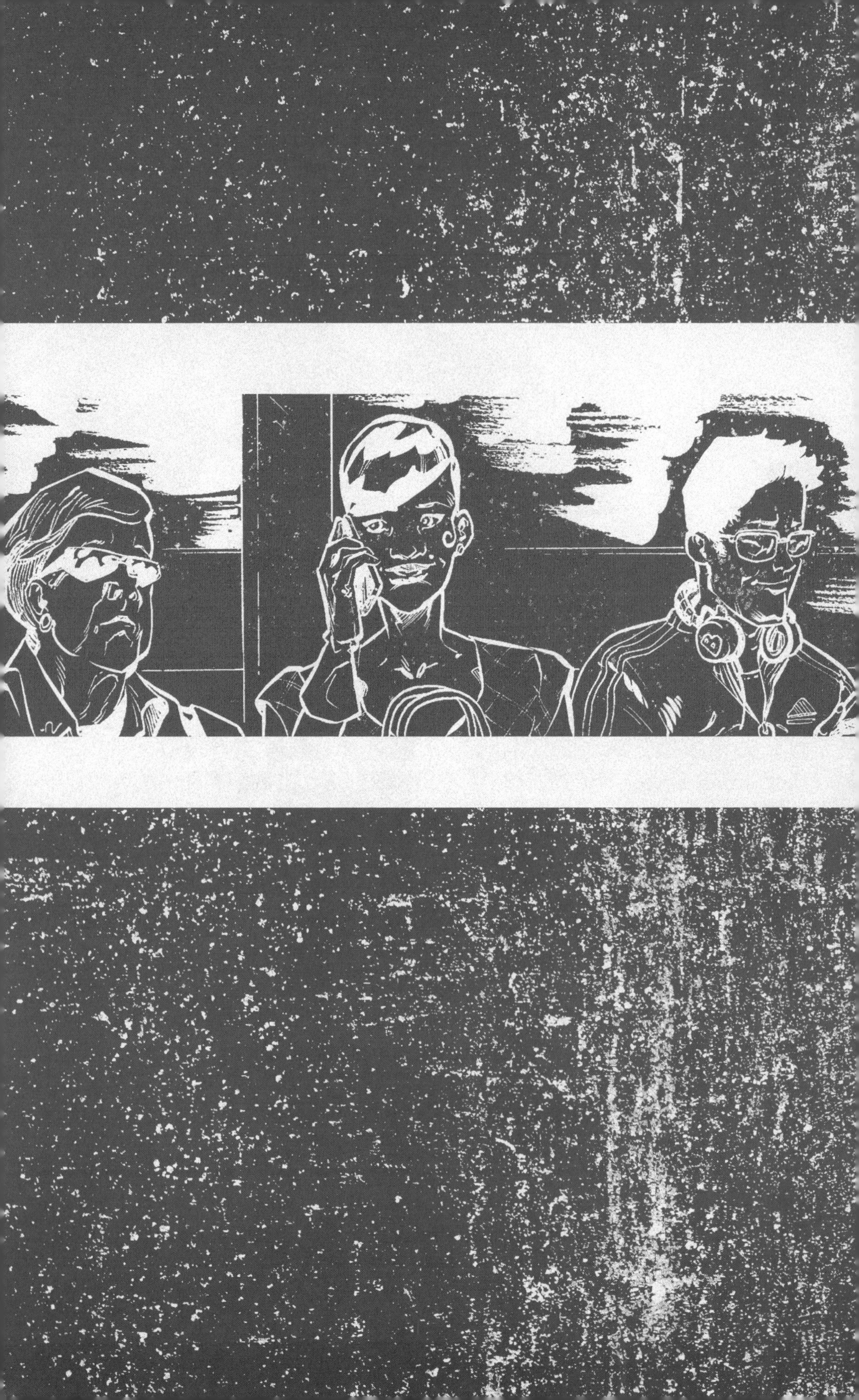

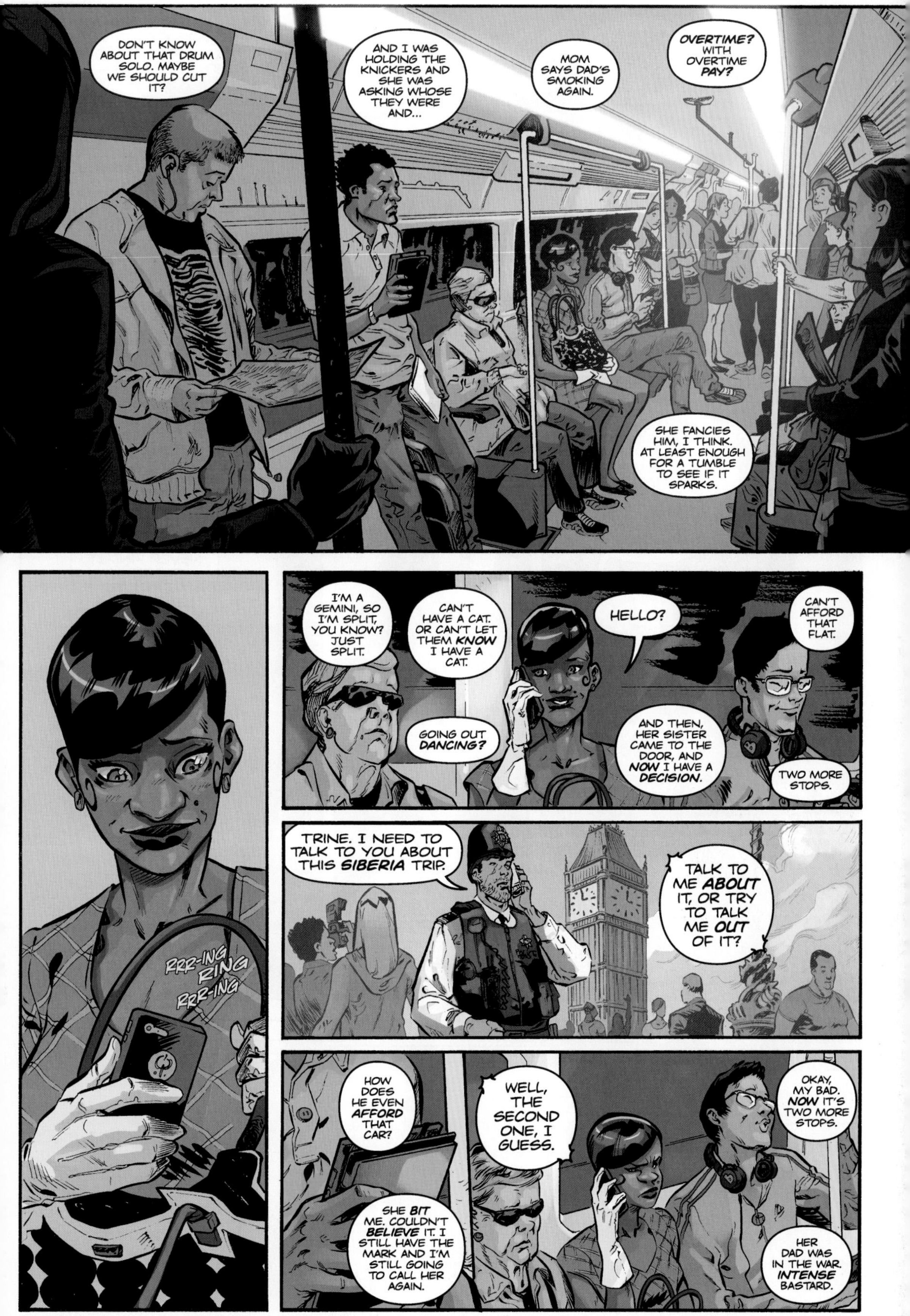
DON'T KNOW ABOUT THAT DRUM SOLO. MAYBE WE SHOULD CUT IT?
AND I WAS HOLDING THE KNICKERS AND SHE WAS ASKING WHOSE THEY WERE AND...
MOM SAYS DAD'S SMOKING AGAIN.
OVERTIME? WITH OVERTIME PAY?
SHE FANCIES HIM, I THINK. AT LEAST ENOUGH FOR A TUMBLE TO SEE IF IT SPARKS.
RRR-ING RING RRR-ING
I'M A GEMINI, SO I'M SPLIT, YOU KNOW? JUST SPLIT.
CAN'T HAVE A CAT. OR CAN'T LET THEM KNOW I HAVE A CAT.
HELLO?
CAN'T AFFORD THAT FLAT.
GOING OUT DANCING?
AND THEN, HER SISTER CAME TO THE DOOR, AND NOW I HAVE A DECISION.
TWO MORE STOPS.
TRINE. I NEED TO TALK TO YOU ABOUT THIS SIBERIA TRIP.
TALK TO ME ABOUT IT, OR TRY TO TALK ME OUT OF IT?
HOW DOES HE EVEN AFFORD THAT CAR?
WELL, THE SECOND ONE, I GUESS.
OKAY, MY BAD. NOW IT'S TWO MORE STOPS.
SHE BIT ME. COULDN'T BELIEVE IT. I STILL HAVE THE MARK AND I'M STILL GOING TO CALL HER AGAIN.
HER DAD WAS IN THE WAR. INTENSE BASTARD.

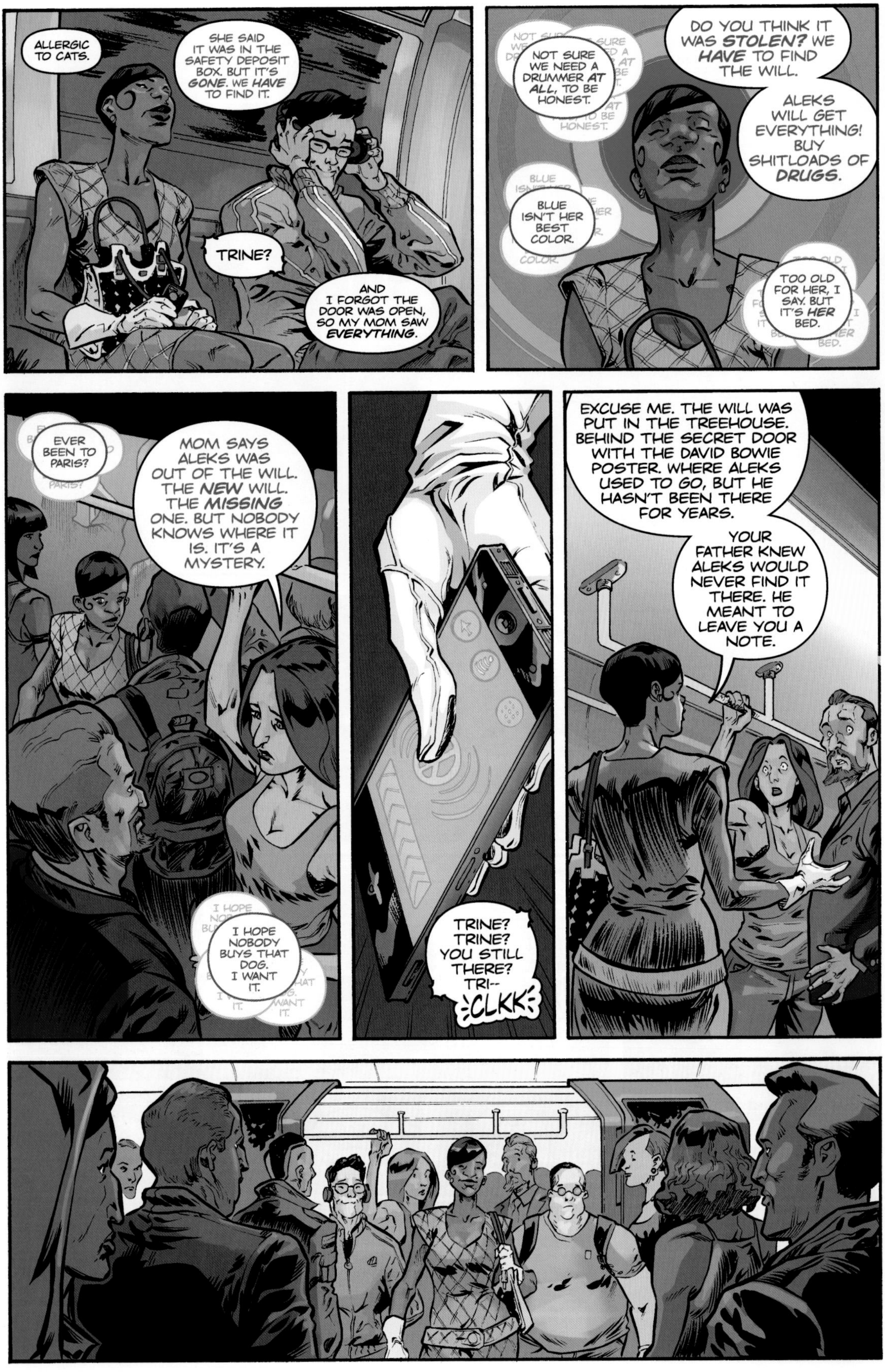

ALLERGIC TO CATS.
SHE SAID IT WAS IN THE SAFETY DEPOSIT BOX. BUT IT'S GONE. WE HAVE TO FIND IT.
TRINE?
AND I FORGOT THE DOOR WAS OPEN, SO MY MOM SAW EVERYTHING.
DO YOU THINK IT WAS STOLEN? WE HAVE TO FIND THE WILL.
NOT SURE WE NEED A DRUMMER AT ALL, TO BE HONEST.
ALEKS WILL GET EVERYTHING! BUY SHITLOADS OF DRUGS.
BLUE ISN'T HER BEST COLOR.
TOO OLD FOR HER, I SAY. BUT IT'S HER BED.
EVER BEEN TO PARIS?
MOM SAYS ALEKS WAS OUT OF THE WILL. THE NEW WILL. THE MISSING ONE. BUT NOBODY KNOWS WHERE IT IS. IT'S A MYSTERY.
I HOPE NOBODY BUYS THAT DOG. I WANT IT.
TRINE? TRINE? YOU STILL THERE? TRI--
CLKK
EXCUSE ME. THE WILL WAS PUT IN THE TREEHOUSE. BEHIND THE SECRET DOOR WITH THE DAVID BOWIE POSTER. WHERE ALEKS USED TO GO, BUT HE HASN'T BEEN THERE FOR YEARS.
YOUR FATHER KNEW ALEKS WOULD NEVER FIND IT THERE. HE MEANT TO LEAVE YOU A NOTE.

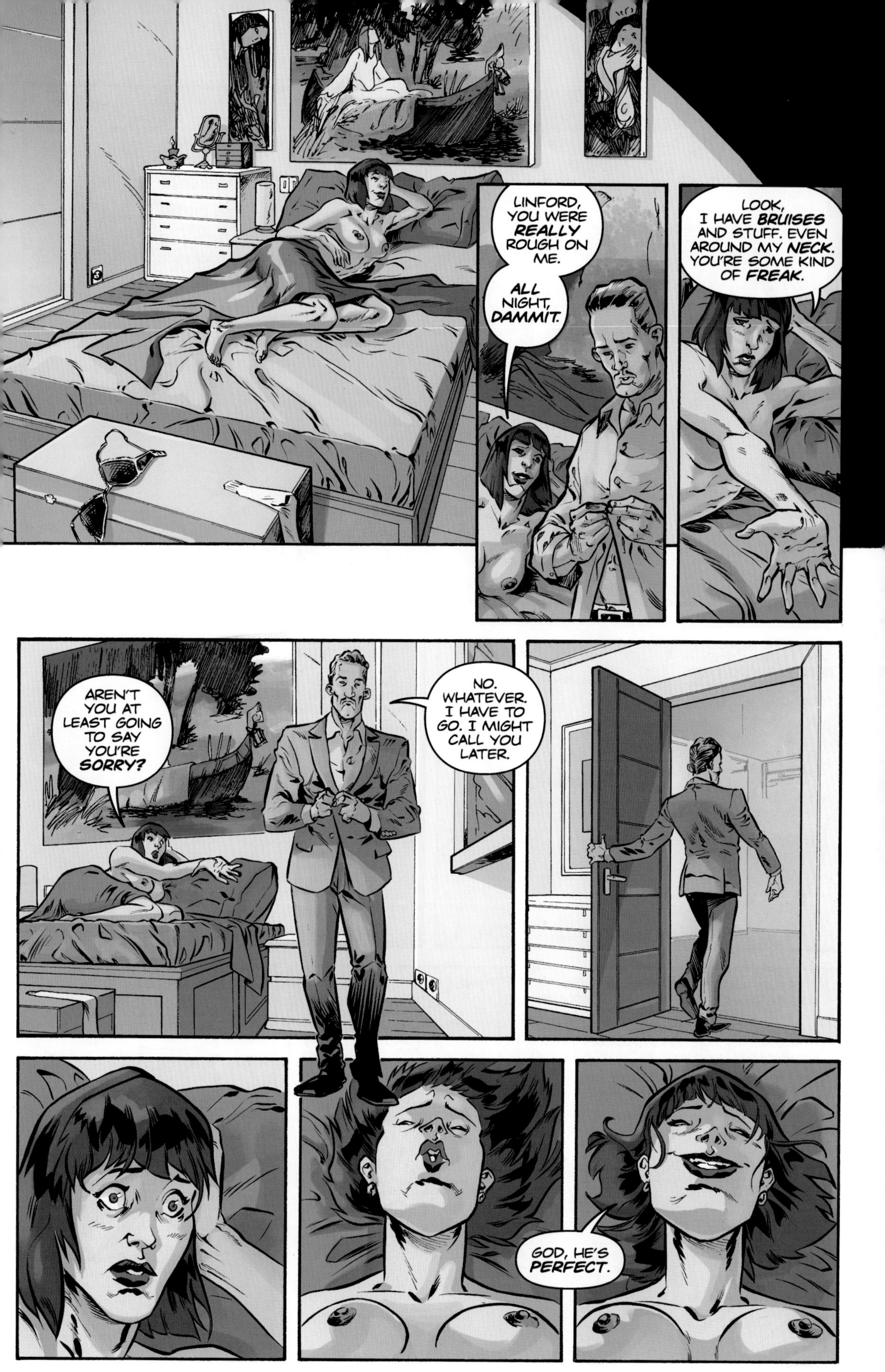
LINFORD, YOU WERE REALLY ROUGH ON ME.
ALL NIGHT, DAMMIT.
LOOK, I HAVE BRUISES AND STUFF. EVEN AROUND MY NECK. YOU'RE SOME KIND OF FREAK.
AREN'T YOU AT LEAST GOING TO SAY YOU'RE SORRY?
NO. WHATEVER. I HAVE TO GO. I MIGHT CALL YOU LATER.
GOD, HE'S PERFECT.

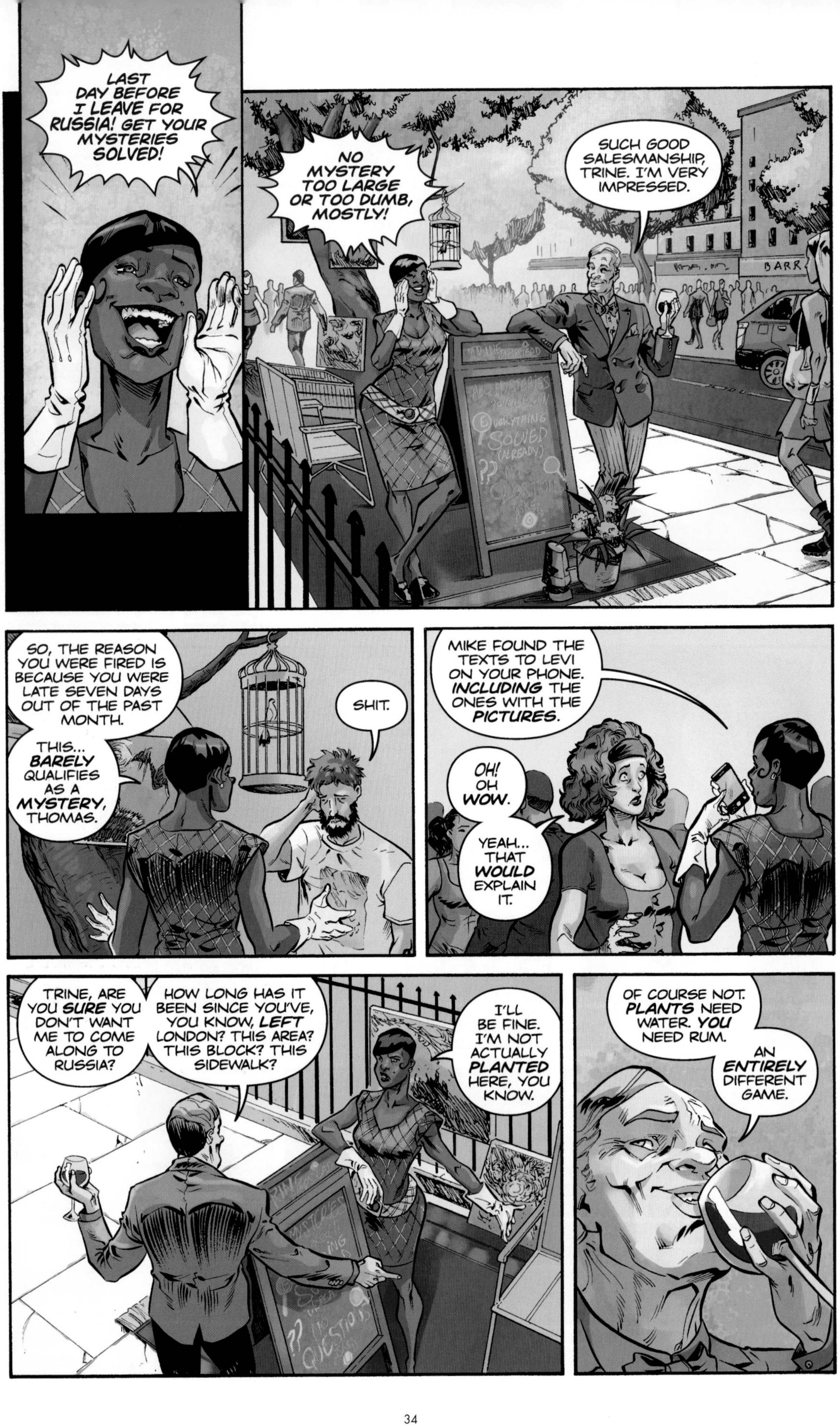
LAST DAY BEFORE I LEAVE FOR RUSSIA! GET YOUR MYSTERIES SOLVED!
NO MYSTERY TOO LARGE OR TOO DUMB, MOSTLY!
SUCH GOOD SALESMANSHIP, TRINE. I'M VERY IMPRESSED.
SO, THE REASON YOU WERE FIRED IS BECAUSE YOU WERE LATE SEVEN DAYS OUT OF THE PAST MONTH.
THIS... BARELY QUALIFIES AS A MYSTERY, THOMAS.
SHIT.
MIKE FOUND THE TEXTS TO LEVI ON YOUR PHONE. INCLUDING THE ONES WITH THE PICTURES.
OH! OH WOW.
YEAH... THAT WOULD EXPLAIN IT.
TRINE, ARE YOU SURE YOU DON'T WANT ME TO COME ALONG TO RUSSIA?
HOW LONG HAS IT BEEN SINCE YOU'VE, YOU KNOW, LEFT LONDON? THIS AREA? THIS BLOCK? THIS SIDEWALK?
I'LL BE FINE. I'M NOT ACTUALLY PLANTED HERE, YOU KNOW.
OF COURSE NOT. PLANTS NEED WATER. YOU NEED RUM.
AN ENTIRELY DIFFERENT GAME.

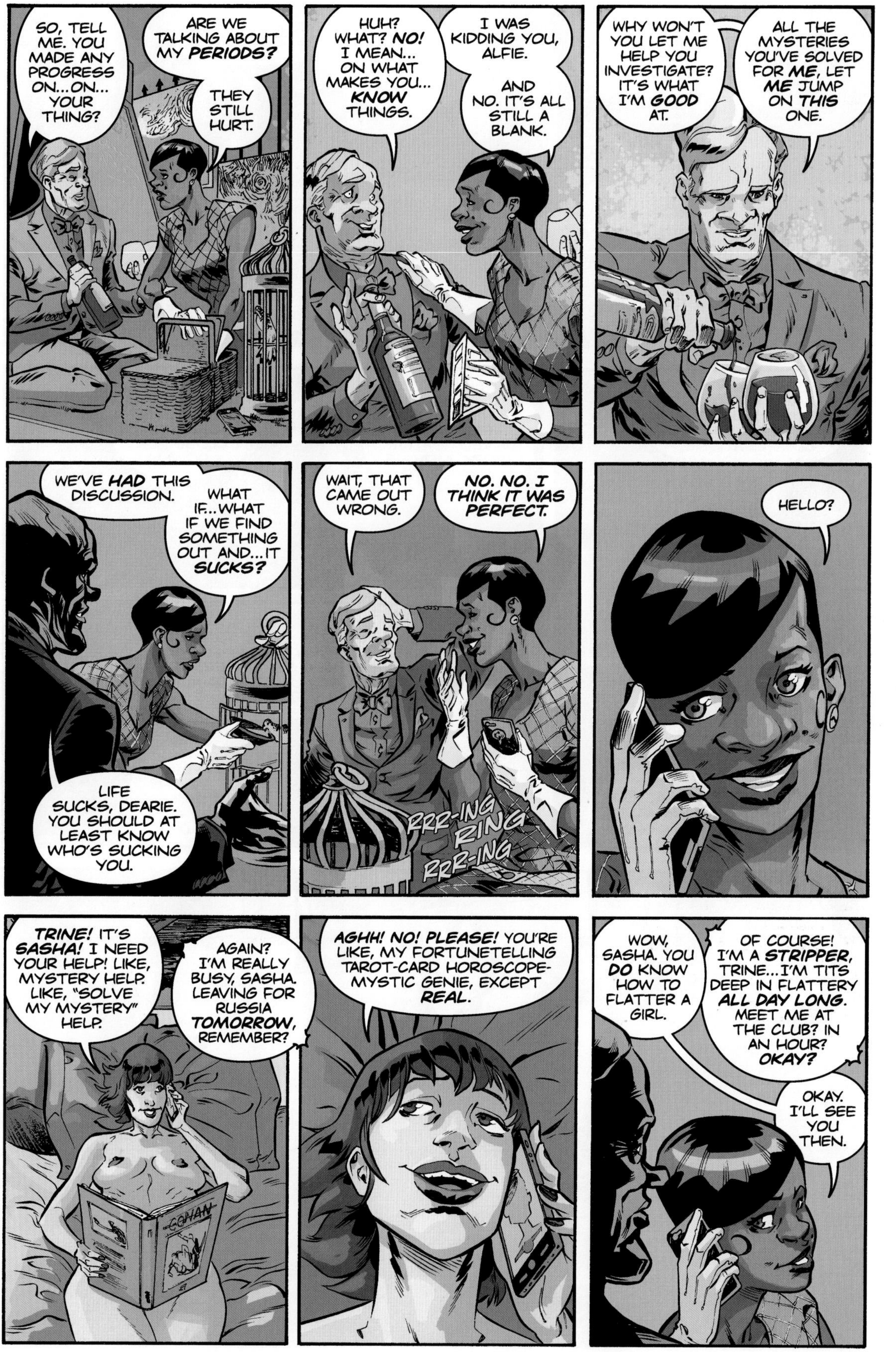
SO, TELL ME. YOU MADE ANY PROGRESS ON...ON... YOUR THING?
ARE WE TALKING ABOUT MY PERIODS?
THEY STILL HURT.
HUH? WHAT? NO! I MEAN... ON WHAT MAKES YOU... KNOW THINGS.
I WAS KIDDING YOU, ALFIE.
AND NO. IT'S ALL STILL A BLANK.
WHY WON'T YOU LET ME HELP YOU INVESTIGATE? IT'S WHAT I'M GOOD AT.
ALL THE MYSTERIES YOU'VE SOLVED FOR ME, LET ME JUMP ON THIS ONE.
WE'VE HAD THIS DISCUSSION.
WHAT IF...WHAT IF WE FIND SOMETHING OUT AND...IT SUCKS?
LIFE SUCKS, DEARIE. YOU SHOULD AT LEAST KNOW WHO'S SUCKING YOU.
WAIT, THAT CAME OUT WRONG.
NO. NO. I THINK IT WAS PERFECT.
RRR-ING RING RRR-ING
HELLO?
TRINE! IT'S SASHA! I NEED YOUR HELP! LIKE, MYSTERY HELP. LIKE, "SOLVE MY MYSTERY" HELP.
AGAIN? I'M REALLY BUSY, SASHA. LEAVING FOR RUSSIA TOMORROW, REMEMBER?
CONAN
AGHH! NO! PLEASE! YOU'RE LIKE, MY FORTUNETELLING TAROT-CARD HOROSCOPE-MYSTIC GENIE, EXCEPT REAL.
WOW, SASHA. YOU DO KNOW HOW TO FLATTER A GIRL.
OF COURSE! I'M A STRIPPER, TRINE...I'M TITS DEEP IN FLATTERY ALL DAY LONG. MEET ME AT THE CLUB? IN AN HOUR? OKAY?
OKAY. I'LL SEE YOU THEN.

Elsewhere.

WHAT I DON'T SEE IS WHY YOU CARE ABOUT MAMMOTHS.

YOU DON'T NEED TO SEE. AND I DON'T CARE ABOUT MAMMOTHS.

THERE'S A...WELL, IT'S COMPLICATED.

ANYWAY, NOW THAT WE HAVE THE JOURNALS, I DON'T WANT THAT WOMAN CAUSING ANY COMPLICATIONS.

YOU SHOULD. COMPLICATIONS ARE INTERESTING.

AND SOME OF WHAT I'VE BEEN HEARING ABOUT THIS TRINE WOMAN...

WELL, LET'S JUST SAY I'VE BEEN DOING SOME PRELIMINARY INVESTIGATIVE WORK, MOVING CLOSER TO TRINE.

I DON'T NEED YOU TO MOVE CLOSER. I NEED YOU TO CLOSE HER DOWN.

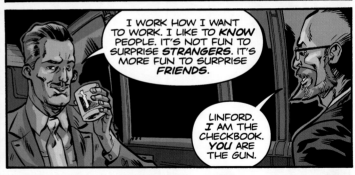

I WORK HOW I WANT TO WORK. I LIKE TO KNOW PEOPLE. IT'S NOT FUN TO SURPRISE STRANGERS. IT'S MORE FUN TO SURPRISE FRIENDS.

LINFORD. I AM THE CHECKBOOK. YOU ARE THE GUN.

WE HAVE THE JOURNALS. WE DON'T NEED THE WOMAN.

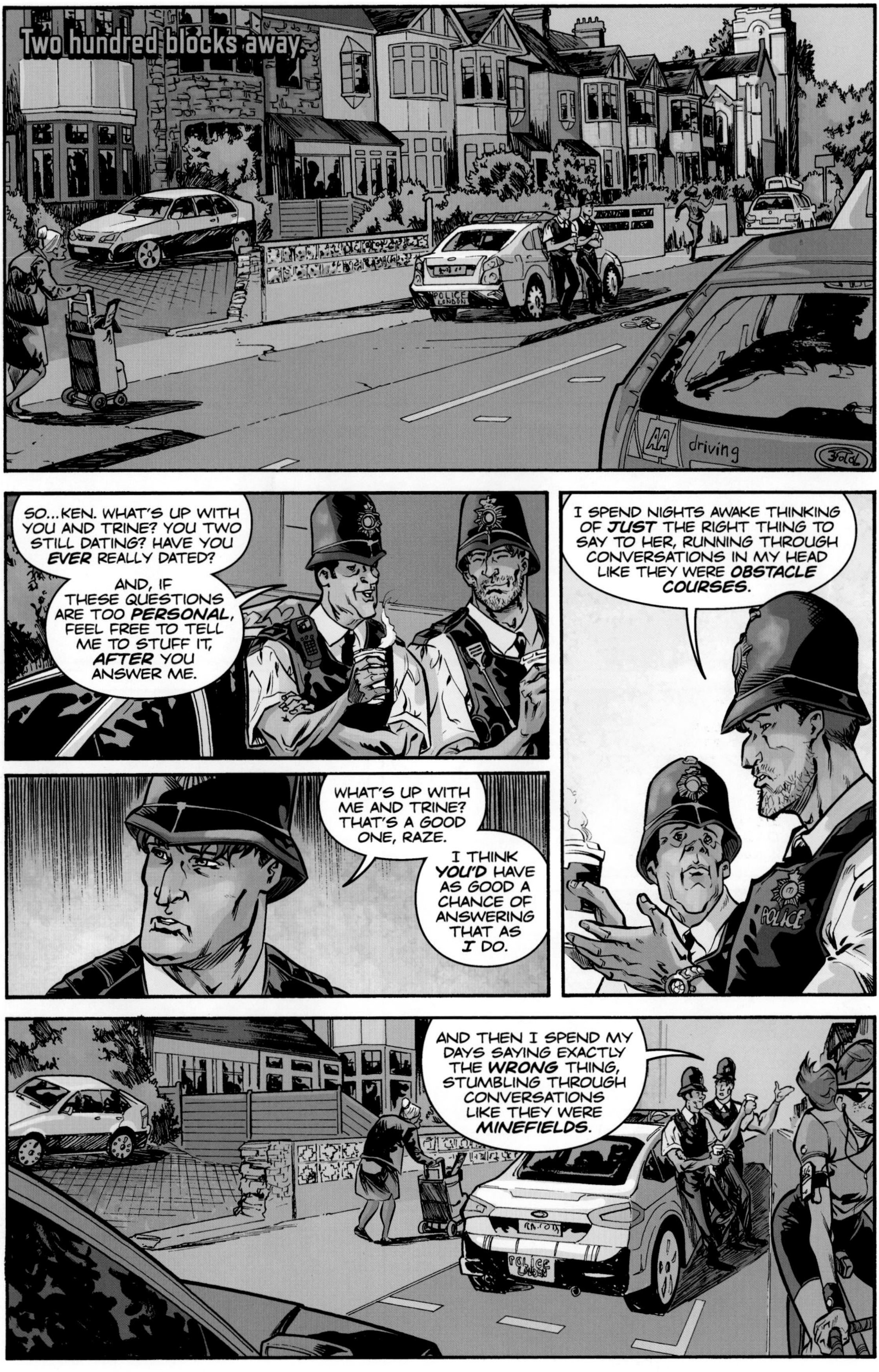
Two hundred blocks away.
driving
SO...KEN. WHAT'S UP WITH YOU AND TRINE? YOU TWO STILL DATING? HAVE YOU EVER REALLY DATED?
AND, IF THESE QUESTIONS ARE TOO PERSONAL, FEEL FREE TO TELL ME TO STUFF IT, AFTER YOU ANSWER ME.
WHAT'S UP WITH ME AND TRINE? THAT'S A GOOD ONE, RAZE.
I THINK YOU'D HAVE AS GOOD A CHANCE OF ANSWERING THAT AS I DO.
I SPEND NIGHTS AWAKE THINKING OF JUST THE RIGHT THING TO SAY TO HER, RUNNING THROUGH CONVERSATIONS IN MY HEAD LIKE THEY WERE OBSTACLE COURSES.
POLICE
AND THEN I SPEND MY DAYS SAYING EXACTLY THE WRONG THING, STUMBLING THROUGH CONVERSATIONS LIKE THEY WERE MINEFIELDS.

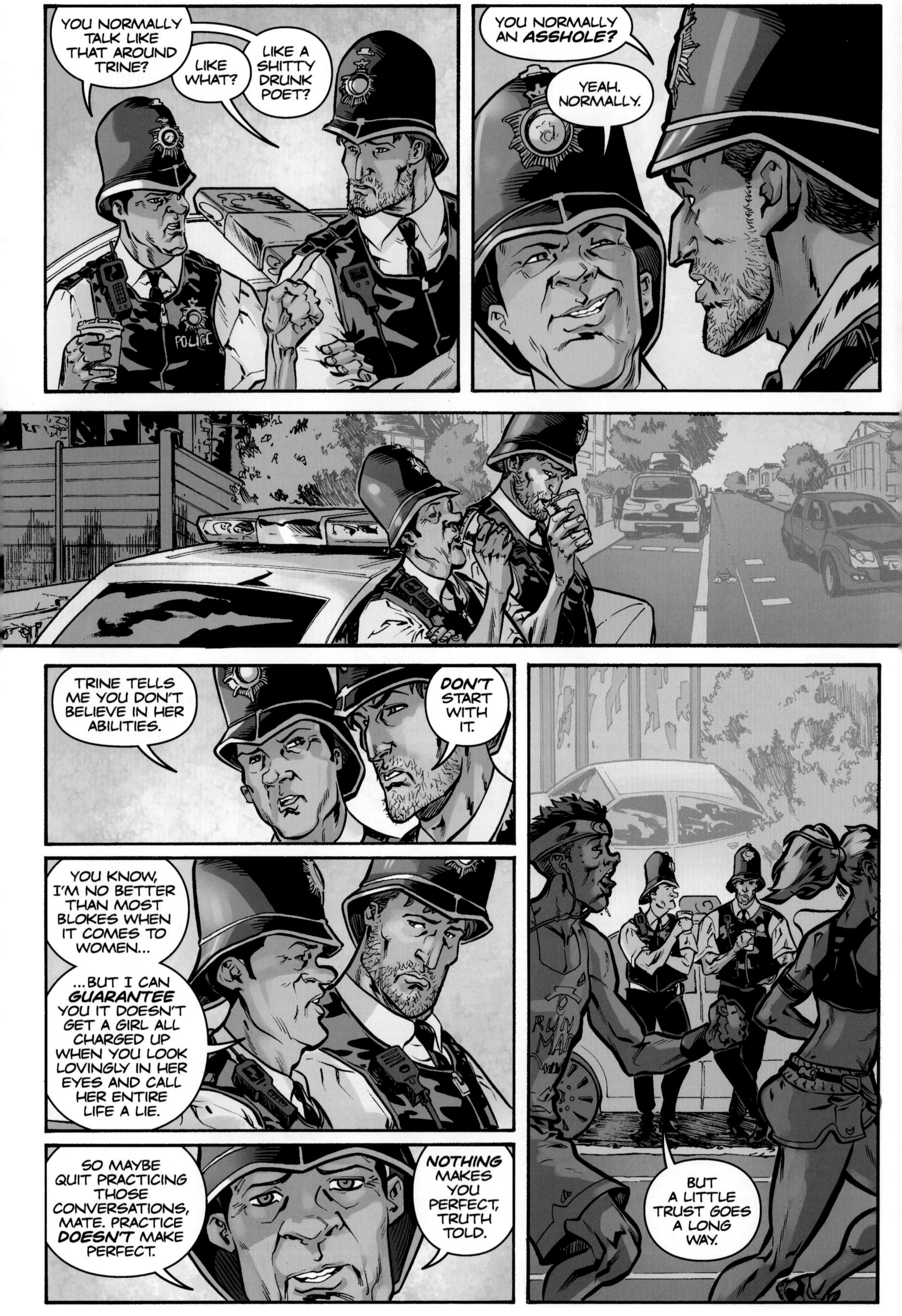
YOU NORMALLY TALK LIKE THAT AROUND TRINE?
LIKE WHAT?
LIKE A SHITTY DRUNK POET?
POLICE
YOU NORMALLY AN ASSHOLE?
YEAH. NORMALLY.
TRINE TELLS ME YOU DON'T BELIEVE IN HER ABILITIES.
DON'T START WITH IT.
YOU KNOW, I'M NO BETTER THAN MOST BLOKES WHEN IT COMES TO WOMEN...
...BUT I CAN GUARANTEE YOU IT DOESN'T GET A GIRL ALL CHARGED UP WHEN YOU LOOK LOVINGLY IN HER EYES AND CALL HER ENTIRE LIFE A LIE.
SO MAYBE QUIT PRACTICING THOSE CONVERSATIONS, MATE. PRACTICE DOESN'T MAKE PERFECT.
NOTHING MAKES YOU PERFECT, TRUTH TOLD.
BUT A LITTLE TRUST GOES A LONG WAY.

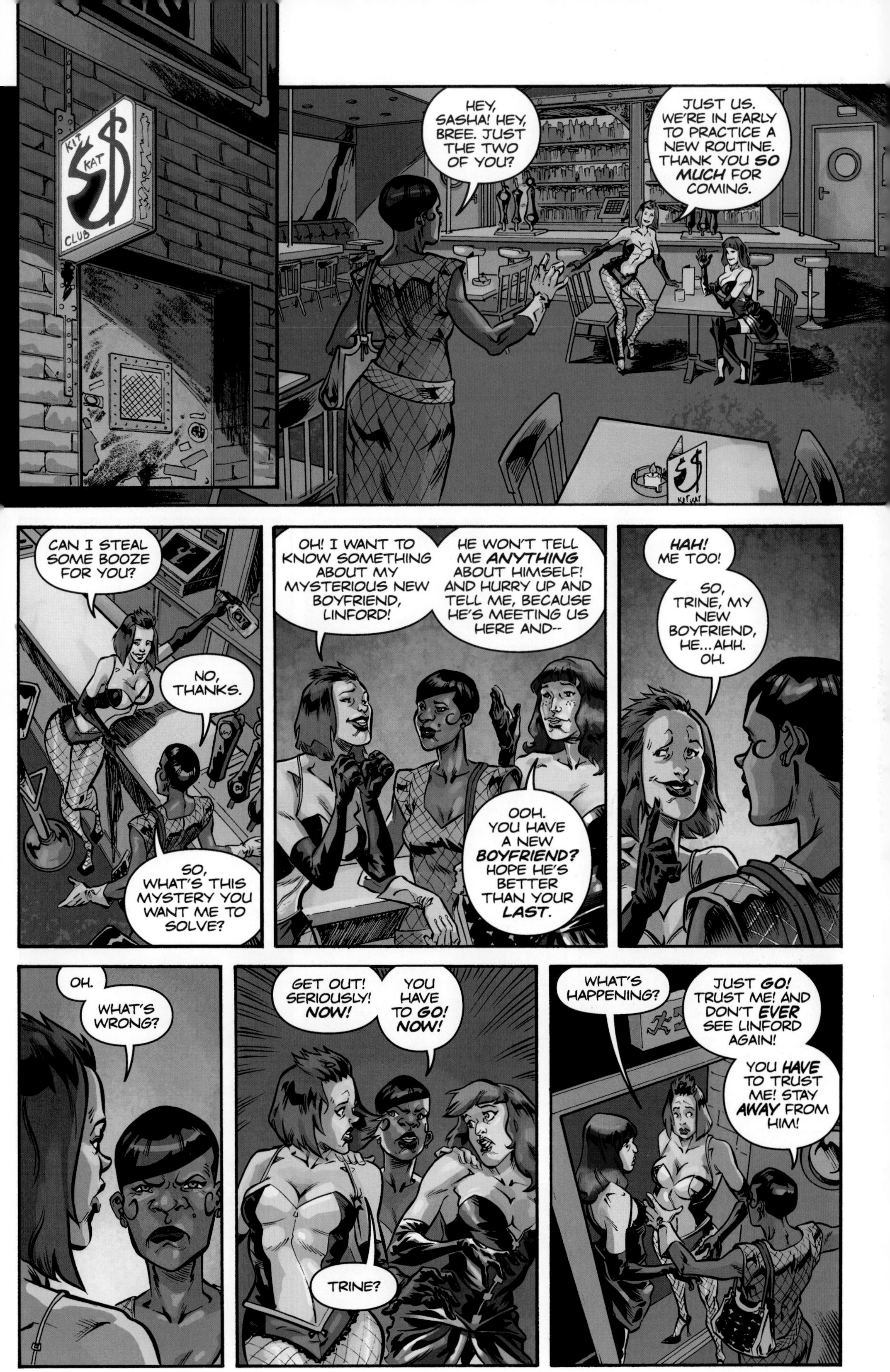
KIT KAT CLUB
HEY, SASHA! HEY, BREE. JUST THE TWO OF YOU?
JUST US. WE'RE IN EARLY TO PRACTICE A NEW ROUTINE. THANK YOU **SO MUCH** FOR COMING.
CAN I STEAL SOME BOOZE FOR YOU?
NO, THANKS.
SO, WHAT'S THIS MYSTERY YOU WANT ME TO SOLVE?
OH! I WANT TO KNOW SOMETHING ABOUT MY MYSTERIOUS NEW BOYFRIEND, LINFORD!
HE WON'T TELL ME **ANYTHING** ABOUT HIMSELF! AND HURRY UP AND TELL ME, BECAUSE HE'S MEETING US HERE AND--
OOH. YOU HAVE A NEW **BOYFRIEND?** HOPE HE'S BETTER THAN YOUR **LAST**.
HAH! ME TOO!
SO, TRINE, MY NEW BOYFRIEND, HE...AHH. OH.
OH.
WHAT'S WRONG?
GET OUT! SERIOUSLY! **NOW!**
YOU HAVE TO **GO! NOW!**
TRINE?
WHAT'S HAPPENING?
JUST **GO!** TRUST ME! AND DON'T **EVER** SEE LINFORD AGAIN!
YOU **HAVE** TO TRUST ME! STAY **AWAY** FROM HIM!

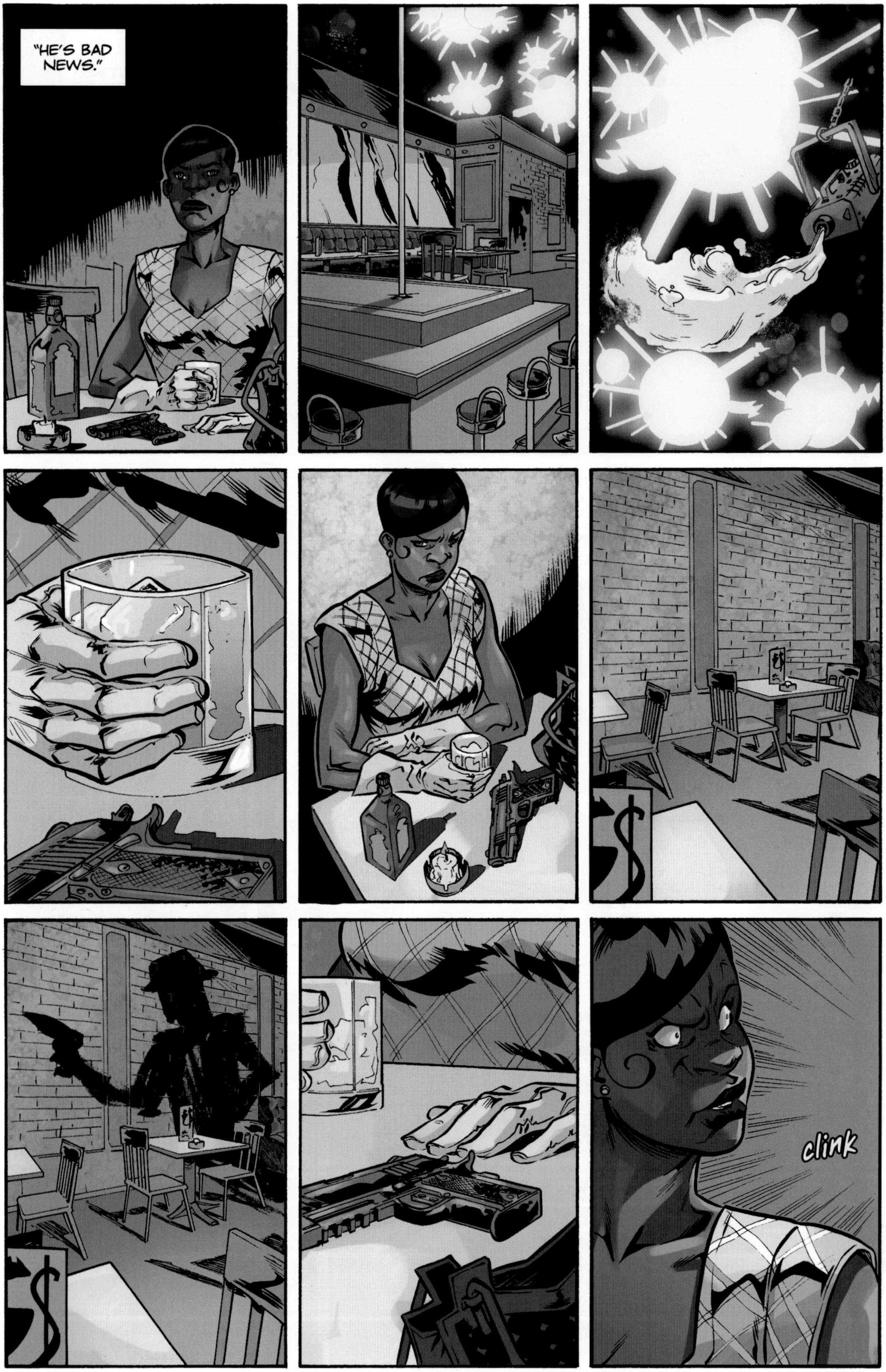
"HE'S BAD NEWS."
clink

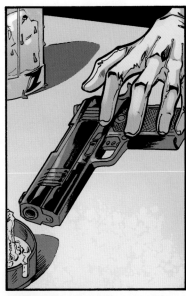

CREAAAAAK

TOKK

clink

COME OUT, LINFORD.

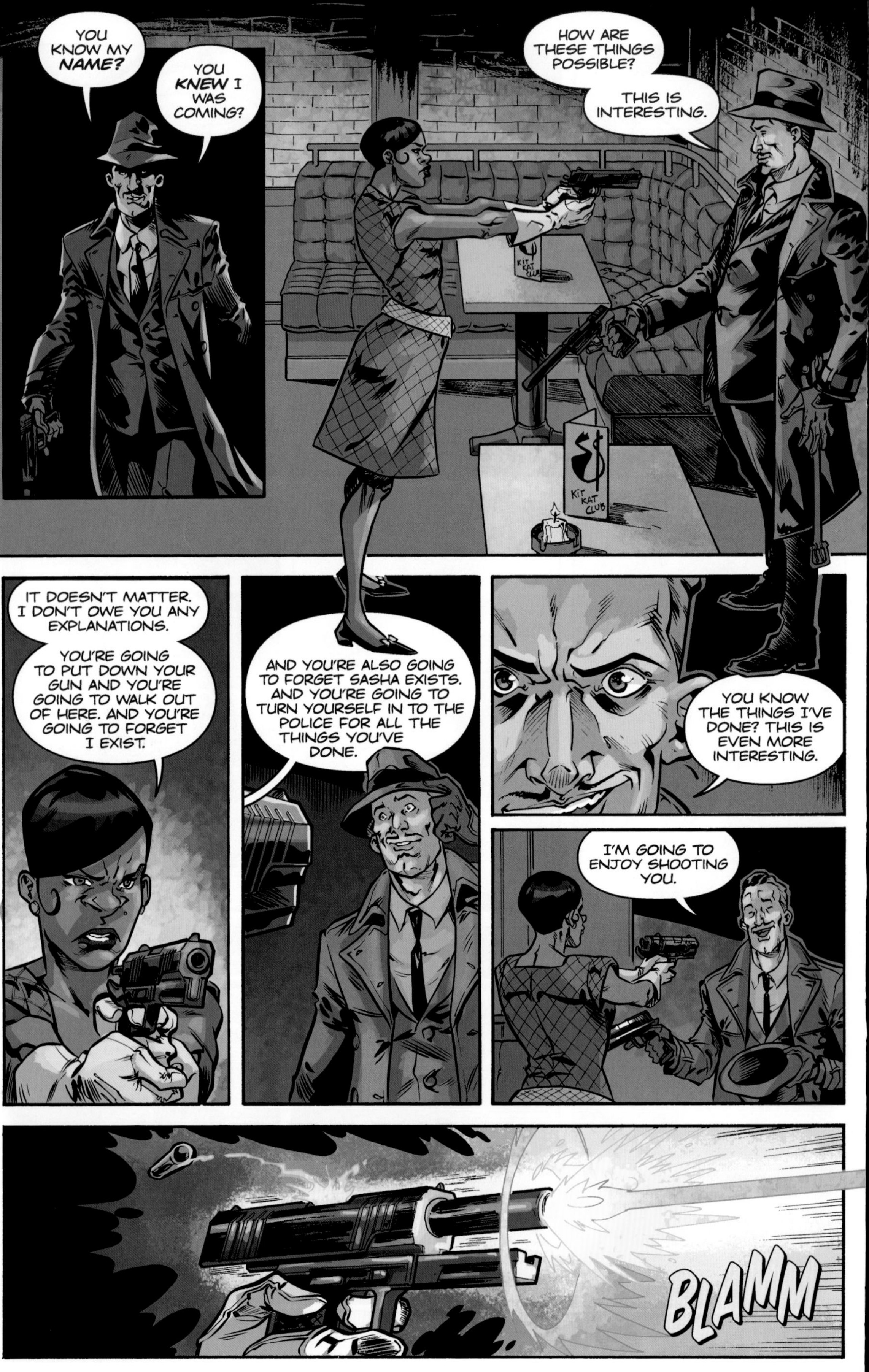
YOU KNOW MY NAME?
YOU KNEW I WAS COMING?
HOW ARE THESE THINGS POSSIBLE?
THIS IS INTERESTING.
KIT KAT CLUB
KIT KAT CLUB
IT DOESN'T MATTER. I DON'T OWE YOU ANY EXPLANATIONS.
YOU'RE GOING TO PUT DOWN YOUR GUN AND YOU'RE GOING TO WALK OUT OF HERE. AND YOU'RE GOING TO FORGET I EXIST.
AND YOU'RE ALSO GOING TO FORGET SASHA EXISTS. AND YOU'RE GOING TO TURN YOURSELF IN TO THE POLICE FOR ALL THE THINGS YOU'VE DONE.
YOU KNOW THE THINGS I'VE DONE? THIS IS EVEN MORE INTERESTING.
I'M GOING TO ENJOY SHOOTING YOU.
BLAMM

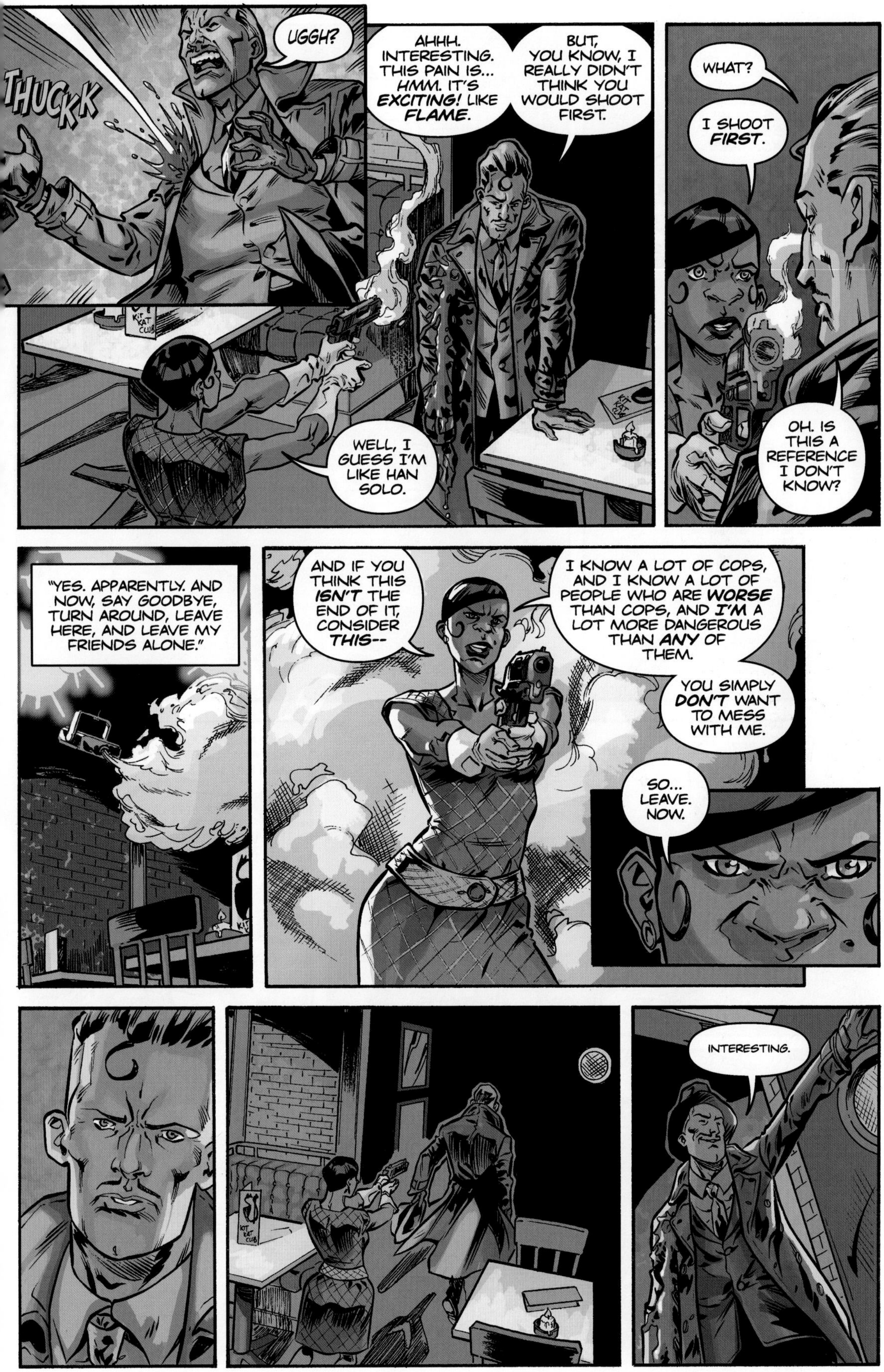
THUCKK
UGGH?
AHHH. INTERESTING. THIS PAIN IS... HMM. IT'S EXCITING! LIKE FLAME.
BUT, YOU KNOW, I REALLY DIDN'T THINK YOU WOULD SHOOT FIRST.
KIT KAT CLUB
WELL, I GUESS I'M LIKE HAN SOLO.
WHAT?
I SHOOT FIRST.
OH. IS THIS A REFERENCE I DON'T KNOW?
"YES. APPARENTLY. AND NOW, SAY GOODBYE, TURN AROUND, LEAVE HERE, AND LEAVE MY FRIENDS ALONE."
AND IF YOU THINK THIS ISN'T THE END OF IT, CONSIDER THIS--
I KNOW A LOT OF COPS, AND I KNOW A LOT OF PEOPLE WHO ARE WORSE THAN COPS, AND I'M A LOT MORE DANGEROUS THAN ANY OF THEM.
YOU SIMPLY DON'T WANT TO MESS WITH ME.
SO... LEAVE. NOW.
KIT KAT CLUB
INTERESTING.

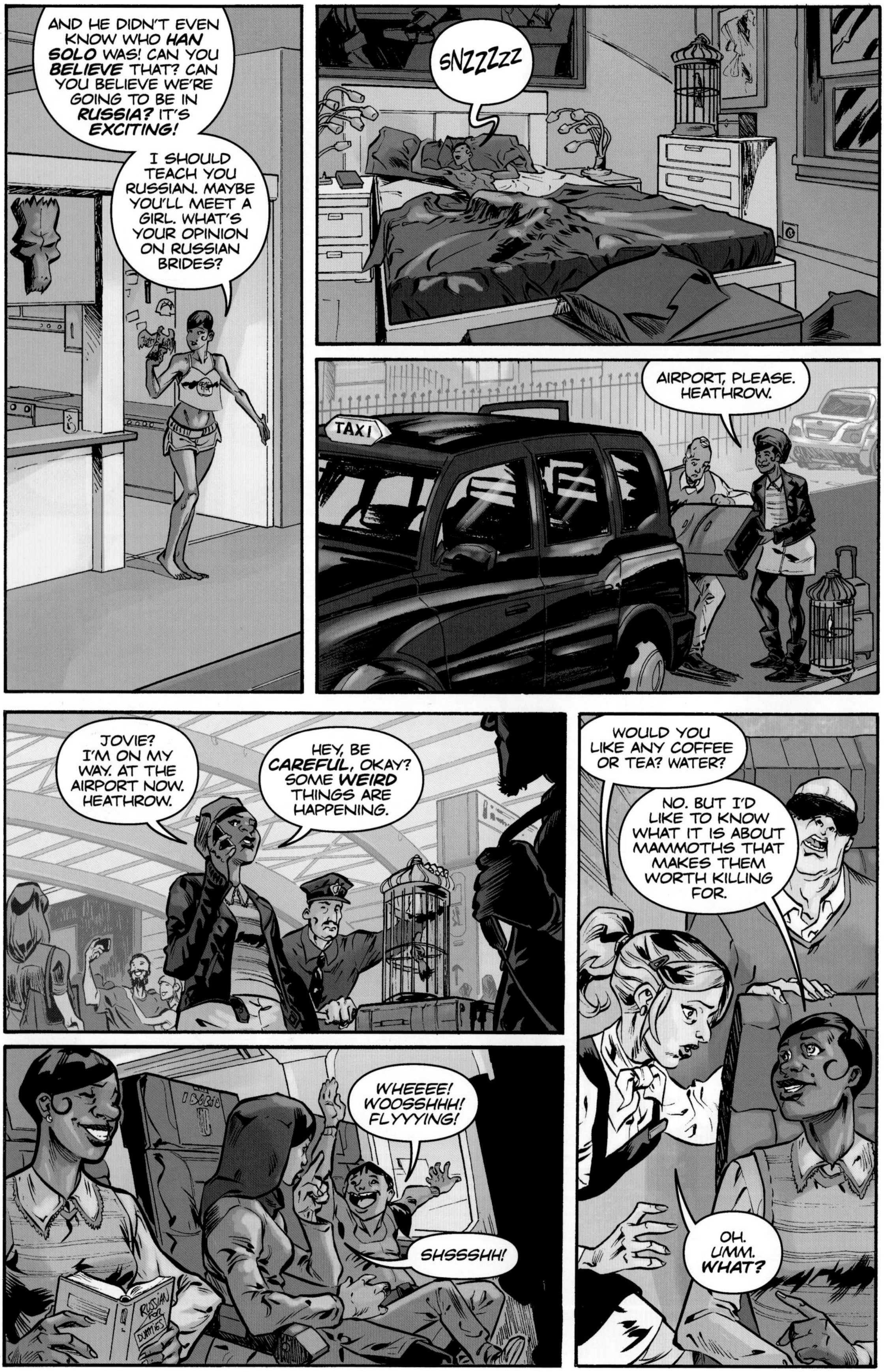
AND HE DIDN'T EVEN KNOW WHO HAN SOLO WAS! CAN YOU BELIEVE THAT? CAN YOU BELIEVE WE'RE GOING TO BE IN RUSSIA? IT'S EXCITING!
I SHOULD TEACH YOU RUSSIAN. MAYBE YOU'LL MEET A GIRL. WHAT'S YOUR OPINION ON RUSSIAN BRIDES?
SNZZZzz
AIRPORT, PLEASE. HEATHROW.
TAXI
JOVIE? I'M ON MY WAY. AT THE AIRPORT NOW. HEATHROW.
HEY, BE CAREFUL, OKAY? SOME WEIRD THINGS ARE HAPPENING.
WOULD YOU LIKE ANY COFFEE OR TEA? WATER?
NO. BUT I'D LIKE TO KNOW WHAT IT IS ABOUT MAMMOTHS THAT MAKES THEM WORTH KILLING FOR.
WHEEEE! WOOSSHHH! FLYYYING!
SHSSSHH!
OH. UMM. WHAT?

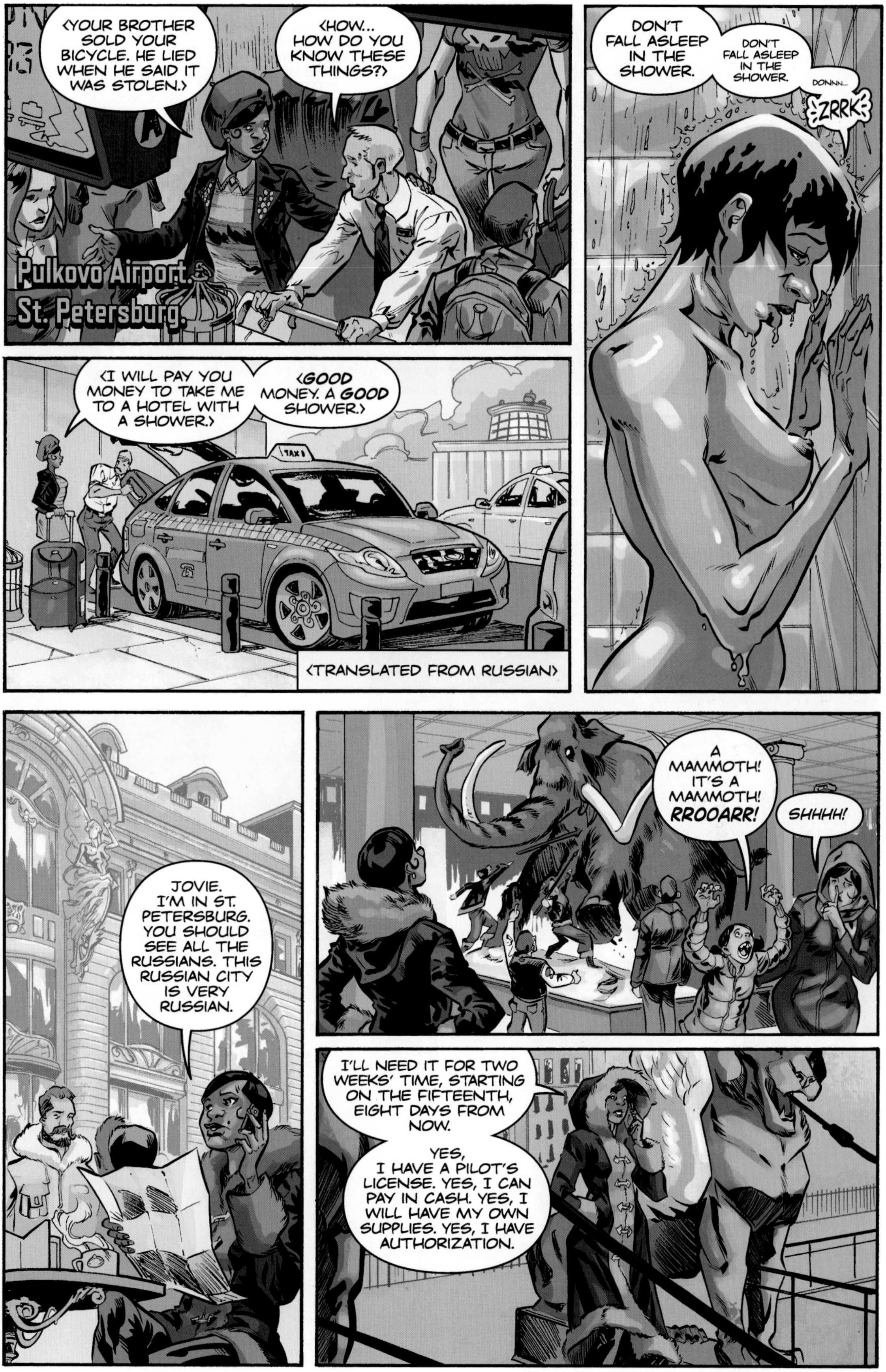
‹YOUR BROTHER SOLD YOUR BICYCLE. HE LIED WHEN HE SAID IT WAS STOLEN.›
‹HOW... HOW DO YOU KNOW THESE THINGS?›
Pulkovo Airport. St. Petersburg.
DON'T FALL ASLEEP IN THE SHOWER.
DON'T FALL ASLEEP IN THE SHOWER.
DONNN...
ZRRK
‹I WILL PAY YOU MONEY TO TAKE ME TO A HOTEL WITH A SHOWER.›
‹GOOD MONEY. A GOOD SHOWER.›
TAXI
‹TRANSLATED FROM RUSSIAN›
JOVIE. I'M IN ST. PETERSBURG. YOU SHOULD SEE ALL THE RUSSIANS. THIS RUSSIAN CITY IS VERY RUSSIAN.
A MAMMOTH! IT'S A MAMMOTH! RROOARR!
SHHHH!
I'LL NEED IT FOR TWO WEEKS' TIME, STARTING ON THE FIFTEENTH, EIGHT DAYS FROM NOW.
YES, I HAVE A PILOT'S LICENSE. YES, I CAN PAY IN CASH. YES, I WILL HAVE MY OWN SUPPLIES. YES, I HAVE AUTHORIZATION.

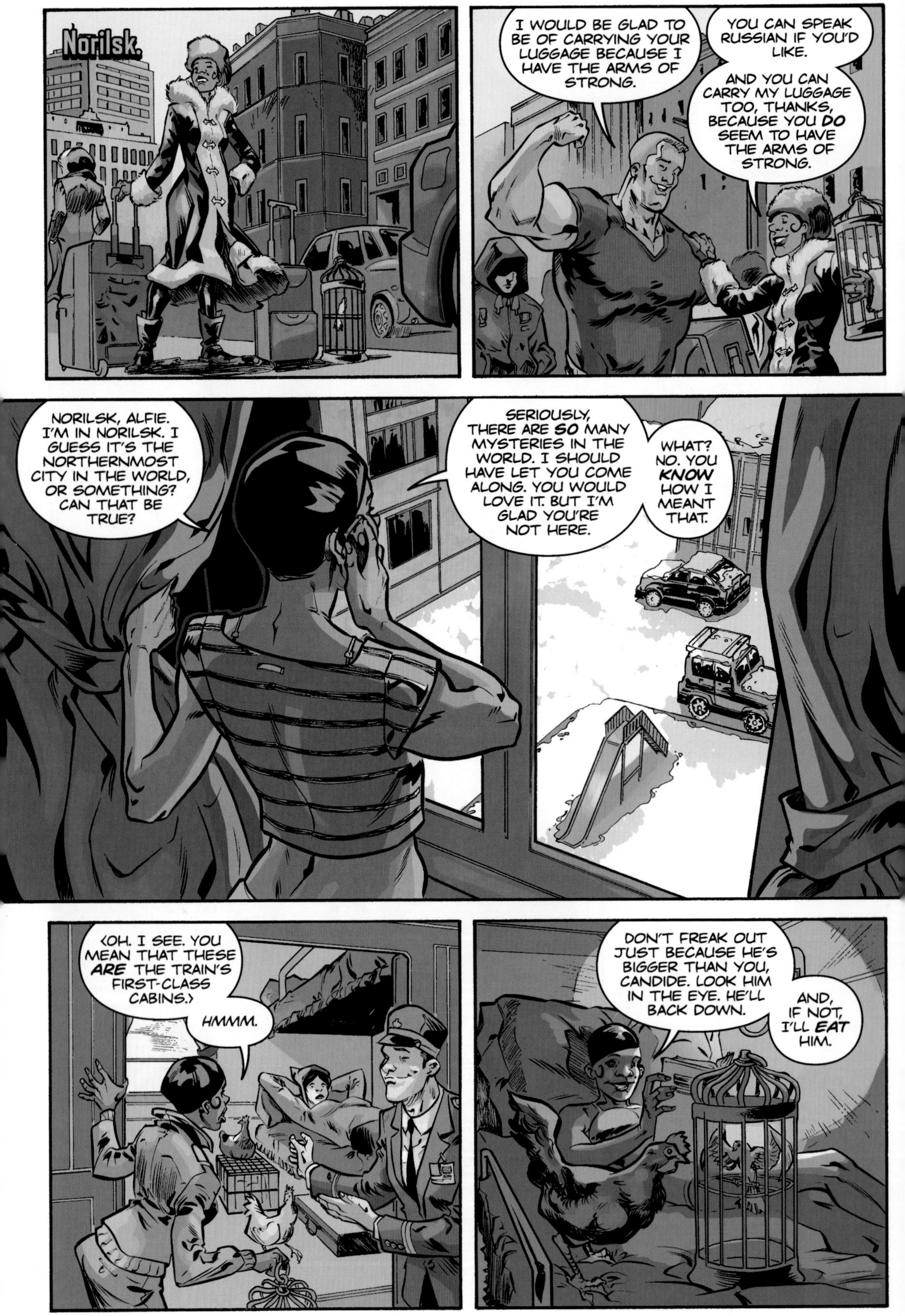

Norilsk.
I WOULD BE GLAD TO BE OF CARRYING YOUR LUGGAGE BECAUSE I HAVE THE ARMS OF STRONG.
YOU CAN SPEAK RUSSIAN IF YOU'D LIKE.
AND YOU CAN CARRY MY LUGGAGE TOO, THANKS, BECAUSE YOU DO SEEM TO HAVE THE ARMS OF STRONG.
NORILSK, ALFIE. I'M IN NORILSK. I GUESS IT'S THE NORTHERNMOST CITY IN THE WORLD, OR SOMETHING? CAN THAT BE TRUE?
SERIOUSLY, THERE ARE SO MANY MYSTERIES IN THE WORLD. I SHOULD HAVE LET YOU COME ALONG. YOU WOULD LOVE IT. BUT I'M GLAD YOU'RE NOT HERE.
WHAT? NO. YOU KNOW HOW I MEANT THAT.
<OH. I SEE. YOU MEAN THAT THESE ARE THE TRAIN'S FIRST-CLASS CABINS.>
HMMM.
DON'T FREAK OUT JUST BECAUSE HE'S BIGGER THAN YOU, CANDIDE. LOOK HIM IN THE EYE. HE'LL BACK DOWN.
AND, IF NOT, I'LL EAT HIM.

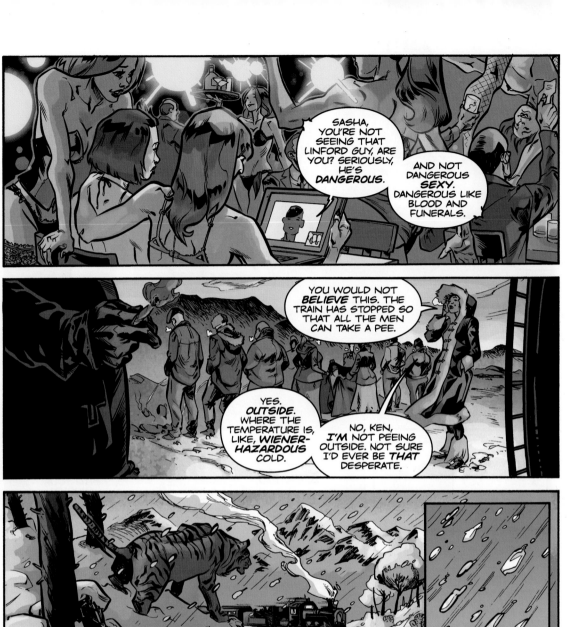

SASHA, YOU'RE NOT SEEING THAT LINFORD GUY, ARE YOU? SERIOUSLY, HE'S *DANGEROUS*.

AND NOT DANGEROUS *SEXY*. DANGEROUS LIKE BLOOD AND FUNERALS.

YOU WOULD NOT *BELIEVE* THIS. THE TRAIN HAS STOPPED SO THAT ALL THE MEN CAN TAKE A PEE.

YES. *OUTSIDE*. WHERE THE TEMPERATURE IS, LIKE, *WIENER-HAZARDOUS* COLD.

NO, KEN, *I'M* NOT PEEING OUTSIDE. NOT SURE I'D EVER BE *THAT* DESPERATE.

OH D-D-DAMN. OH IT'SsssO COLD.

OH S-SHIT, I HOPE YOU D-DON'T SPEAK ENGLISH. I HOPE Y-YOU DIDN'T UNDERsssSTAND THAT.

OH S-SHIT IT'S COLD.

TH-THANK YOU F-FOR HOLDING THE BLANKET.

THANK YOU T-T-THANK YOU OH DAMN IT'S SO C-COLD.

I FEEL L-LIKE I'M GOING REVERSE C-COWBOY ON A SssSNOWMAN!

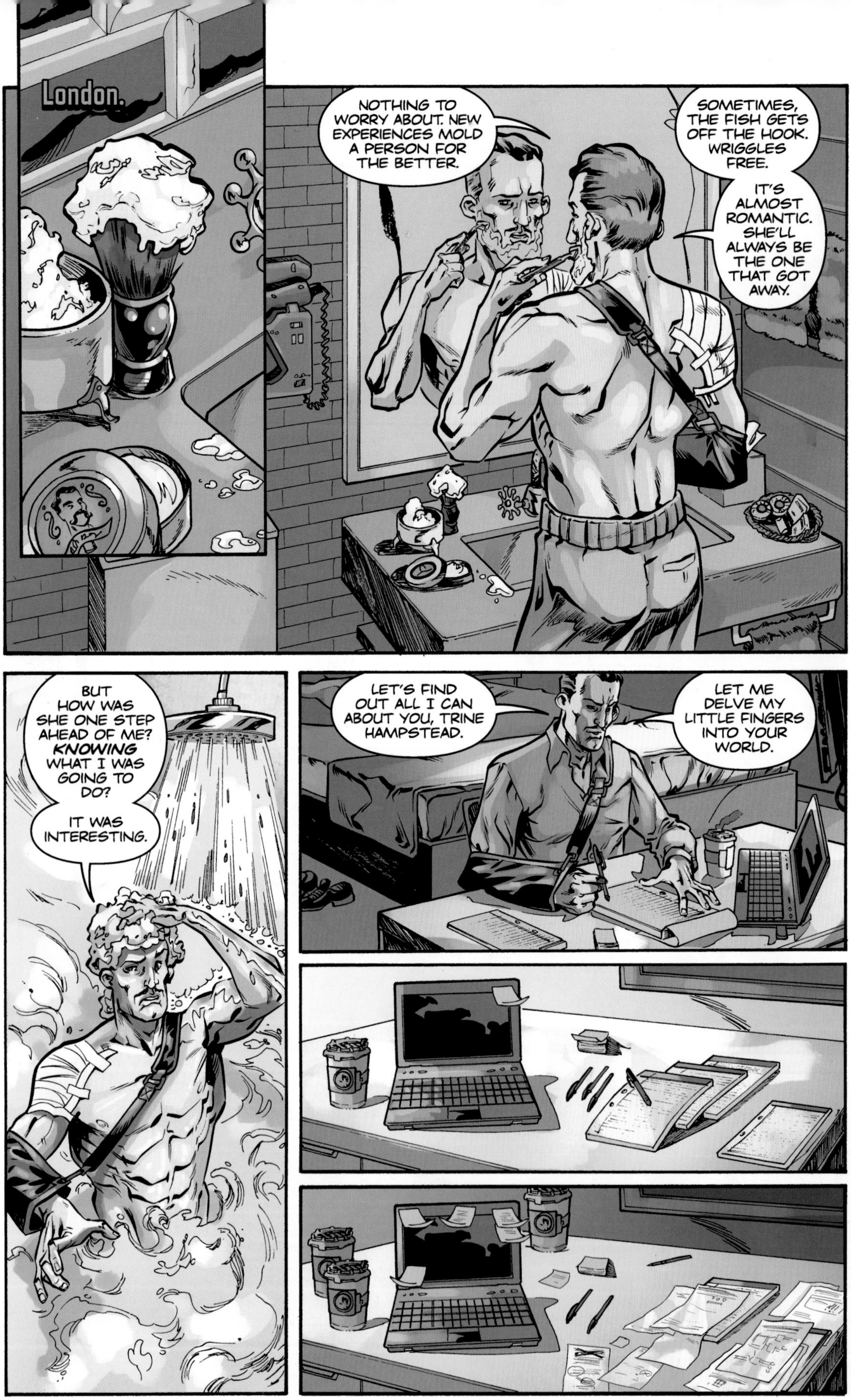
London.
NOTHING TO WORRY ABOUT. NEW EXPERIENCES MOLD A PERSON FOR THE BETTER.
SOMETIMES, THE FISH GETS OFF THE HOOK. WRIGGLES FREE.
IT'S ALMOST ROMANTIC. SHE'LL ALWAYS BE THE ONE THAT GOT AWAY.
BUT HOW WAS SHE ONE STEP AHEAD OF ME? *KNOWING* WHAT I WAS GOING TO DO?
IT WAS INTERESTING.
LET'S FIND OUT ALL I CAN ABOUT YOU, TRINE HAMPSTEAD.
LET ME DELVE MY LITTLE FINGERS INTO YOUR WORLD.

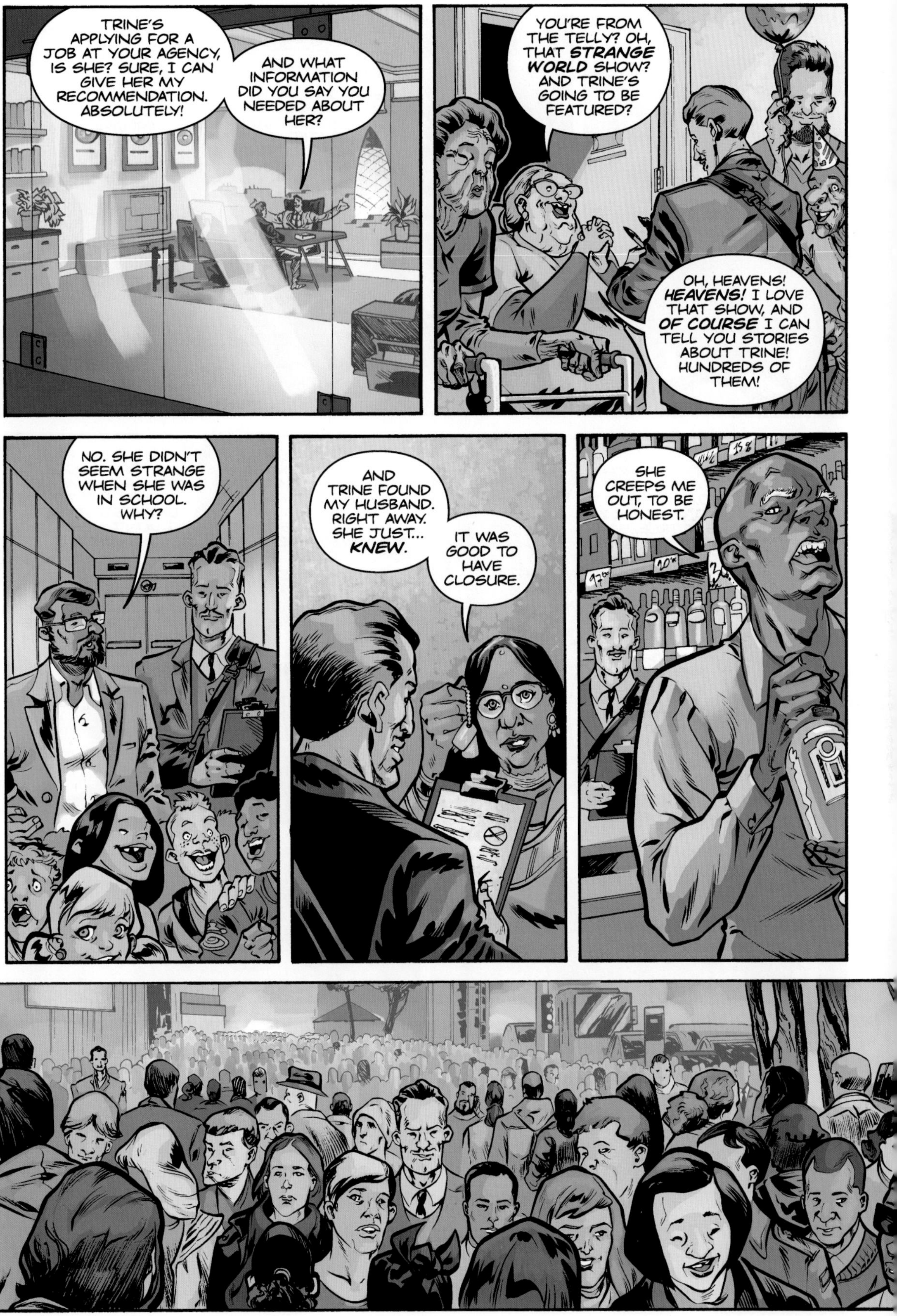
TRINE'S APPLYING FOR A JOB AT YOUR AGENCY, IS SHE? SURE, I CAN GIVE HER MY RECOMMENDATION. ABSOLUTELY!
AND WHAT INFORMATION DID YOU SAY YOU NEEDED ABOUT HER?
YOU'RE FROM THE TELLY? OH, THAT STRANGE WORLD SHOW? AND TRINE'S GOING TO BE FEATURED?
OH, HEAVENS! HEAVENS! I LOVE THAT SHOW, AND OF COURSE I CAN TELL YOU STORIES ABOUT TRINE! HUNDREDS OF THEM!
NO. SHE DIDN'T SEEM STRANGE WHEN SHE WAS IN SCHOOL. WHY?
AND TRINE FOUND MY HUSBAND. RIGHT AWAY. SHE JUST... KNEW.
IT WAS GOOD TO HAVE CLOSURE.
SHE CREEPS ME OUT, TO BE HONEST.

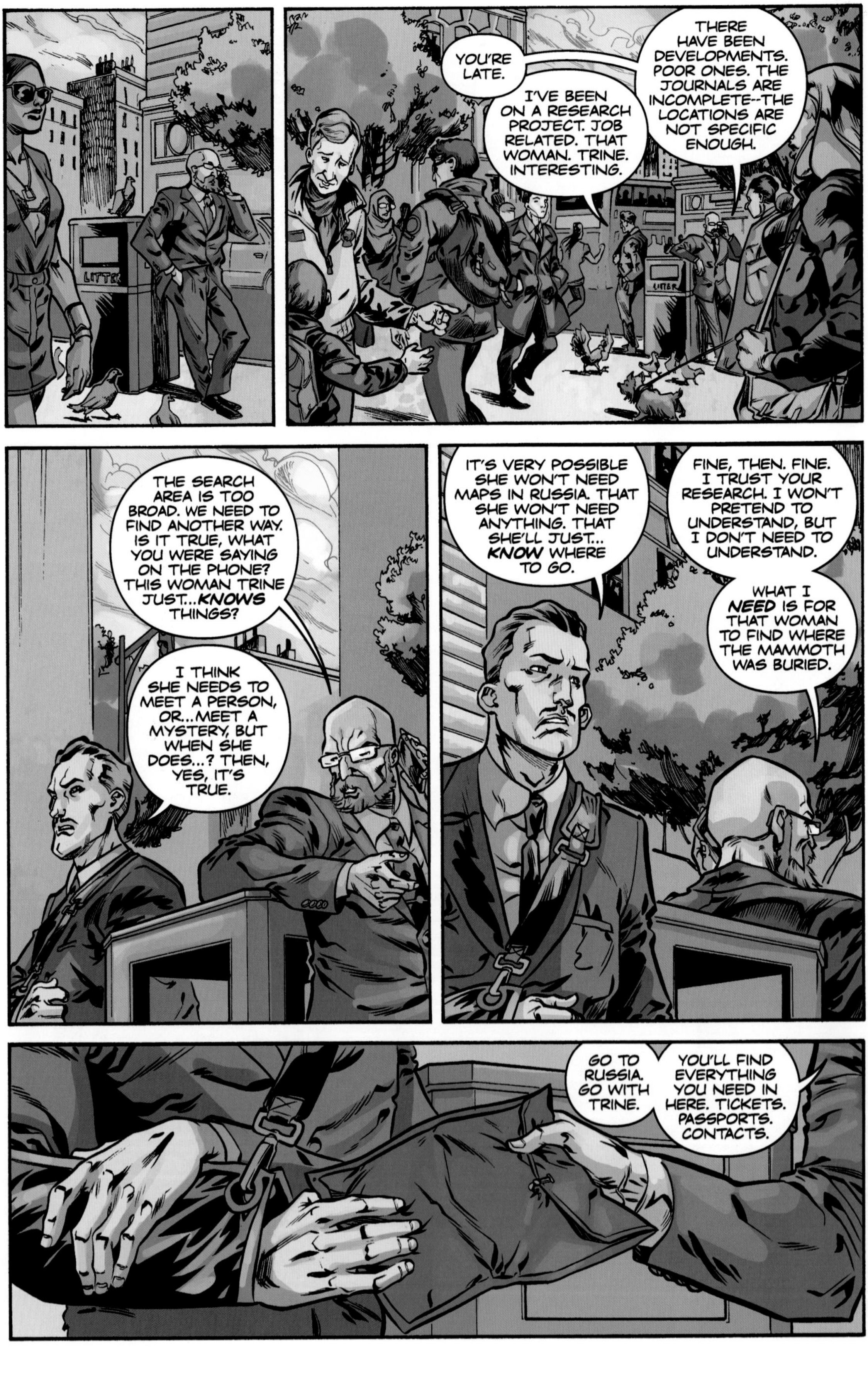
YOU'RE LATE.
I'VE BEEN ON A RESEARCH PROJECT. JOB RELATED. THAT WOMAN. TRINE. INTERESTING.
THERE HAVE BEEN DEVELOPMENTS. POOR ONES. THE JOURNALS ARE INCOMPLETE--THE LOCATIONS ARE NOT SPECIFIC ENOUGH.
LITTER
THE SEARCH AREA IS TOO BROAD. WE NEED TO FIND ANOTHER WAY. IS IT TRUE, WHAT YOU WERE SAYING ON THE PHONE? THIS WOMAN TRINE JUST...KNOWS THINGS?
I THINK SHE NEEDS TO MEET A PERSON, OR...MEET A MYSTERY, BUT WHEN SHE DOES...? THEN, YES, IT'S TRUE.
IT'S VERY POSSIBLE SHE WON'T NEED MAPS IN RUSSIA. THAT SHE WON'T NEED ANYTHING. THAT SHE'LL JUST... KNOW WHERE TO GO.
FINE, THEN. FINE. I TRUST YOUR RESEARCH. I WON'T PRETEND TO UNDERSTAND, BUT I DON'T NEED TO UNDERSTAND.
WHAT I NEED IS FOR THAT WOMAN TO FIND WHERE THE MAMMOTH WAS BURIED.
GO TO RUSSIA. GO WITH TRINE.
YOU'LL FIND EVERYTHING YOU NEED IN HERE. TICKETS. PASSPORTS. CONTACTS.

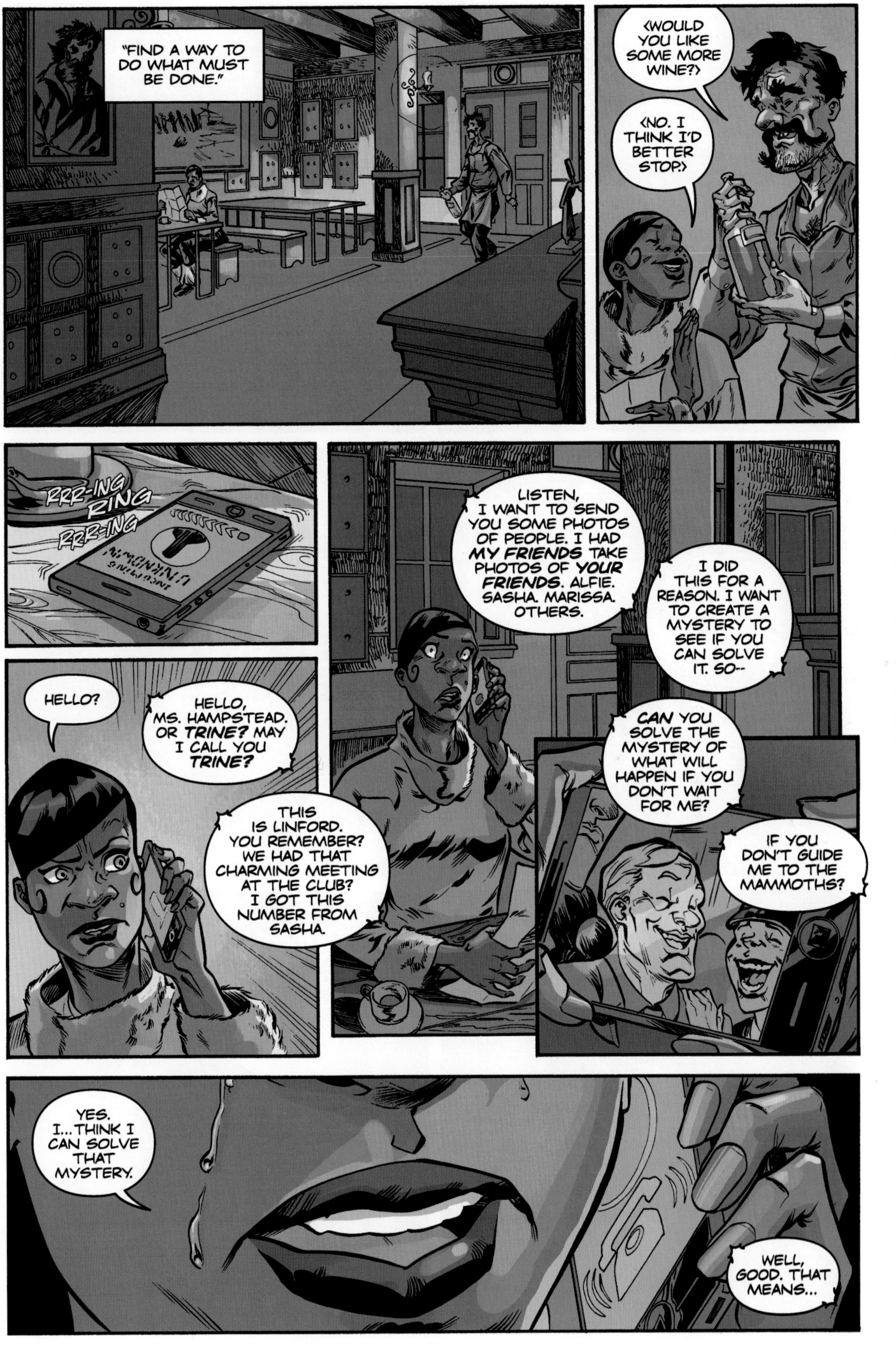
"FIND A WAY TO DO WHAT MUST BE DONE."
‹WOULD YOU LIKE SOME MORE WINE?›
‹NO. I THINK I'D BETTER STOP.›
RRR-ING RING RRR-ING
HELLO?
HELLO, MS. HAMPSTEAD. OR TRINE? MAY I CALL YOU TRINE?
THIS IS LINFORD. YOU REMEMBER? WE HAD THAT CHARMING MEETING AT THE CLUB? I GOT THIS NUMBER FROM SASHA.
LISTEN, I WANT TO SEND YOU SOME PHOTOS OF PEOPLE. I HAD MY FRIENDS TAKE PHOTOS OF YOUR FRIENDS. ALFIE. SASHA. MARISSA. OTHERS.
I DID THIS FOR A REASON. I WANT TO CREATE A MYSTERY TO SEE IF YOU CAN SOLVE IT. SO--
CAN YOU SOLVE THE MYSTERY OF WHAT WILL HAPPEN IF YOU DON'T WAIT FOR ME?
IF YOU DON'T GUIDE ME TO THE MAMMOTHS?
YES. I...THINK I CAN SOLVE THAT MYSTERY.
WELL, GOOD. THAT MEANS...

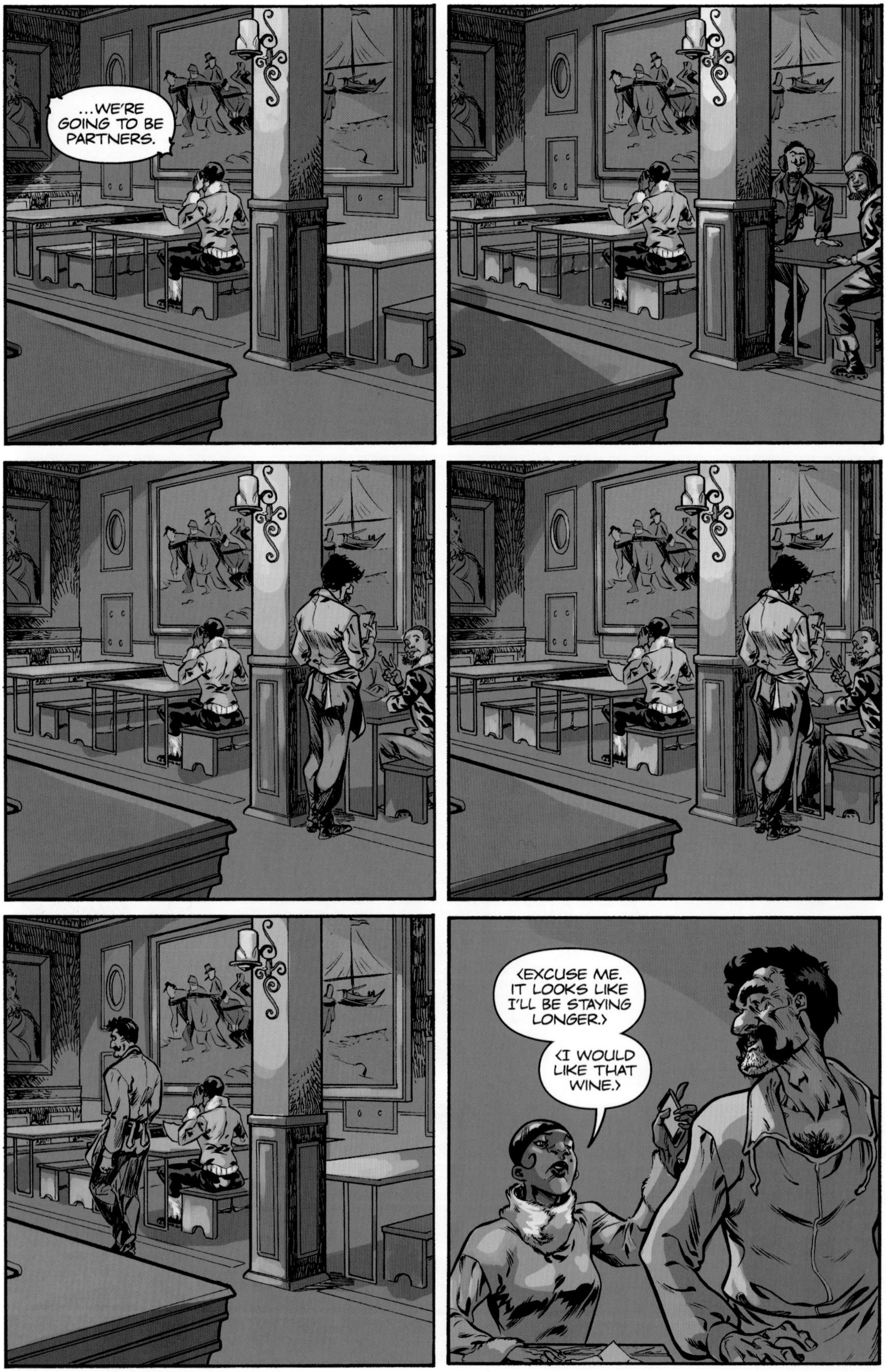
...WE'RE GOING TO BE PARTNERS.
<EXCUSE ME. IT LOOKS LIKE I'LL BE STAYING LONGER.>
<I WOULD LIKE THAT WINE.>

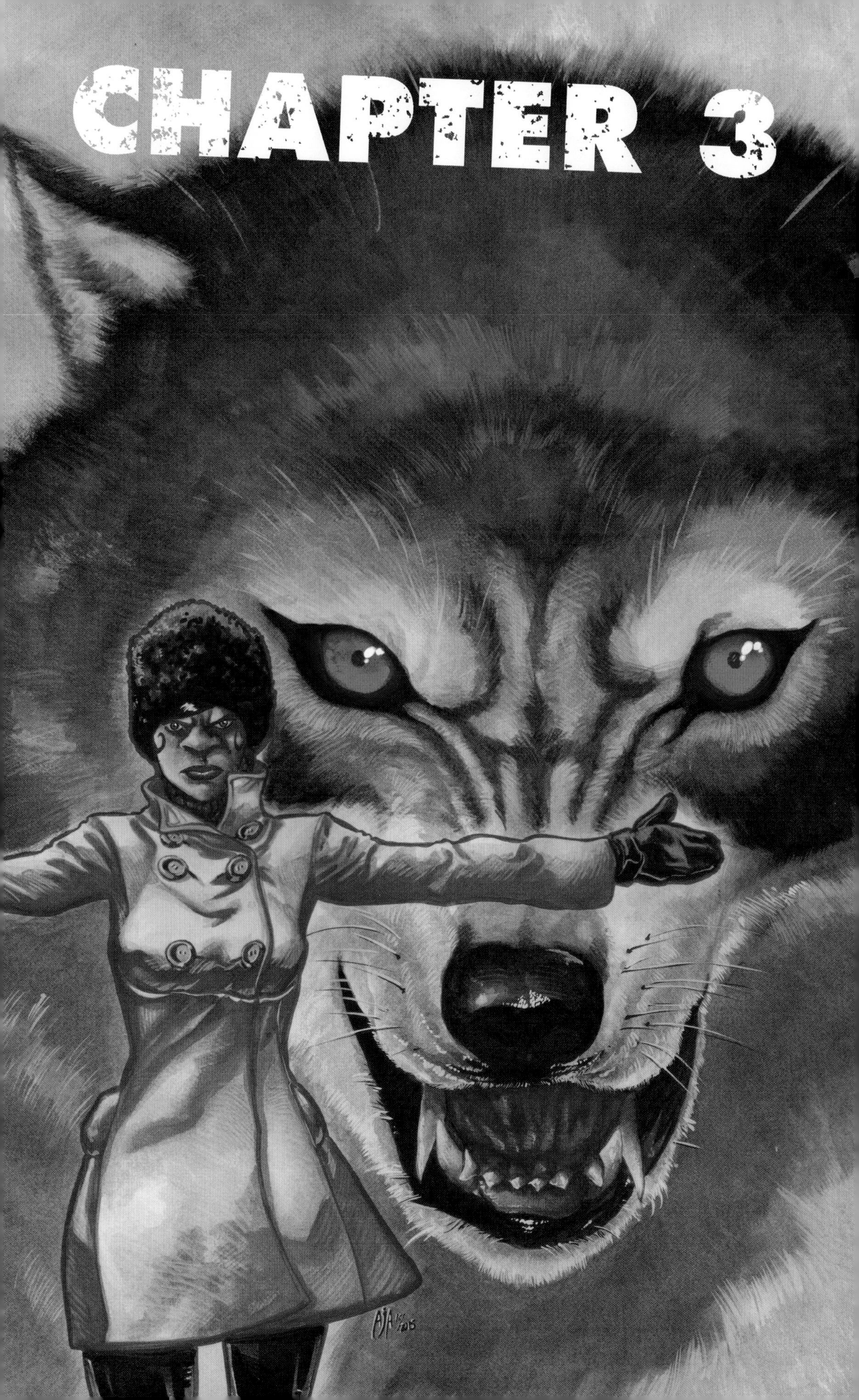
CHAPTER 3

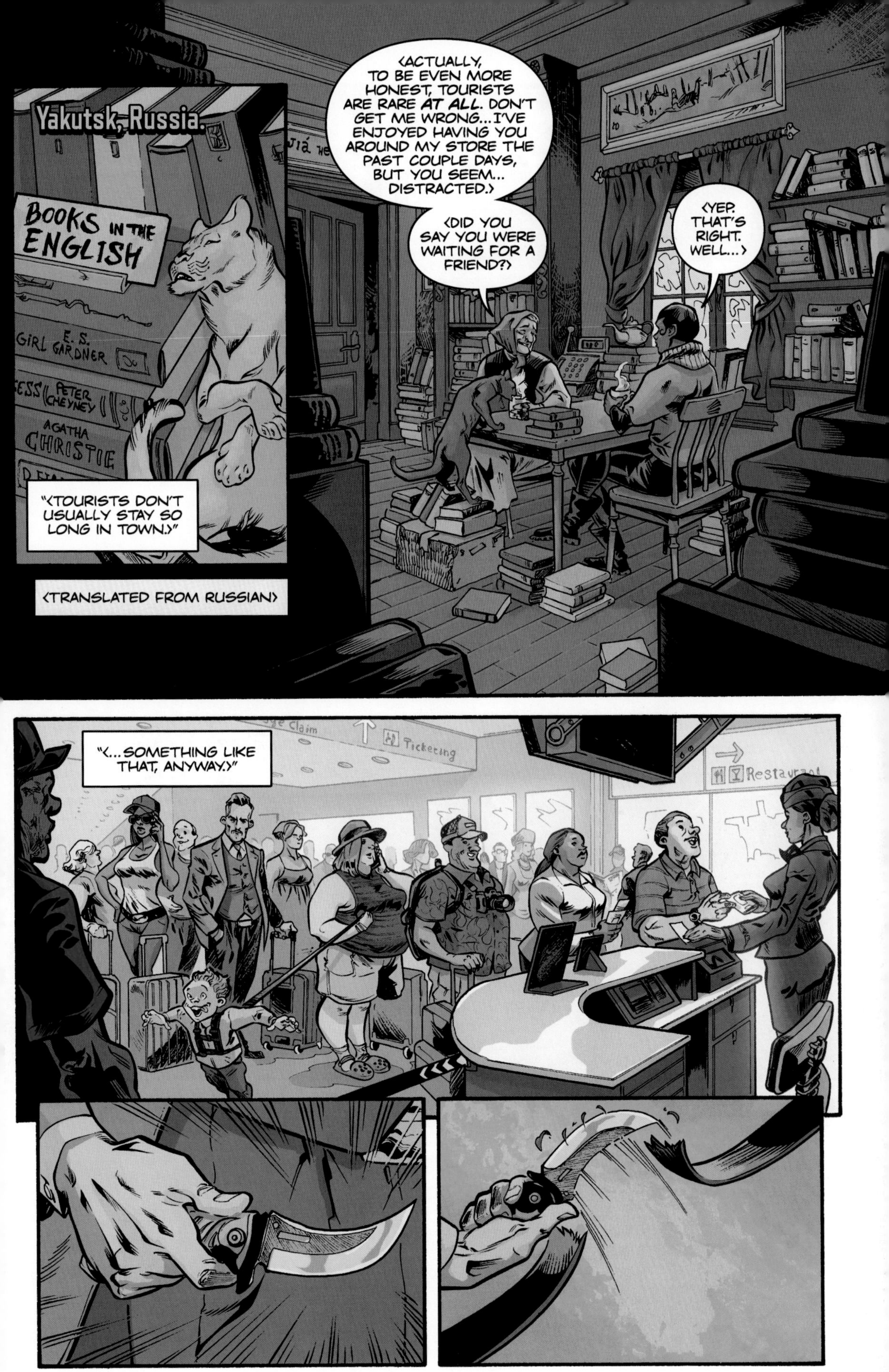
Yakutsk, Russia.
BOOKS IN THE ENGLISH
GIRL
E. S. GARDNER
PETER CHEYNEY
AGATHA CHRISTIE
"<TOURISTS DON'T USUALLY STAY SO LONG IN TOWN.>"
<TRANSLATED FROM RUSSIAN>
<ACTUALLY, TO BE EVEN MORE HONEST, TOURISTS ARE RARE **AT ALL**. DON'T GET ME WRONG...I'VE ENJOYED HAVING YOU AROUND MY STORE THE PAST COUPLE DAYS, BUT YOU SEEM... DISTRACTED.>
<DID YOU SAY YOU WERE WAITING FOR A FRIEND?>
<YEP. THAT'S RIGHT. WELL...>
"<...SOMETHING LIKE THAT, ANYWAY.>"
Ticketing

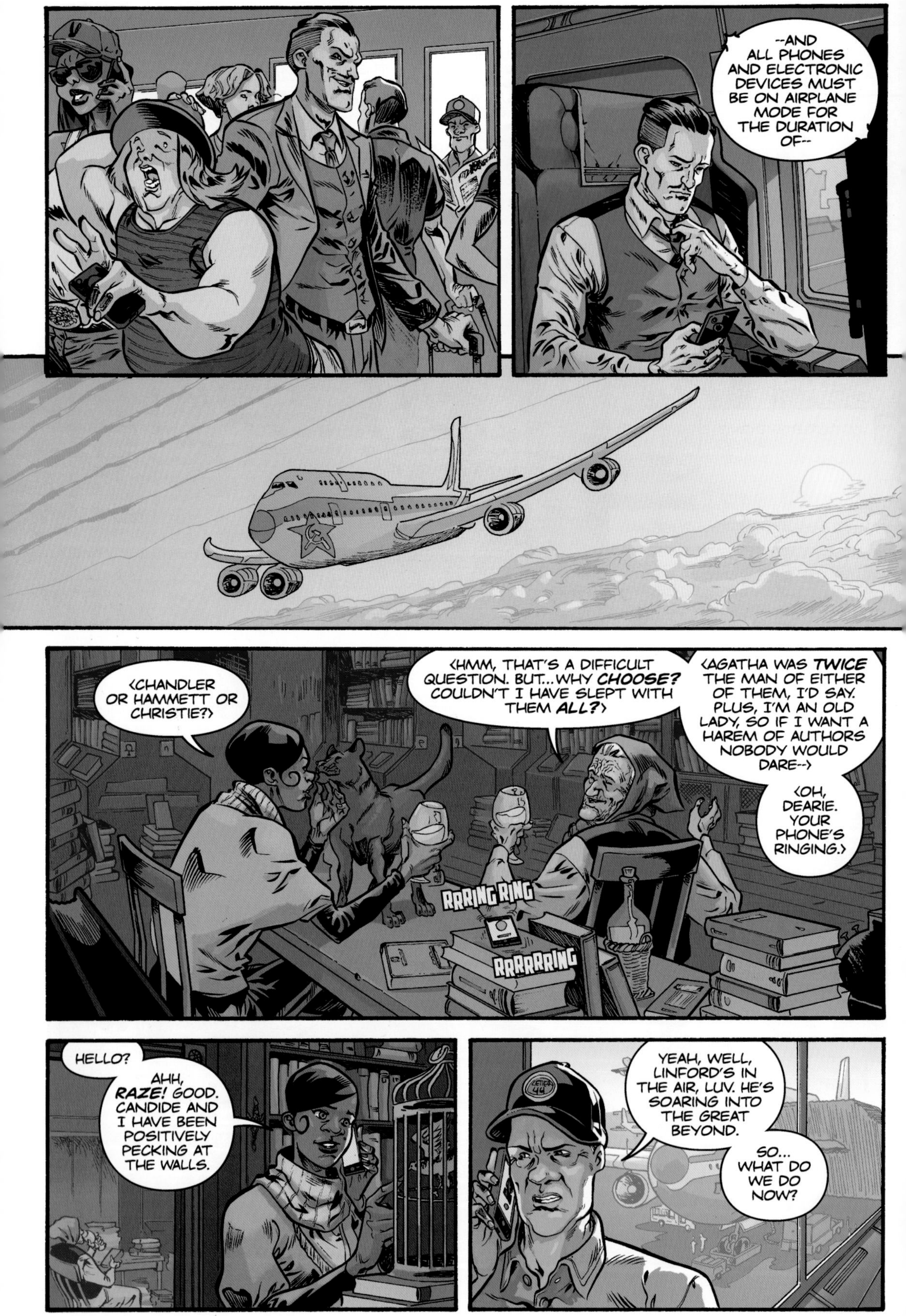
--AND ALL PHONES AND ELECTRONIC DEVICES MUST BE ON AIRPLANE MODE FOR THE DURATION OF--
‹CHANDLER OR HAMMETT OR CHRISTIE?›
‹HMM, THAT'S A DIFFICULT QUESTION. BUT...WHY CHOOSE? COULDN'T I HAVE SLEPT WITH THEM ALL?›
‹AGATHA WAS TWICE THE MAN OF EITHER OF THEM, I'D SAY. PLUS, I'M AN OLD LADY, SO IF I WANT A HAREM OF AUTHORS NOBODY WOULD DARE--›
‹OH, DEARIE. YOUR PHONE'S RINGING.›
RRRING RING
RRRRRRING
HELLO?
AHH, RAZE! GOOD. CANDIDE AND I HAVE BEEN POSITIVELY PECKING AT THE WALLS.
YEAH, WELL, LINFORD'S IN THE AIR, LUV. HE'S SOARING INTO THE GREAT BEYOND.
SO... WHAT DO WE DO NOW?

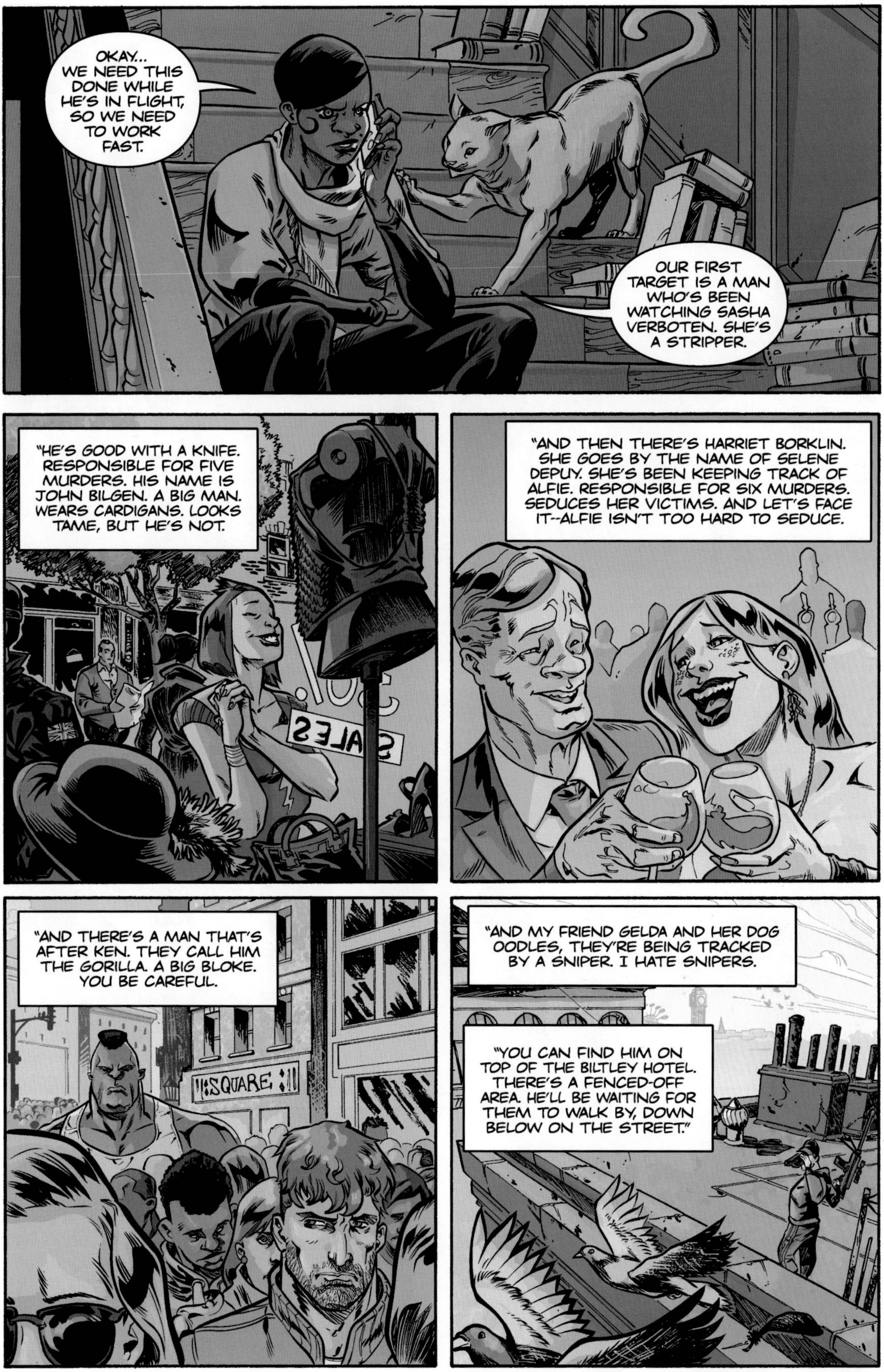
OKAY... WE NEED THIS DONE WHILE HE'S IN FLIGHT, SO WE NEED TO WORK FAST.
OUR FIRST TARGET IS A MAN WHO'S BEEN WATCHING SASHA VERBOTEN. SHE'S A STRIPPER.
"HE'S GOOD WITH A KNIFE. RESPONSIBLE FOR FIVE MURDERS. HIS NAME IS JOHN BILGEN. A BIG MAN. WEARS CARDIGANS. LOOKS TAME, BUT HE'S NOT.
SALES
"AND THEN THERE'S HARRIET BORKLIN. SHE GOES BY THE NAME OF SELENE DEPUY. SHE'S BEEN KEEPING TRACK OF ALFIE. RESPONSIBLE FOR SIX MURDERS. SEDUCES HER VICTIMS. AND LET'S FACE IT--ALFIE ISN'T TOO HARD TO SEDUCE.
"AND THERE'S A MAN THAT'S AFTER KEN. THEY CALL HIM THE GORILLA. A BIG BLOKE. YOU BE CAREFUL.
SQUARE
"AND MY FRIEND GELDA AND HER DOG OODLES, THEY'RE BEING TRACKED BY A SNIPER. I HATE SNIPERS.
"YOU CAN FIND HIM ON TOP OF THE BILTLEY HOTEL. THERE'S A FENCED-OFF AREA. HE'LL BE WAITING FOR THEM TO WALK BY, DOWN BELOW ON THE STREET."

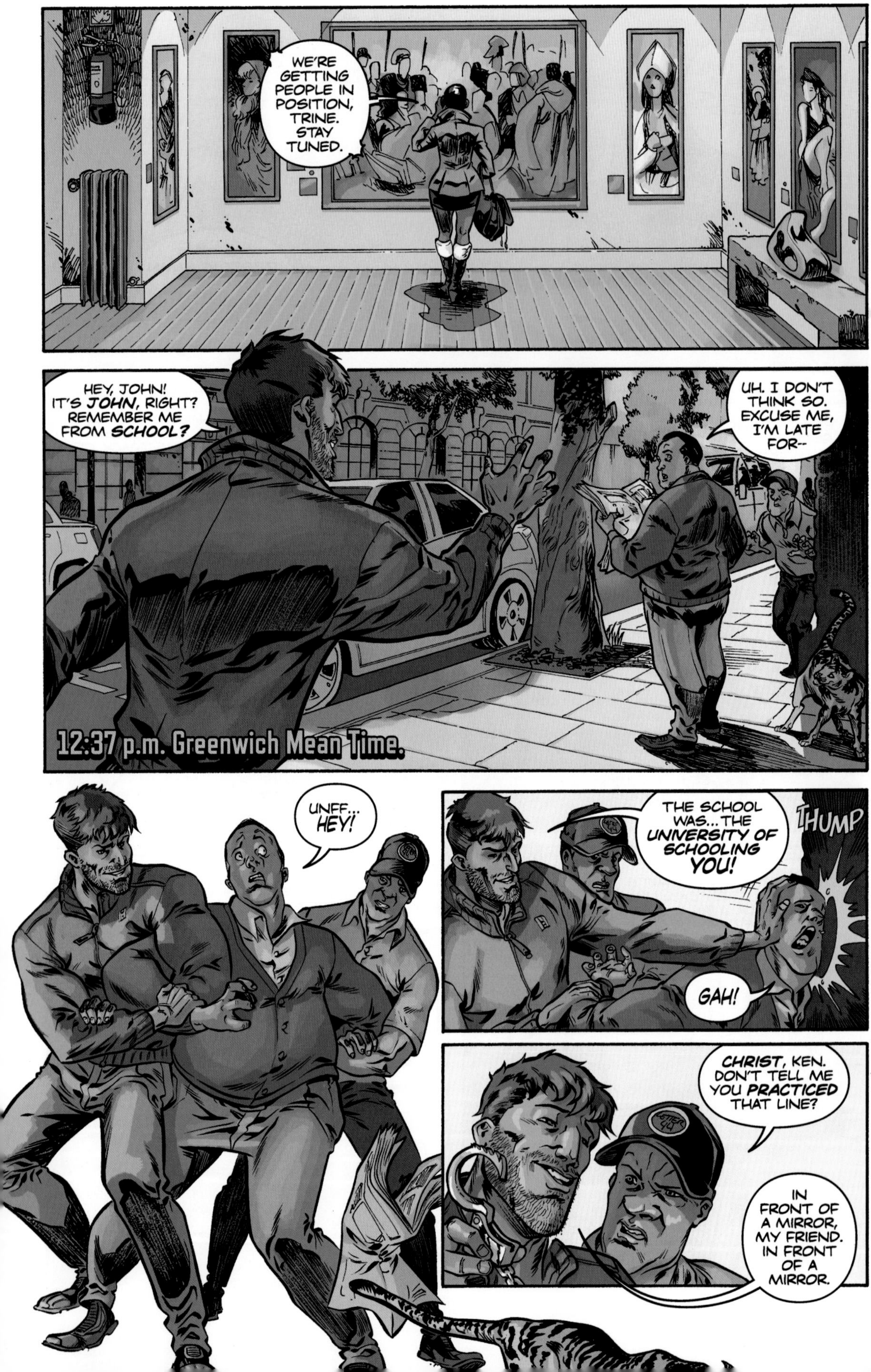
WE'RE GETTING PEOPLE IN POSITION, TRINE. STAY TUNED.
HEY, JOHN! IT'S JOHN, RIGHT? REMEMBER ME FROM SCHOOL?
UH. I DON'T THINK SO. EXCUSE ME, I'M LATE FOR--
12:37 p.m. Greenwich Mean Time.
UNFF... HEY!
THE SCHOOL WAS... THE UNIVERSITY OF SCHOOLING YOU!
THUMP
GAH!
CHRIST, KEN. DON'T TELL ME YOU PRACTICED THAT LINE?
IN FRONT OF A MIRROR, MY FRIEND. IN FRONT OF A MIRROR.

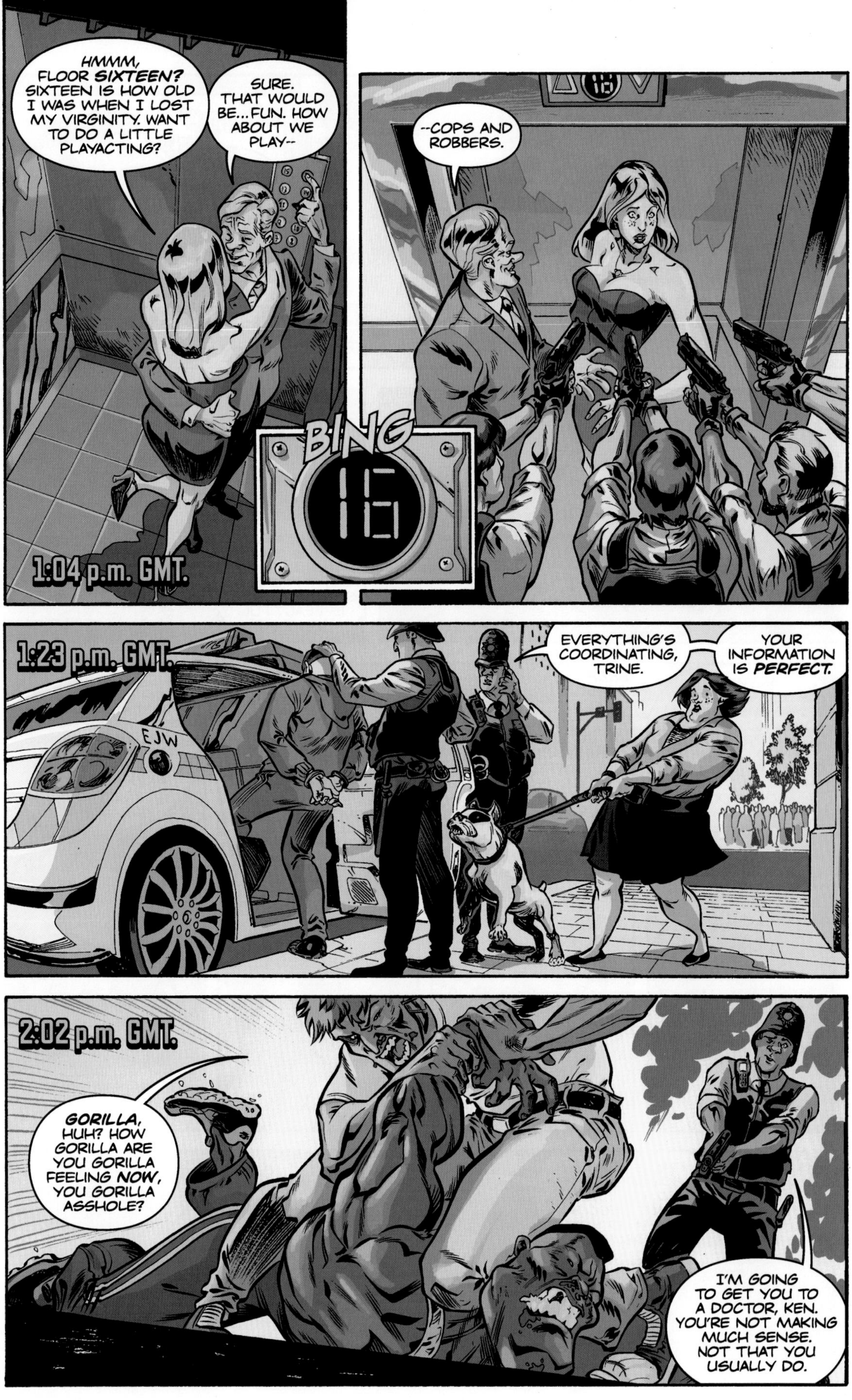
HMMM, FLOOR SIXTEEN? SIXTEEN IS HOW OLD I WAS WHEN I LOST MY VIRGINITY. WANT TO DO A LITTLE PLAYACTING?
SURE. THAT WOULD BE...FUN. HOW ABOUT WE PLAY--
1:04 p.m. GMT.
BING
16
--COPS AND ROBBERS.
1:23 p.m. GMT.
EJW
EVERYTHING'S COORDINATING, TRINE.
YOUR INFORMATION IS PERFECT.
2:02 p.m. GMT.
GORILLA, HUH? HOW GORILLA ARE YOU GORILLA FEELING NOW, YOU GORILLA ASSHOLE?
I'M GOING TO GET YOU TO A DOCTOR, KEN. YOU'RE NOT MAKING MUCH SENSE. NOT THAT YOU USUALLY DO.

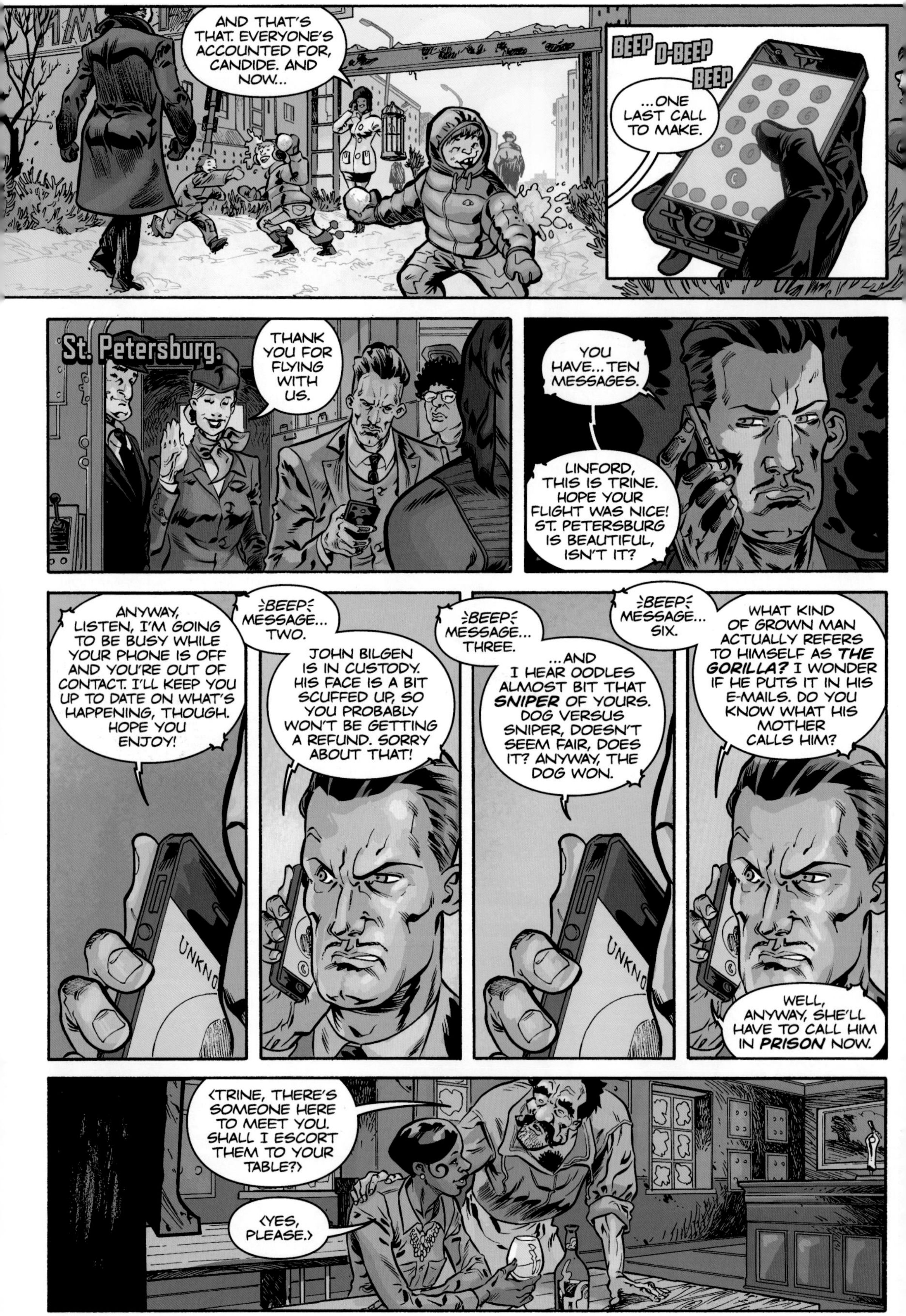
AND THAT'S THAT. EVERYONE'S ACCOUNTED FOR, CANDIDE. AND NOW...
BEEP D-BEEP BEEP
...ONE LAST CALL TO MAKE.
St. Petersburg.
THANK YOU FOR FLYING WITH US.
YOU HAVE... TEN MESSAGES.
LINFORD, THIS IS TRINE. HOPE YOUR FLIGHT WAS NICE! ST. PETERSBURG IS BEAUTIFUL, ISN'T IT?
ANYWAY, LISTEN, I'M GOING TO BE BUSY WHILE YOUR PHONE IS OFF AND YOU'RE OUT OF CONTACT. I'LL KEEP YOU UP TO DATE ON WHAT'S HAPPENING, THOUGH. HOPE YOU ENJOY!
BEEP MESSAGE... TWO.
JOHN BILGEN IS IN CUSTODY. HIS FACE IS A BIT SCUFFED UP, SO YOU PROBABLY WON'T BE GETTING A REFUND. SORRY ABOUT THAT!
BEEP MESSAGE... THREE.
...AND I HEAR OODLES ALMOST BIT THAT SNIPER OF YOURS. DOG VERSUS SNIPER, DOESN'T SEEM FAIR, DOES IT? ANYWAY, THE DOG WON.
BEEP MESSAGE... SIX.
WHAT KIND OF GROWN MAN ACTUALLY REFERS TO HIMSELF AS THE GORILLA? I WONDER IF HE PUTS IT IN HIS E-MAILS. DO YOU KNOW WHAT HIS MOTHER CALLS HIM?
WELL, ANYWAY, SHE'LL HAVE TO CALL HIM IN PRISON NOW.
<TRINE, THERE'S SOMEONE HERE TO MEET YOU. SHALL I ESCORT THEM TO YOUR TABLE?>
<YES, PLEASE.>

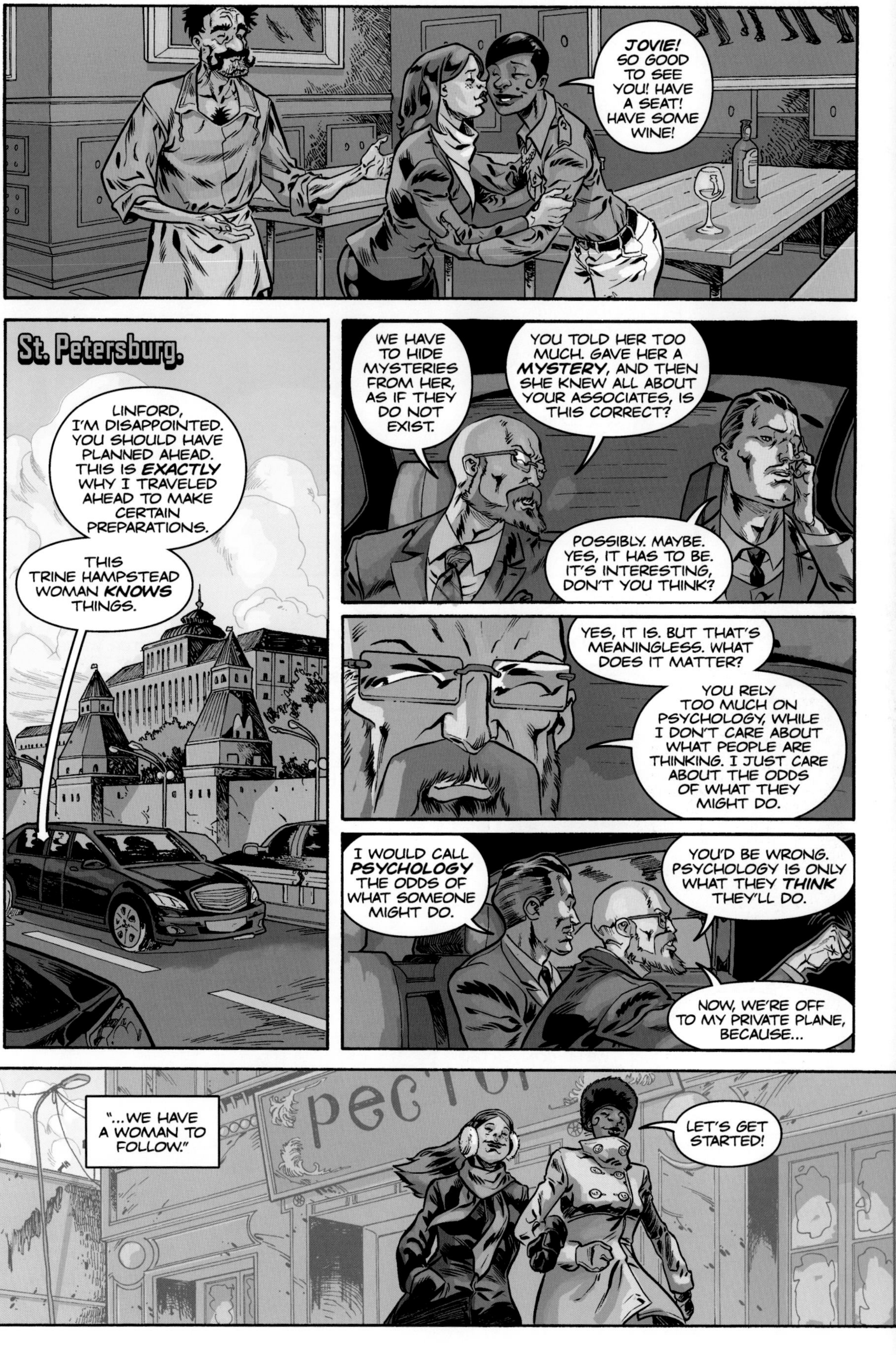
JOVIE! SO GOOD TO SEE YOU! HAVE A SEAT! HAVE SOME WINE!
St. Petersburg.
LINFORD, I'M DISAPPOINTED. YOU SHOULD HAVE PLANNED AHEAD. THIS IS EXACTLY WHY I TRAVELED AHEAD TO MAKE CERTAIN PREPARATIONS.
THIS TRINE HAMPSTEAD WOMAN KNOWS THINGS.
WE HAVE TO HIDE MYSTERIES FROM HER, AS IF THEY DO NOT EXIST.
YOU TOLD HER TOO MUCH. GAVE HER A MYSTERY, AND THEN SHE KNEW ALL ABOUT YOUR ASSOCIATES, IS THIS CORRECT?
POSSIBLY. MAYBE. YES, IT HAS TO BE. IT'S INTERESTING, DON'T YOU THINK?
YES, IT IS. BUT THAT'S MEANINGLESS. WHAT DOES IT MATTER?
YOU RELY TOO MUCH ON PSYCHOLOGY, WHILE I DON'T CARE ABOUT WHAT PEOPLE ARE THINKING. I JUST CARE ABOUT THE ODDS OF WHAT THEY MIGHT DO.
I WOULD CALL PSYCHOLOGY THE ODDS OF WHAT SOMEONE MIGHT DO.
YOU'D BE WRONG. PSYCHOLOGY IS ONLY WHAT THEY THINK THEY'LL DO.
NOW, WE'RE OFF TO MY PRIVATE PLANE, BECAUSE...
"...WE HAVE A WOMAN TO FOLLOW."
LET'S GET STARTED!

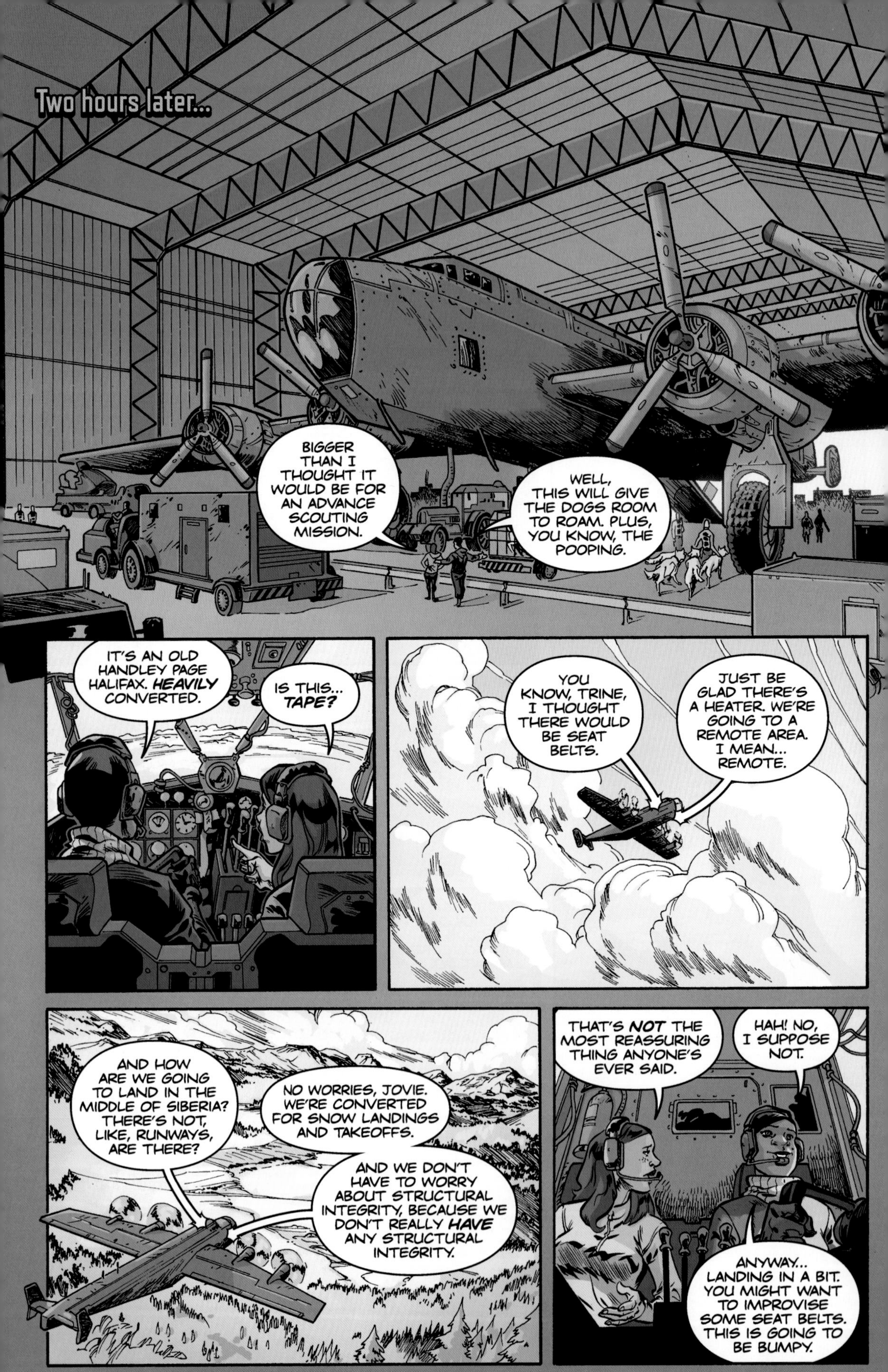
Two hours later...
BIGGER THAN I THOUGHT IT WOULD BE FOR AN ADVANCE SCOUTING MISSION.
WELL, THIS WILL GIVE THE DOGS ROOM TO ROAM. PLUS, YOU KNOW, THE POOPING.
IT'S AN OLD HANDLEY PAGE HALIFAX. HEAVILY CONVERTED.
IS THIS... TAPE?
YOU KNOW, TRINE, I THOUGHT THERE WOULD BE SEAT BELTS.
JUST BE GLAD THERE'S A HEATER. WE'RE GOING TO A REMOTE AREA. I MEAN... REMOTE.
AND HOW ARE WE GOING TO LAND IN THE MIDDLE OF SIBERIA? THERE'S NOT, LIKE, RUNWAYS, ARE THERE?
NO WORRIES, JOVIE. WE'RE CONVERTED FOR SNOW LANDINGS AND TAKEOFFS.
AND WE DON'T HAVE TO WORRY ABOUT STRUCTURAL INTEGRITY, BECAUSE WE DON'T REALLY HAVE ANY STRUCTURAL INTEGRITY.
THAT'S NOT THE MOST REASSURING THING ANYONE'S EVER SAID.
HAH! NO, I SUPPOSE NOT.
ANYWAY... LANDING IN A BIT. YOU MIGHT WANT TO IMPROVISE SOME SEAT BELTS. THIS IS GOING TO BE BUMPY.

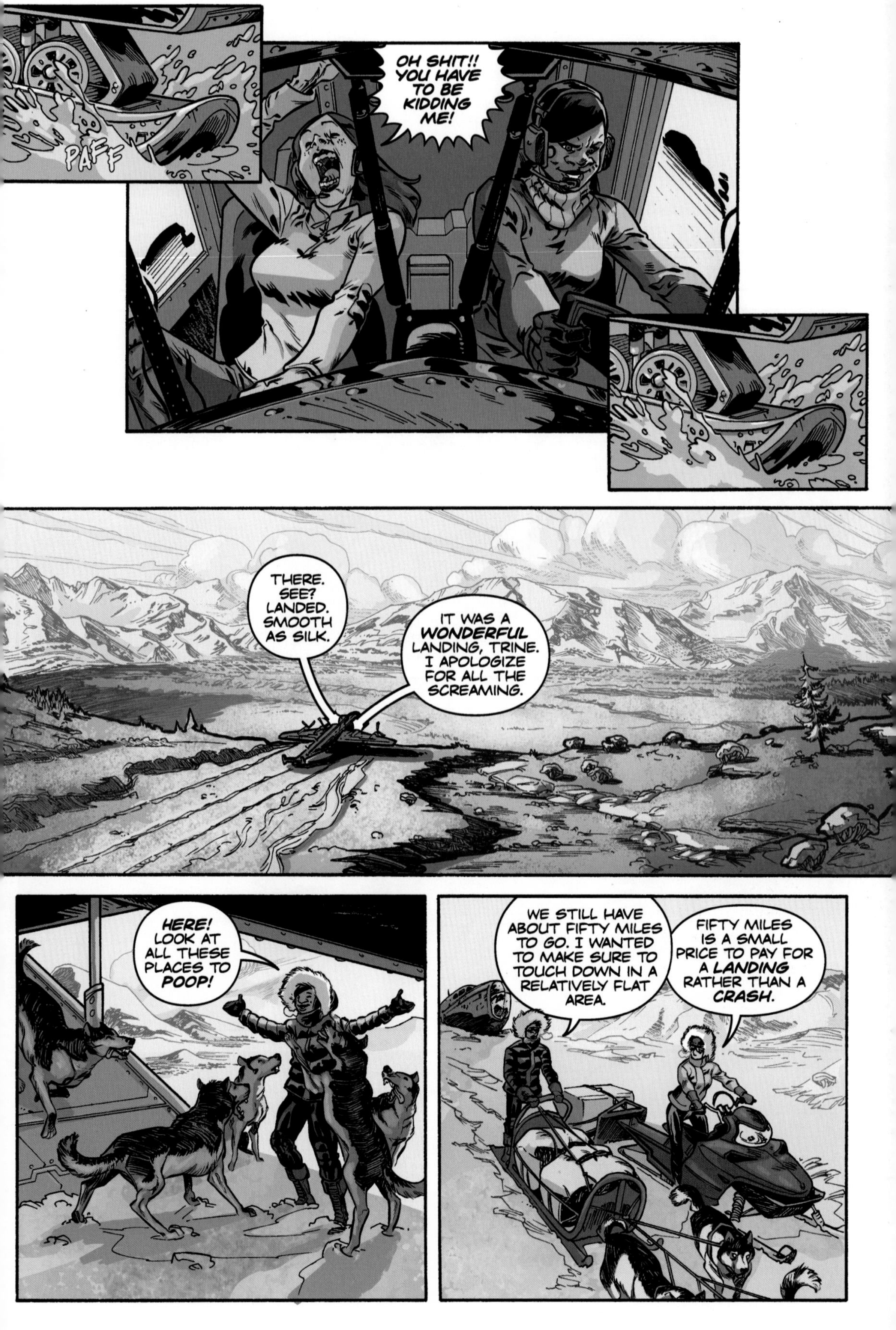
PAFF
OH SHIT!! YOU HAVE TO BE KIDDING ME!
THERE. SEE? LANDED. SMOOTH AS SILK.
IT WAS A WONDERFUL LANDING, TRINE. I APOLOGIZE FOR ALL THE SCREAMING.
HERE! LOOK AT ALL THESE PLACES TO POOP!
WE STILL HAVE ABOUT FIFTY MILES TO GO. I WANTED TO MAKE SURE TO TOUCH DOWN IN A RELATIVELY FLAT AREA.
FIFTY MILES IS A SMALL PRICE TO PAY FOR A LANDING RATHER THAN A CRASH.

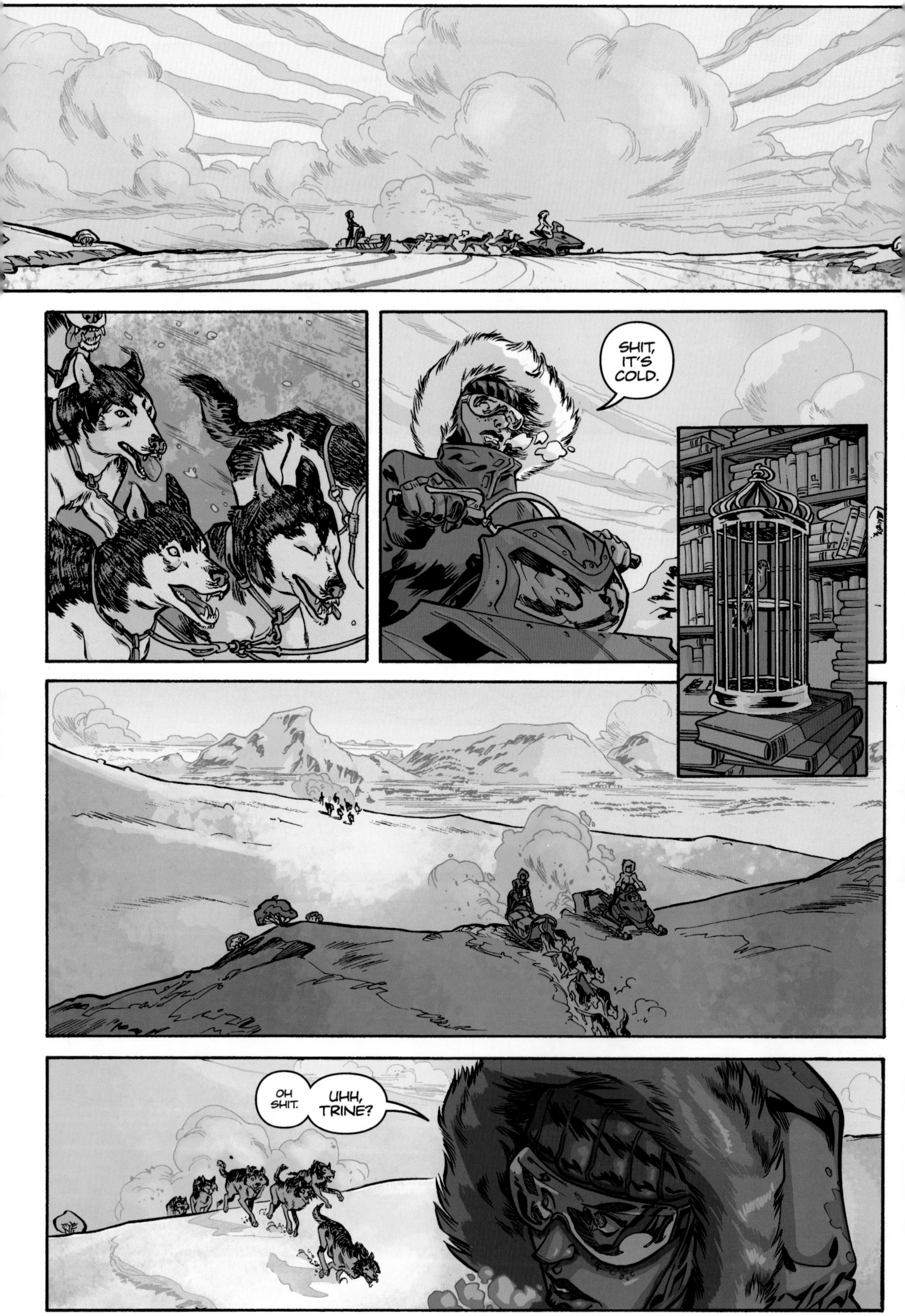
SHIT, IT'S COLD.
OH SHIT.
UHH, TRINE?

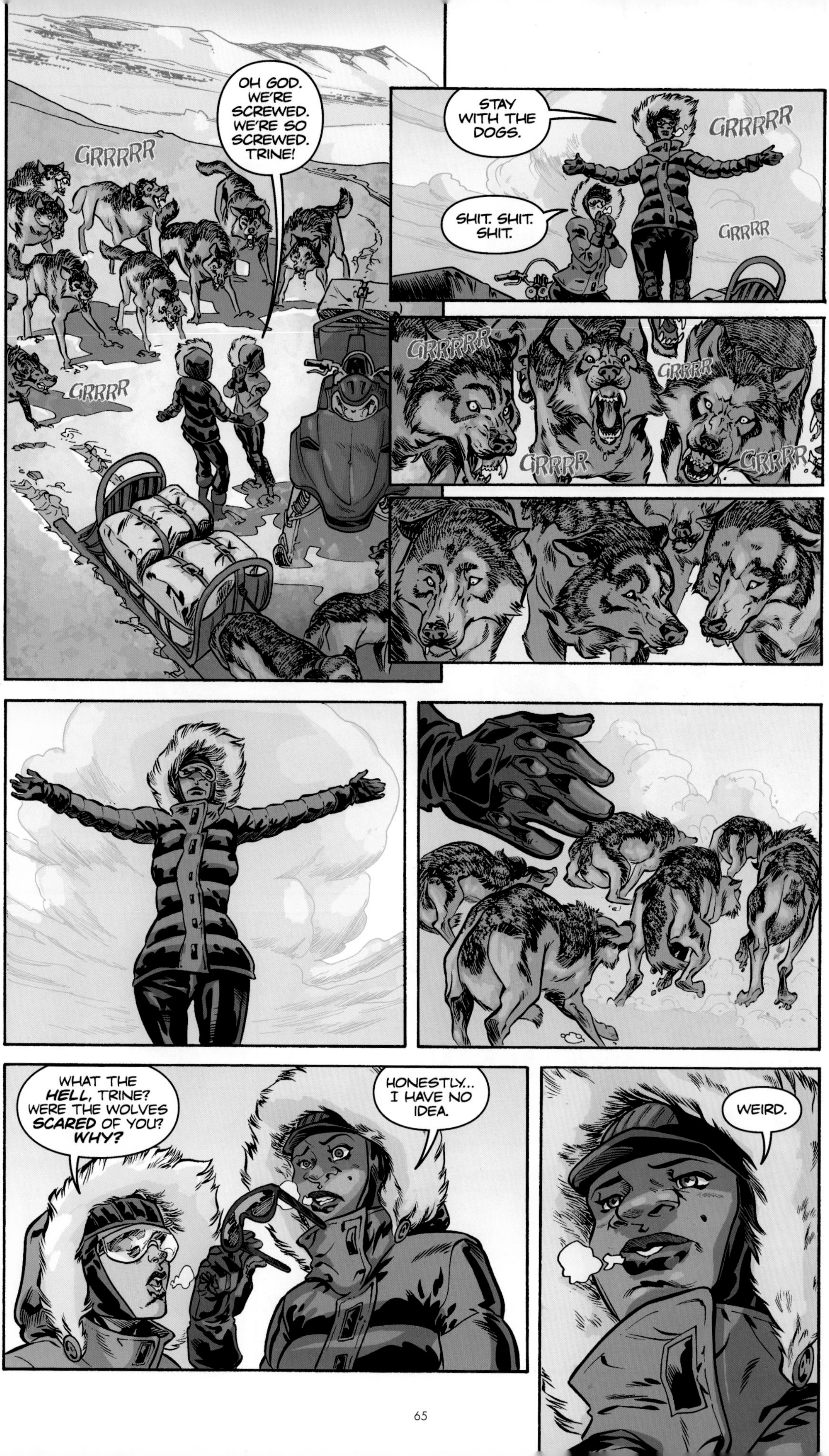
GRRRRR
OH GOD. WE'RE SCREWED. WE'RE SO SCREWED. TRINE!
GRRRR
STAY WITH THE DOGS.
GRRRRR
SHIT. SHIT. SHIT.
GRRRR
GRRRRR
GRRRR
GRRRR
GRRRR
WHAT THE HELL, TRINE? WERE THE WOLVES SCARED OF YOU? WHY?
HONESTLY... I HAVE NO IDEA.
WEIRD.

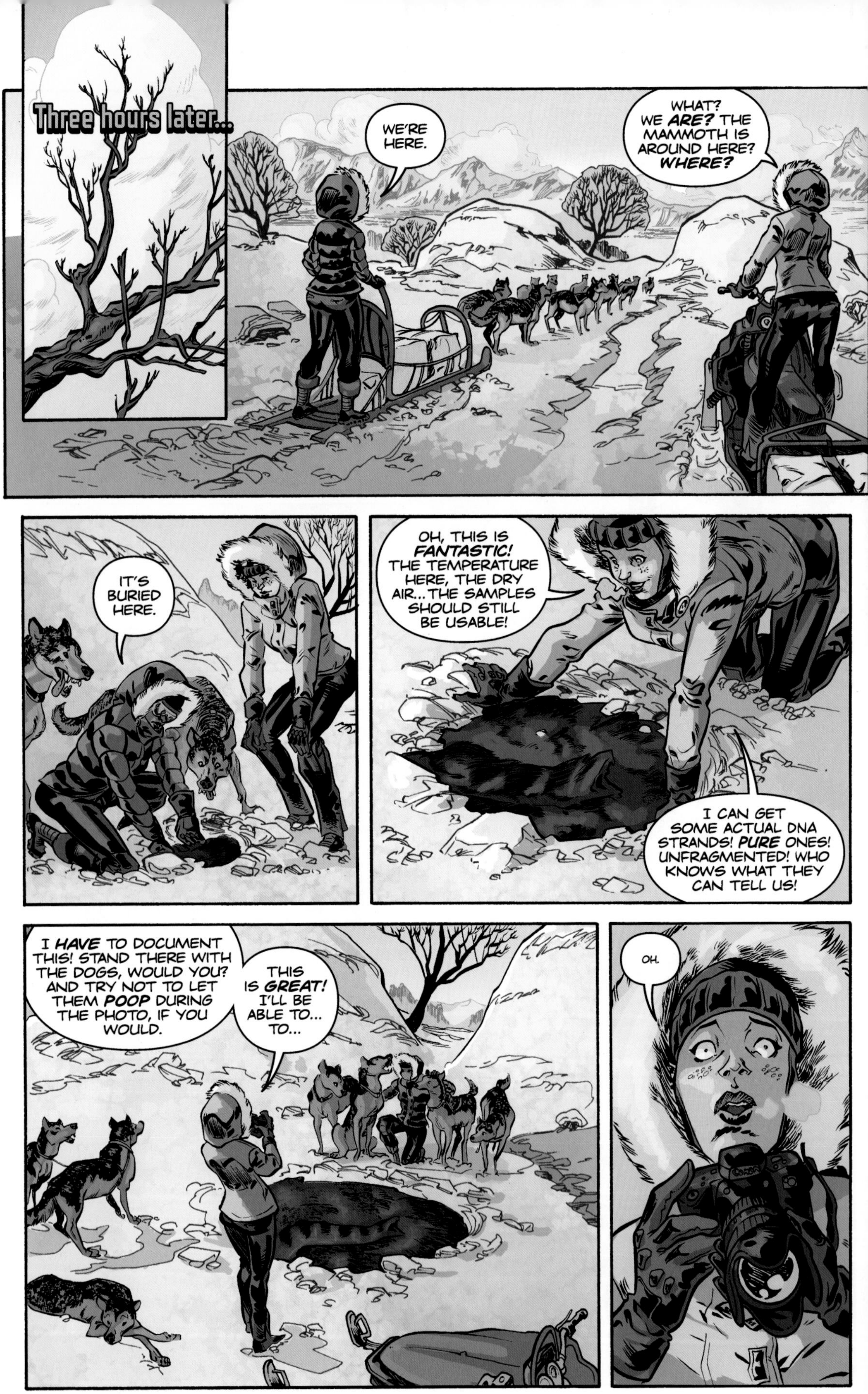

Three hours later...
WE'RE HERE.
WHAT? WE ARE? THE MAMMOTH IS AROUND HERE? WHERE?
IT'S BURIED HERE.
OH, THIS IS FANTASTIC! THE TEMPERATURE HERE, THE DRY AIR... THE SAMPLES SHOULD STILL BE USABLE!
I CAN GET SOME ACTUAL DNA STRANDS! PURE ONES! UNFRAGMENTED! WHO KNOWS WHAT THEY CAN TELL US!
I HAVE TO DOCUMENT THIS! STAND THERE WITH THE DOGS, WOULD YOU? AND TRY NOT TO LET THEM POOP DURING THE PHOTO, IF YOU WOULD.
THIS IS GREAT! I'LL BE ABLE TO... TO...
OH.

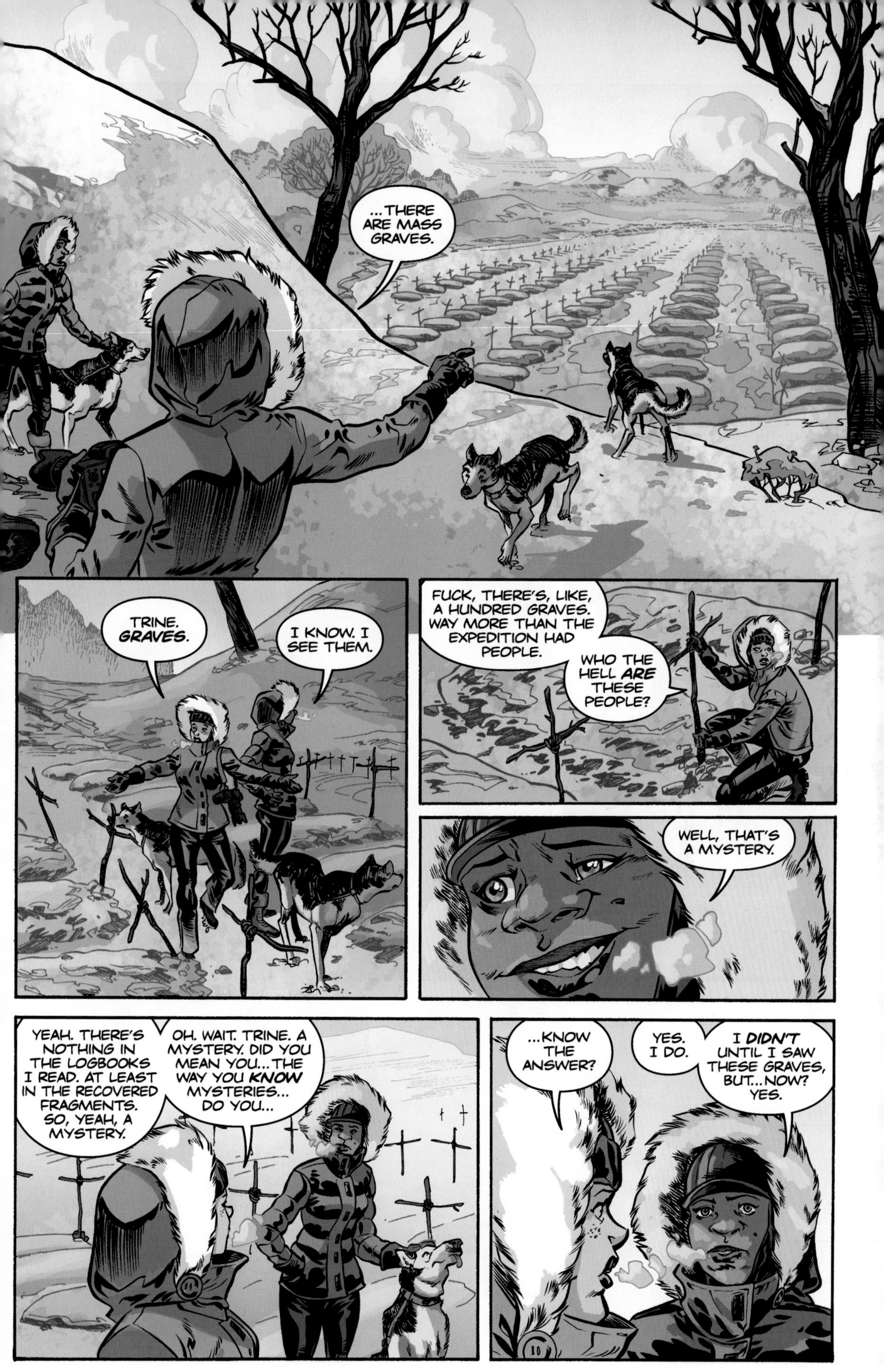
...THERE ARE MASS GRAVES.
TRINE. GRAVES.
I KNOW. I SEE THEM.
FUCK, THERE'S, LIKE, A HUNDRED GRAVES. WAY MORE THAN THE EXPEDITION HAD PEOPLE.
WHO THE HELL ARE THESE PEOPLE?
WELL, THAT'S A MYSTERY.
YEAH. THERE'S NOTHING IN THE LOGBOOKS I READ. AT LEAST IN THE RECOVERED FRAGMENTS. SO, YEAH, A MYSTERY.
OH. WAIT. TRINE. A MYSTERY. DID YOU MEAN YOU...THE WAY YOU KNOW MYSTERIES... DO YOU...
...KNOW THE ANSWER?
YES. I DO.
I DIDN'T UNTIL I SAW THESE GRAVES, BUT...NOW? YES.

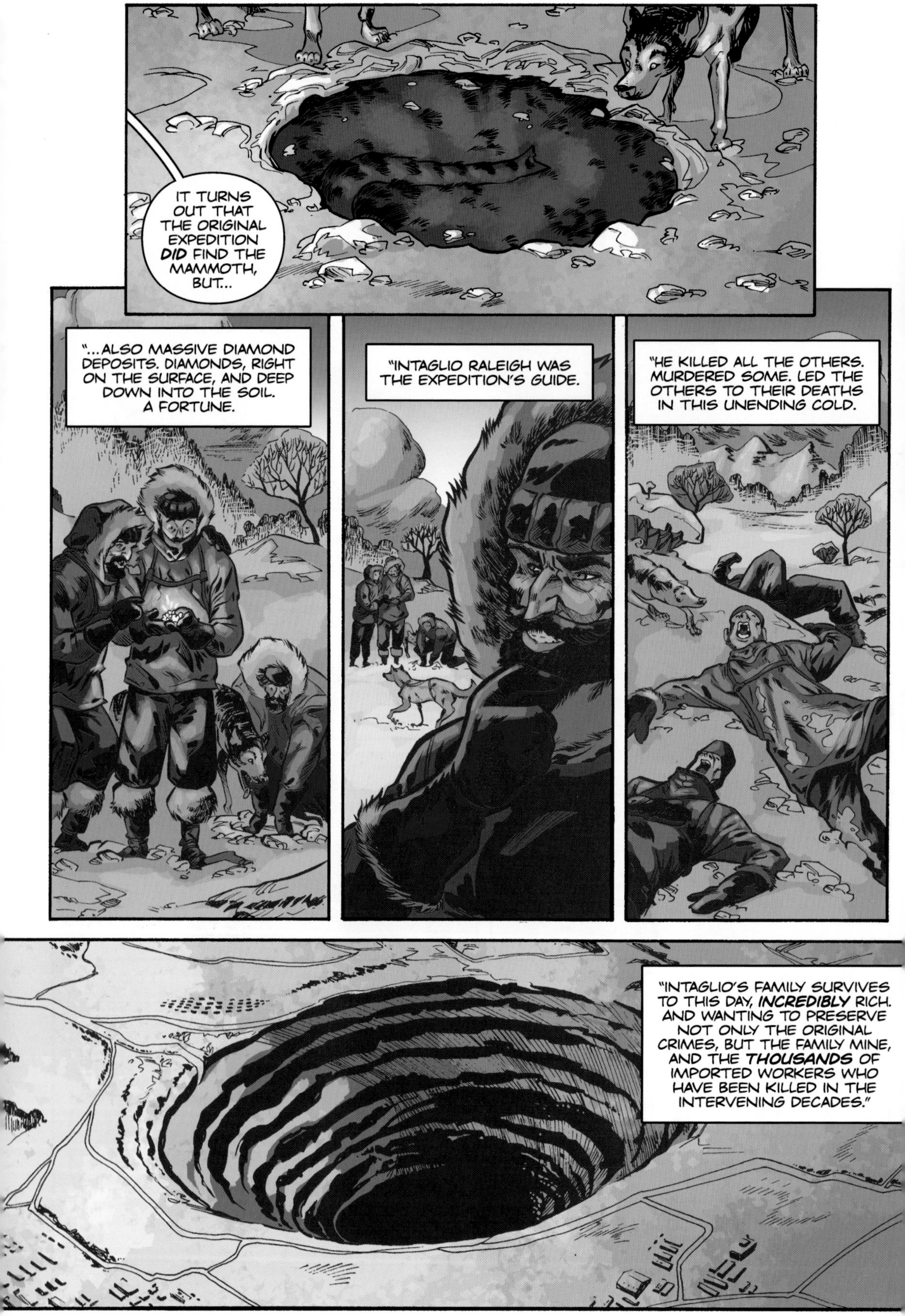
IT TURNS OUT THAT THE ORIGINAL EXPEDITION *DID* FIND THE MAMMOTH, BUT...
"...ALSO MASSIVE DIAMOND DEPOSITS. DIAMONDS, RIGHT ON THE SURFACE, AND DEEP DOWN INTO THE SOIL. A FORTUNE.
"INTAGLIO RALEIGH WAS THE EXPEDITION'S GUIDE.
"HE KILLED ALL THE OTHERS. MURDERED SOME. LED THE OTHERS TO THEIR DEATHS IN THIS UNENDING COLD.
"INTAGLIO'S FAMILY SURVIVES TO THIS DAY, *INCREDIBLY* RICH. AND WANTING TO PRESERVE NOT ONLY THE ORIGINAL CRIMES, BUT THE FAMILY MINE, AND THE *THOUSANDS* OF IMPORTED WORKERS WHO HAVE BEEN KILLED IN THE INTERVENING DECADES."

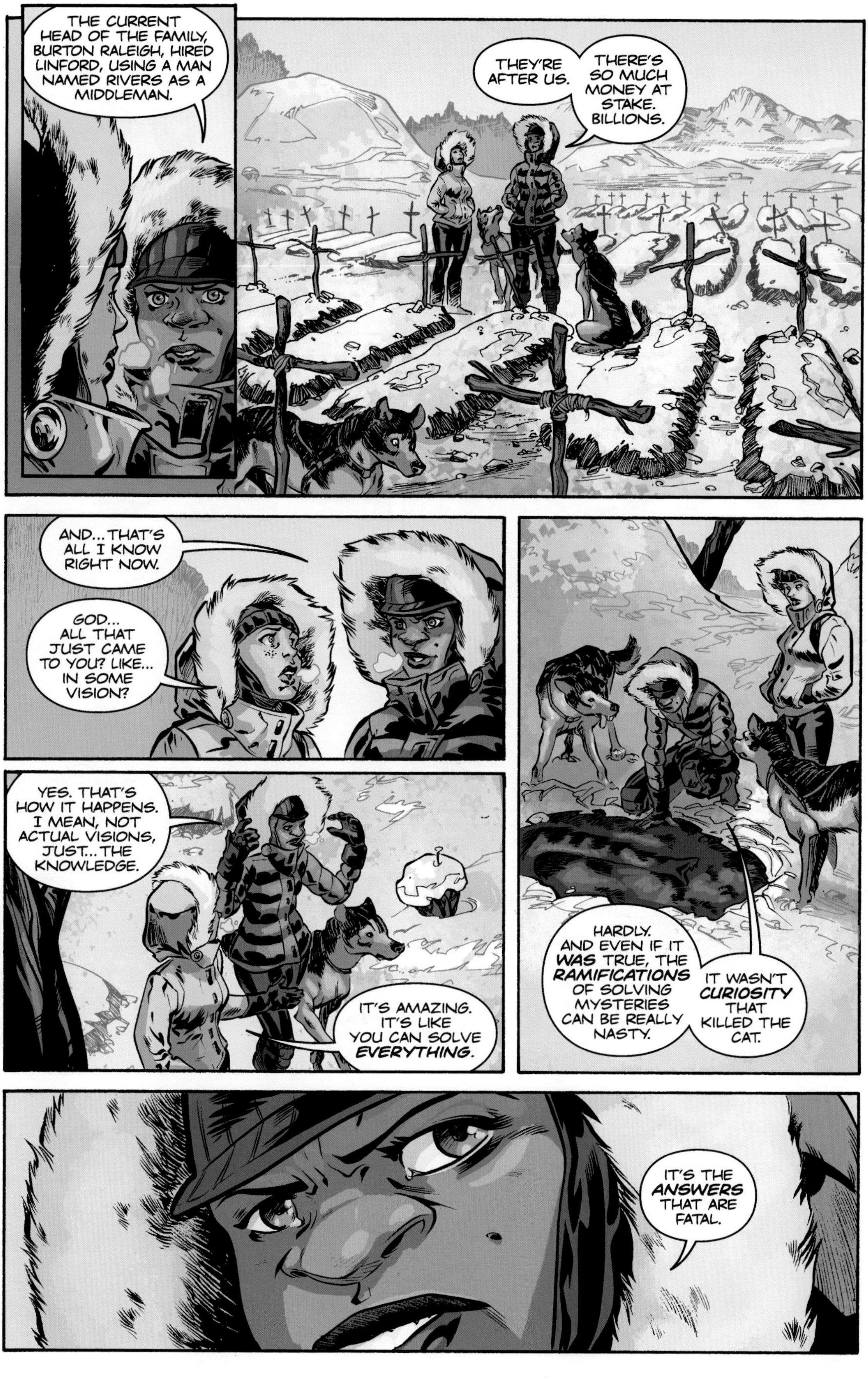
THE CURRENT HEAD OF THE FAMILY, BURTON RALEIGH, HIRED LINFORD, USING A MAN NAMED RIVERS AS A MIDDLEMAN.
THEY'RE AFTER US.
THERE'S SO MUCH MONEY AT STAKE. BILLIONS.
AND... THAT'S ALL I KNOW RIGHT NOW.
GOD... ALL THAT JUST CAME TO YOU? LIKE... IN SOME VISION?
YES. THAT'S HOW IT HAPPENS. I MEAN, NOT ACTUAL VISIONS, JUST... THE KNOWLEDGE.
IT'S AMAZING. IT'S LIKE YOU CAN SOLVE EVERYTHING.
HARDLY. AND EVEN IF IT WAS TRUE, THE RAMIFICATIONS OF SOLVING MYSTERIES CAN BE REALLY NASTY.
IT WASN'T CURIOSITY THAT KILLED THE CAT.
IT'S THE ANSWERS THAT ARE FATAL.

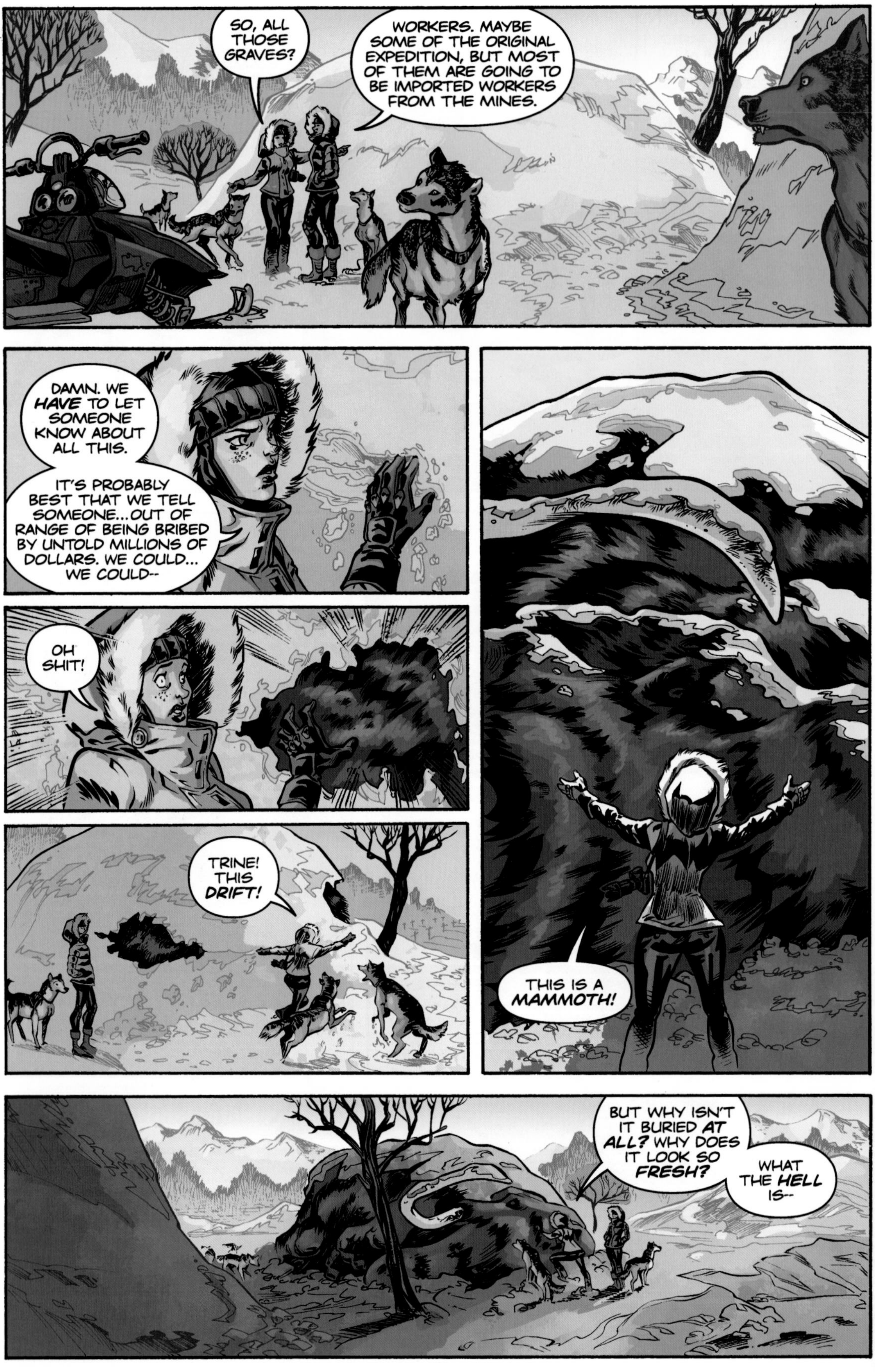
SO, ALL THOSE GRAVES?
WORKERS. MAYBE SOME OF THE ORIGINAL EXPEDITION, BUT MOST OF THEM ARE GOING TO BE IMPORTED WORKERS FROM THE MINES.
DAMN. WE HAVE TO LET SOMEONE KNOW ABOUT ALL THIS.
IT'S PROBABLY BEST THAT WE TELL SOMEONE...OUT OF RANGE OF BEING BRIBED BY UNTOLD MILLIONS OF DOLLARS. WE COULD... WE COULD--
OH SHIT!
TRINE! THIS DRIFT!
THIS IS A MAMMOTH!
BUT WHY ISN'T IT BURIED AT ALL? WHY DOES IT LOOK SO FRESH?
WHAT THE HELL IS--

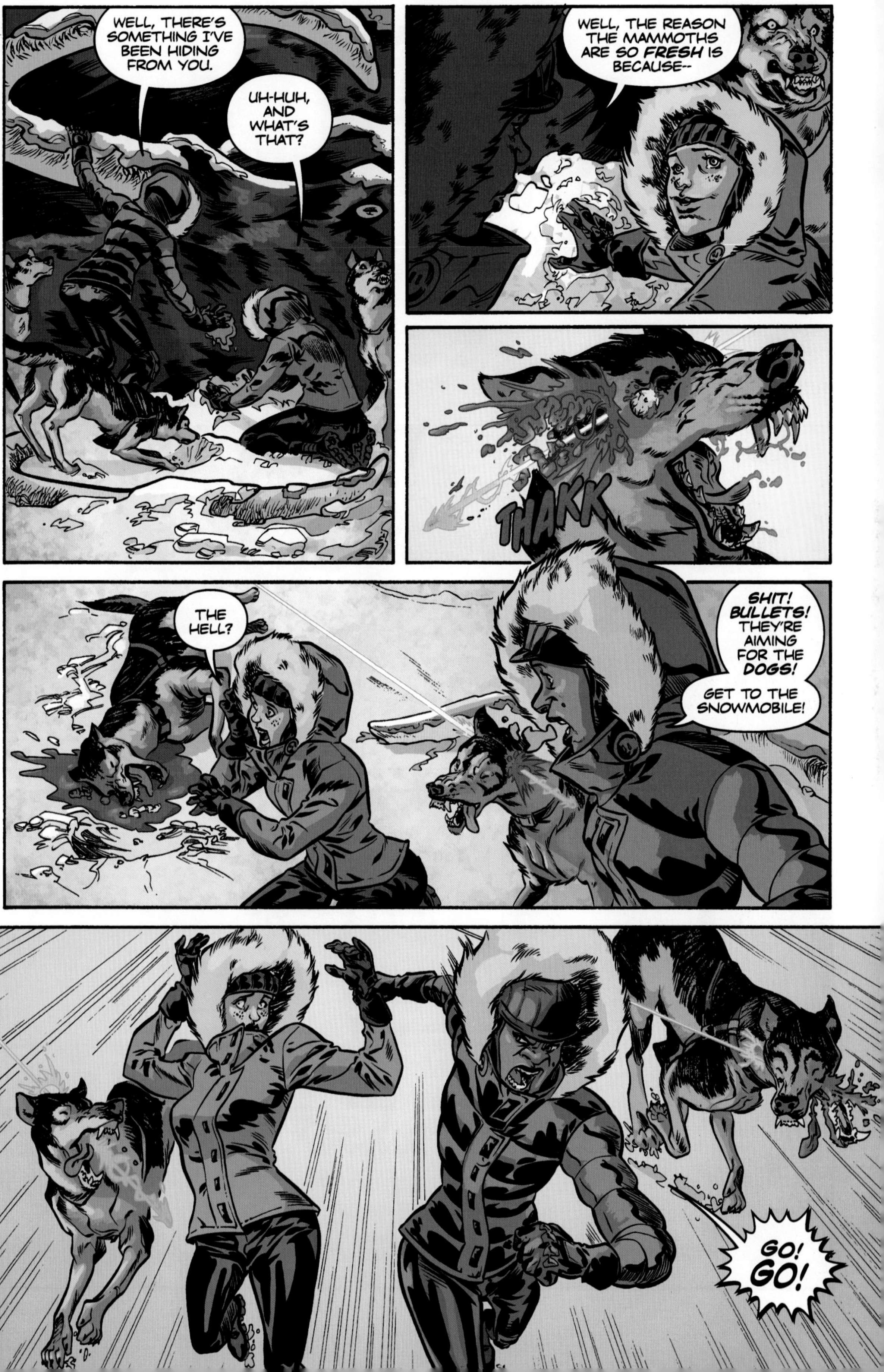
WELL, THERE'S SOMETHING I'VE BEEN HIDING FROM YOU.
UH-HUH, AND WHAT'S THAT?
WELL, THE REASON THE MAMMOTHS ARE SO FRESH IS BECAUSE--
THAKK
THE HELL?
SHIT! BULLETS! THEY'RE AIMING FOR THE DOGS!
GET TO THE SNOWMOBILE!
GO! GO!

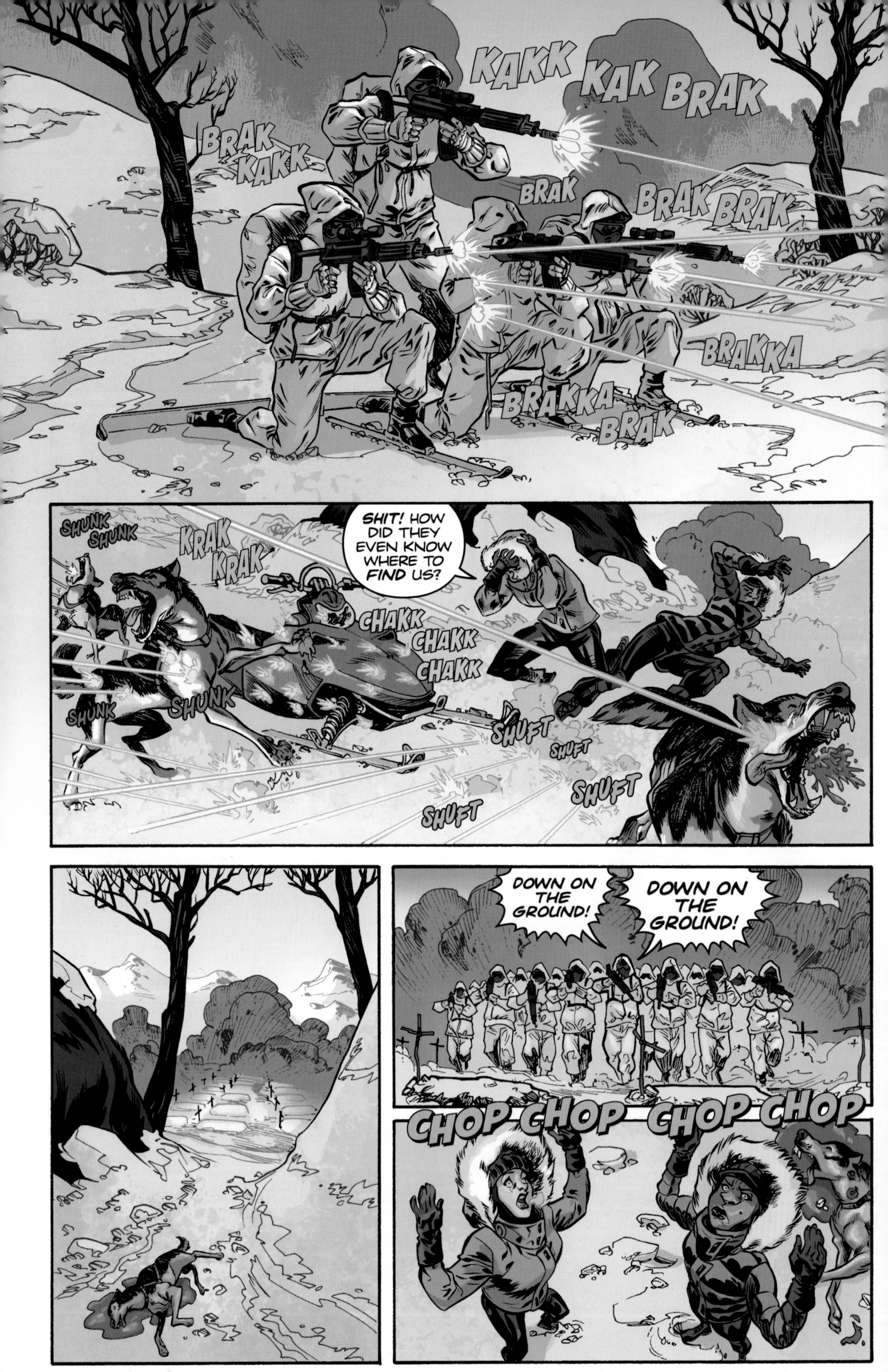
BRAK KAKK
KAKK KAK BRAK
BRAK
BRAK BRAK
BRAKKA
BRAKKA BRAK
SHUNK SHUNK
KRAK KRAK
SHIT! HOW DID THEY EVEN KNOW WHERE TO FIND US?
CHAKK CHAKK CHAKK
SHUNK
SHUNK
SHUFT
SHUFT
SHUFT
SHUFT
DOWN ON THE GROUND!
DOWN ON THE GROUND!
CHOP CHOP CHOP CHOP

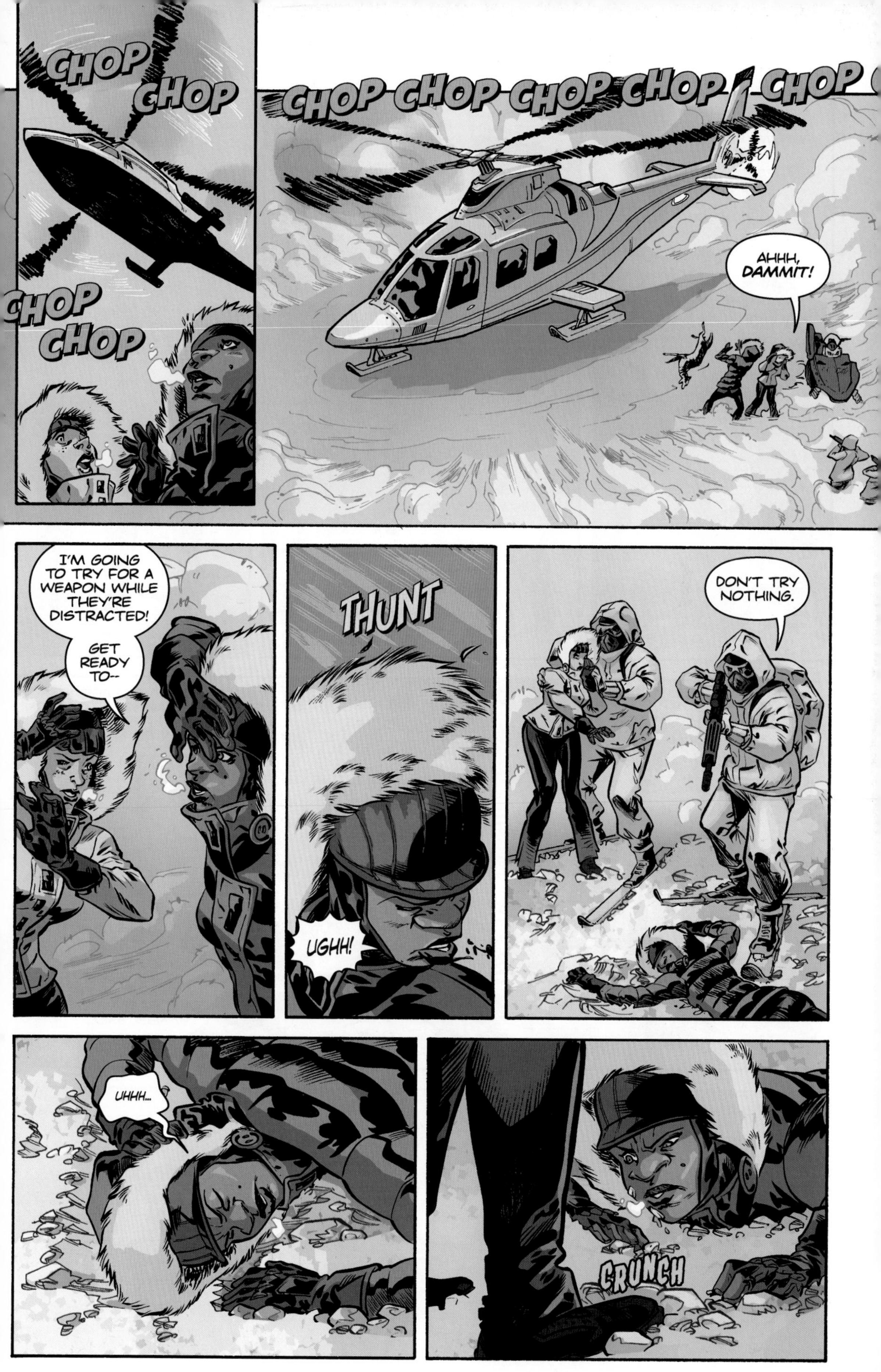
CHOP
CHOP
CHOP
CHOP
CHOP CHOP CHOP CHOP CHOP
AHHH, DAMMIT!
I'M GOING TO TRY FOR A WEAPON WHILE THEY'RE DISTRACTED!
GET READY TO--
THUNT
UGHH!
DON'T TRY NOTHING.
UHHH...
CRUNCH

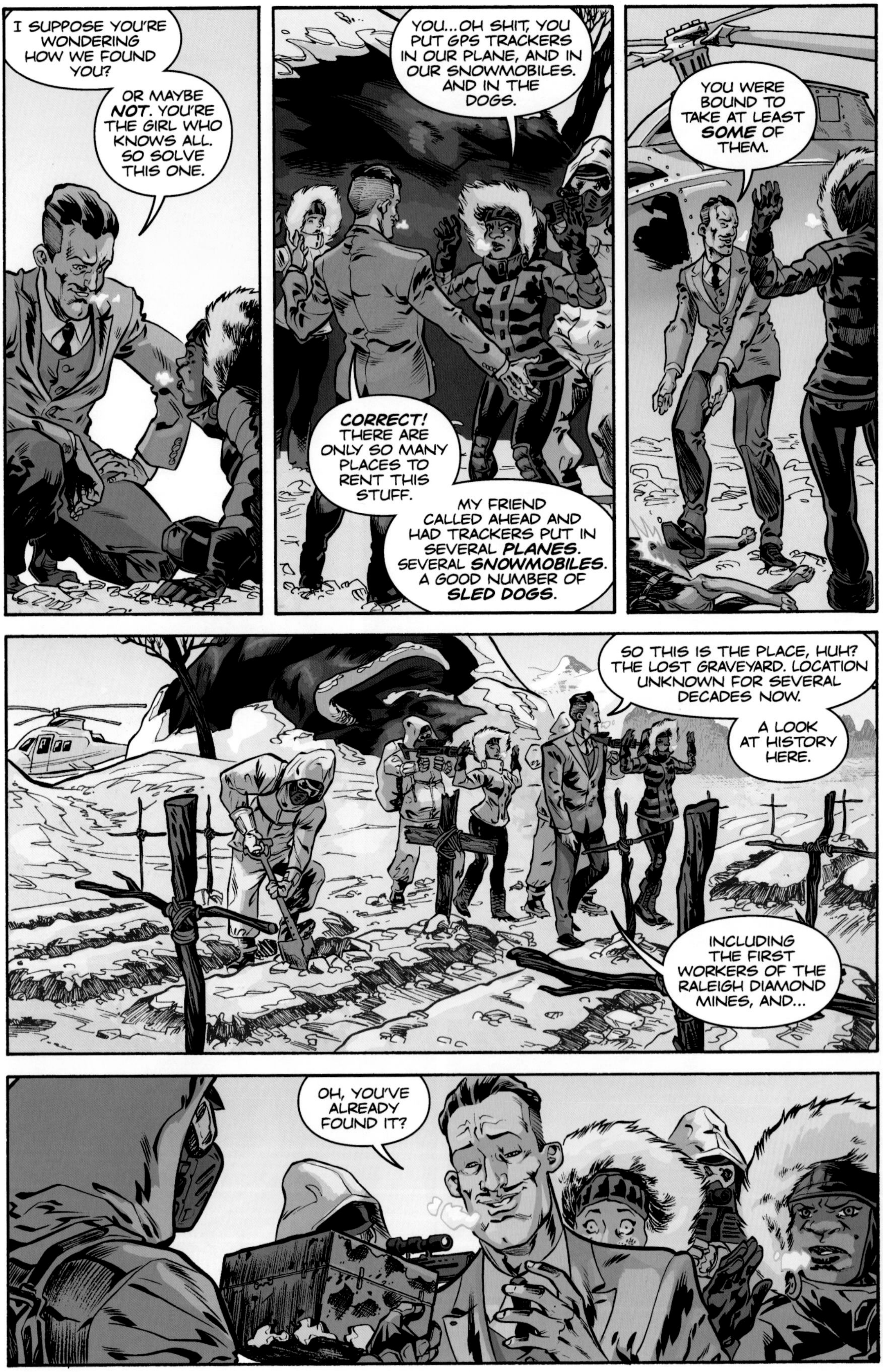
I SUPPOSE YOU'RE WONDERING HOW WE FOUND YOU?
OR MAYBE **NOT**. YOU'RE THE GIRL WHO KNOWS ALL. SO SOLVE THIS ONE.
YOU...OH SHIT, YOU PUT GPS TRACKERS IN OUR PLANE, AND IN OUR SNOWMOBILES. AND IN THE DOGS.
CORRECT! THERE ARE ONLY SO MANY PLACES TO RENT THIS STUFF.
MY FRIEND CALLED AHEAD AND HAD TRACKERS PUT IN SEVERAL ***PLANES***. SEVERAL ***SNOWMOBILES***. A GOOD NUMBER OF ***SLED DOGS***.
YOU WERE BOUND TO TAKE AT LEAST ***SOME*** OF THEM.
SO THIS IS THE PLACE, HUH? THE LOST GRAVEYARD. LOCATION UNKNOWN FOR SEVERAL DECADES NOW.
A LOOK AT HISTORY HERE.
INCLUDING THE FIRST WORKERS OF THE RALEIGH DIAMOND MINES, AND...
OH, YOU'VE ALREADY FOUND IT?

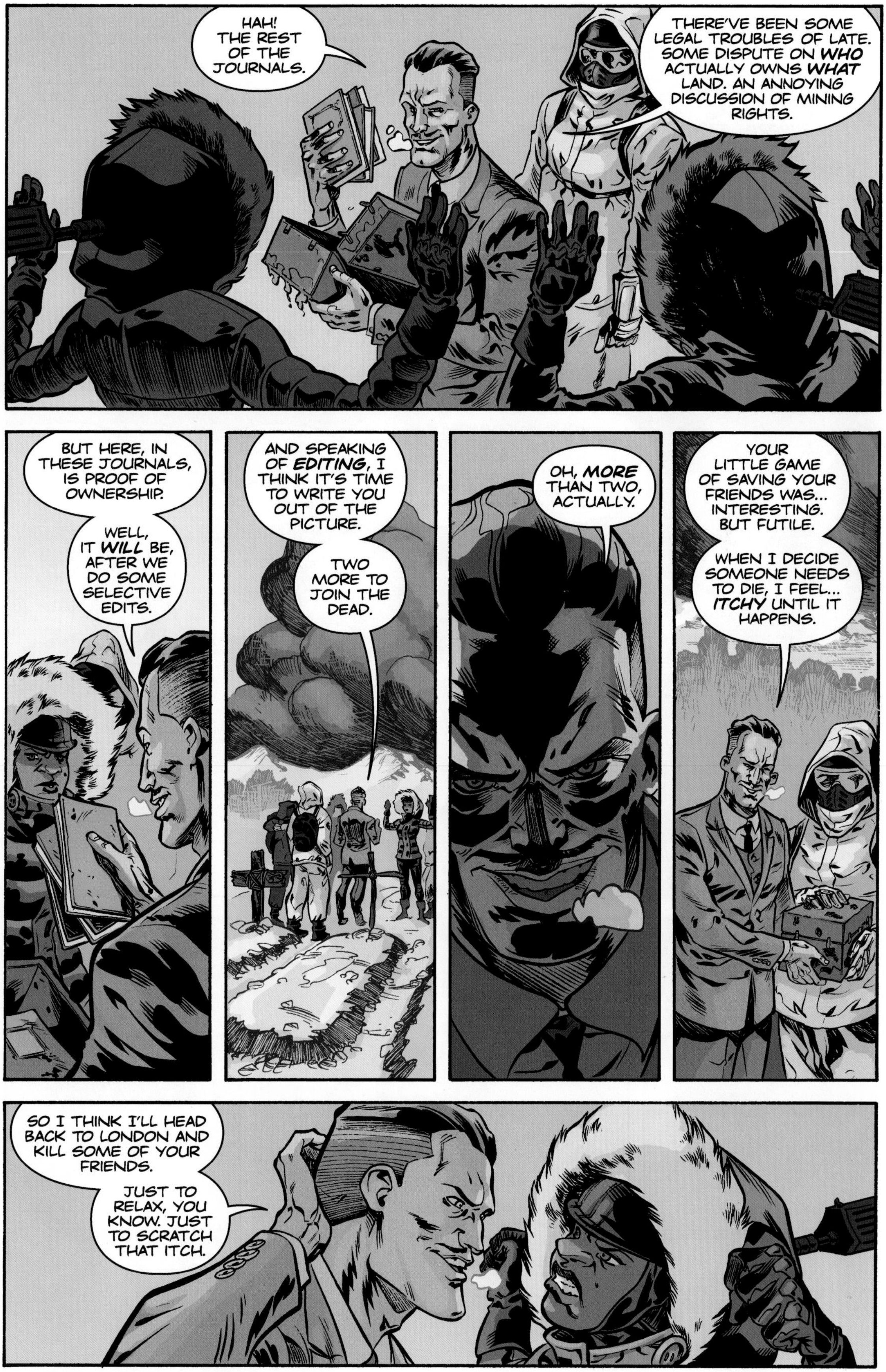
HAH! THE REST OF THE JOURNALS.
THERE'VE BEEN SOME LEGAL TROUBLES OF LATE. SOME DISPUTE ON WHO ACTUALLY OWNS WHAT LAND. AN ANNOYING DISCUSSION OF MINING RIGHTS.
BUT HERE, IN THESE JOURNALS, IS PROOF OF OWNERSHIP.
WELL, IT WILL BE, AFTER WE DO SOME SELECTIVE EDITS.
AND SPEAKING OF EDITING, I THINK IT'S TIME TO WRITE YOU OUT OF THE PICTURE.
TWO MORE TO JOIN THE DEAD.
OH, MORE THAN TWO, ACTUALLY.
YOUR LITTLE GAME OF SAVING YOUR FRIENDS WAS... INTERESTING. BUT FUTILE.
WHEN I DECIDE SOMEONE NEEDS TO DIE, I FEEL... ITCHY UNTIL IT HAPPENS.
SO I THINK I'LL HEAD BACK TO LONDON AND KILL SOME OF YOUR FRIENDS.
JUST TO RELAX, YOU KNOW. JUST TO SCRATCH THAT ITCH.

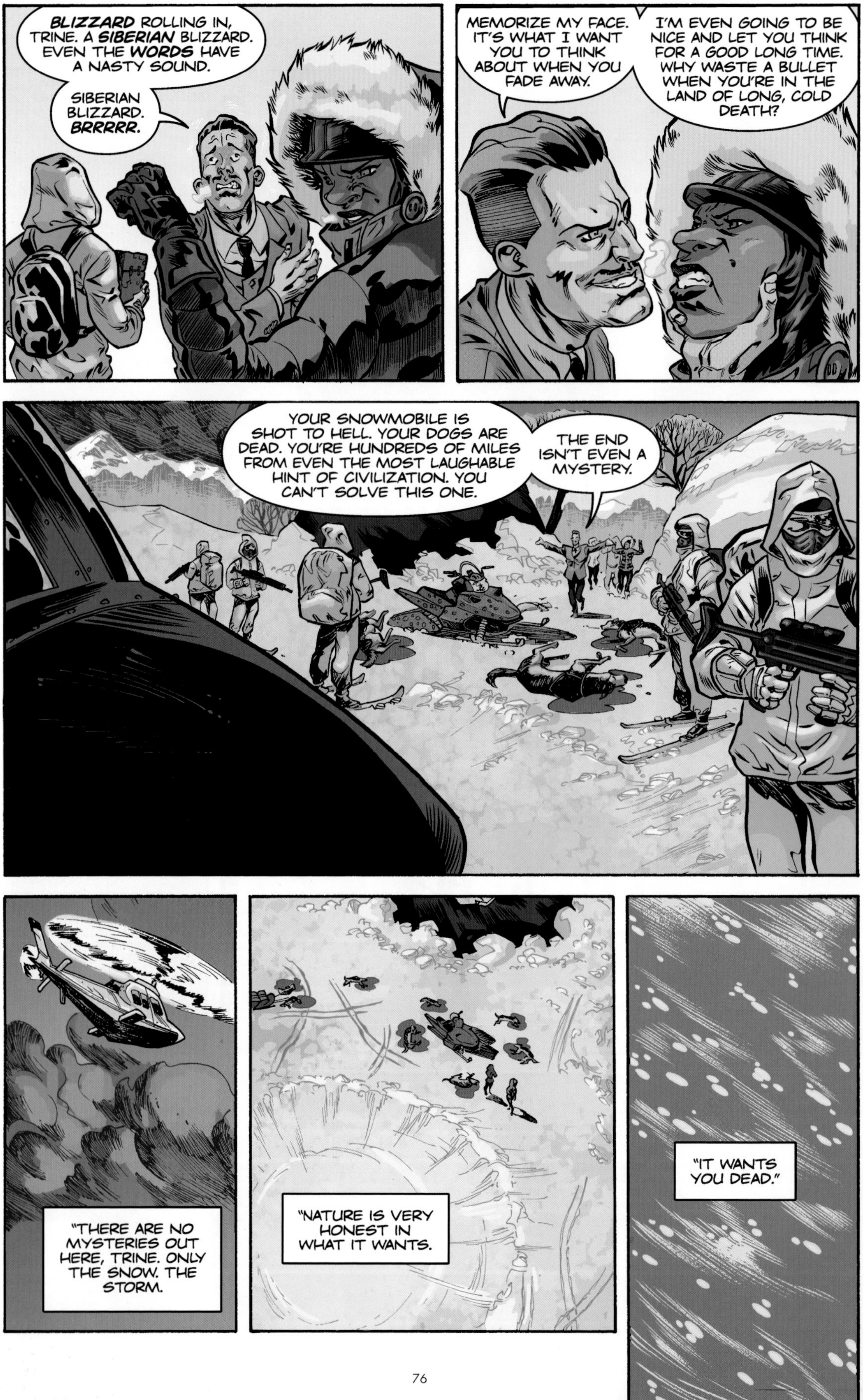

BLIZZARD ROLLING IN, TRINE. A **SIBERIAN** BLIZZARD. EVEN THE **WORDS** HAVE A NASTY SOUND.
SIBERIAN BLIZZARD. **BRRRRR.**
MEMORIZE MY FACE. IT'S WHAT I WANT YOU TO THINK ABOUT WHEN YOU FADE AWAY.
I'M EVEN GOING TO BE NICE AND LET YOU THINK FOR A GOOD LONG TIME. WHY WASTE A BULLET WHEN YOU'RE IN THE LAND OF LONG, COLD DEATH?
YOUR SNOWMOBILE IS SHOT TO HELL. YOUR DOGS ARE DEAD. YOU'RE HUNDREDS OF MILES FROM EVEN THE MOST LAUGHABLE HINT OF CIVILIZATION. YOU CAN'T SOLVE THIS ONE.
THE END ISN'T EVEN A MYSTERY.
"THERE ARE NO MYSTERIES OUT HERE, TRINE. ONLY THE SNOW. THE STORM.
"NATURE IS VERY HONEST IN WHAT IT WANTS.
"IT WANTS YOU DEAD."

CHAPTER 4

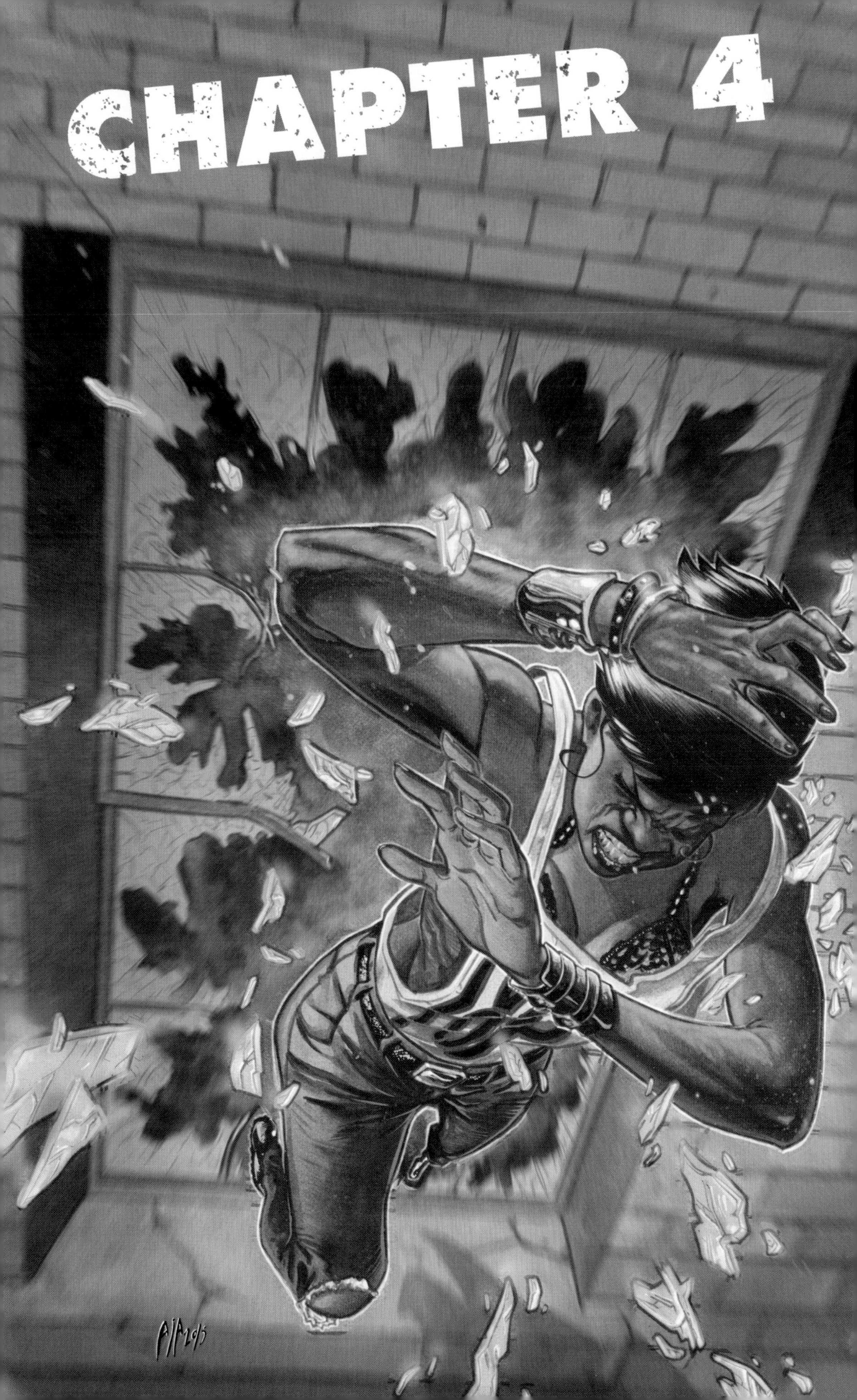

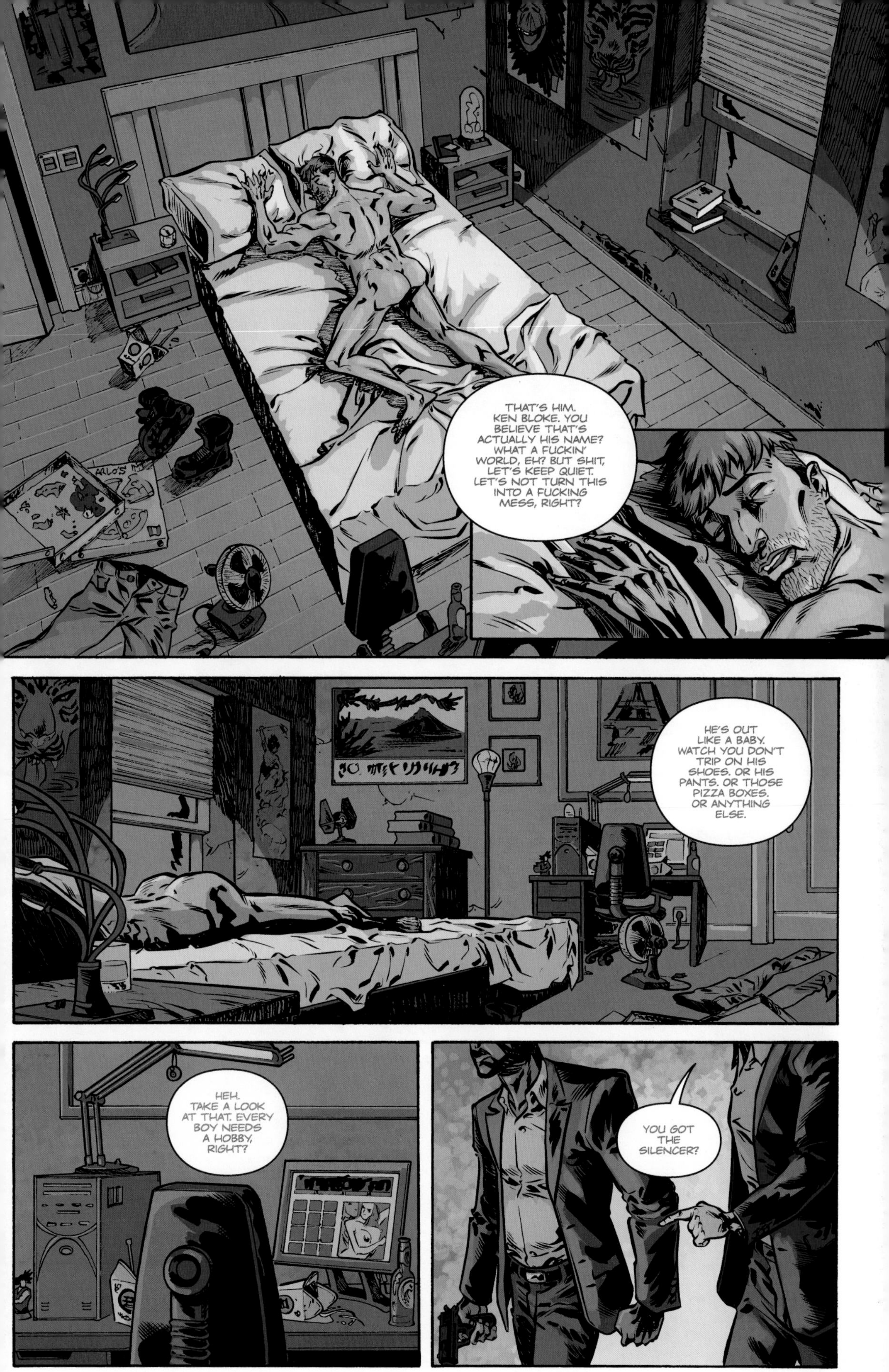
THAT'S HIM. KEN BLOKE. YOU BELIEVE THAT'S ACTUALLY HIS NAME? WHAT A FUCKIN' WORLD, EH? BUT SHIT, LET'S KEEP QUIET. LET'S NOT TURN THIS INTO A FUCKING MESS, RIGHT?
HE'S OUT LIKE A BABY. WATCH YOU DON'T TRIP ON HIS SHOES. OR HIS PANTS. OR THOSE PIZZA BOXES. OR ANYTHING ELSE.
HEH. TAKE A LOOK AT THAT. EVERY BOY NEEDS A HOBBY, RIGHT?
YOU GOT THE SILENCER?

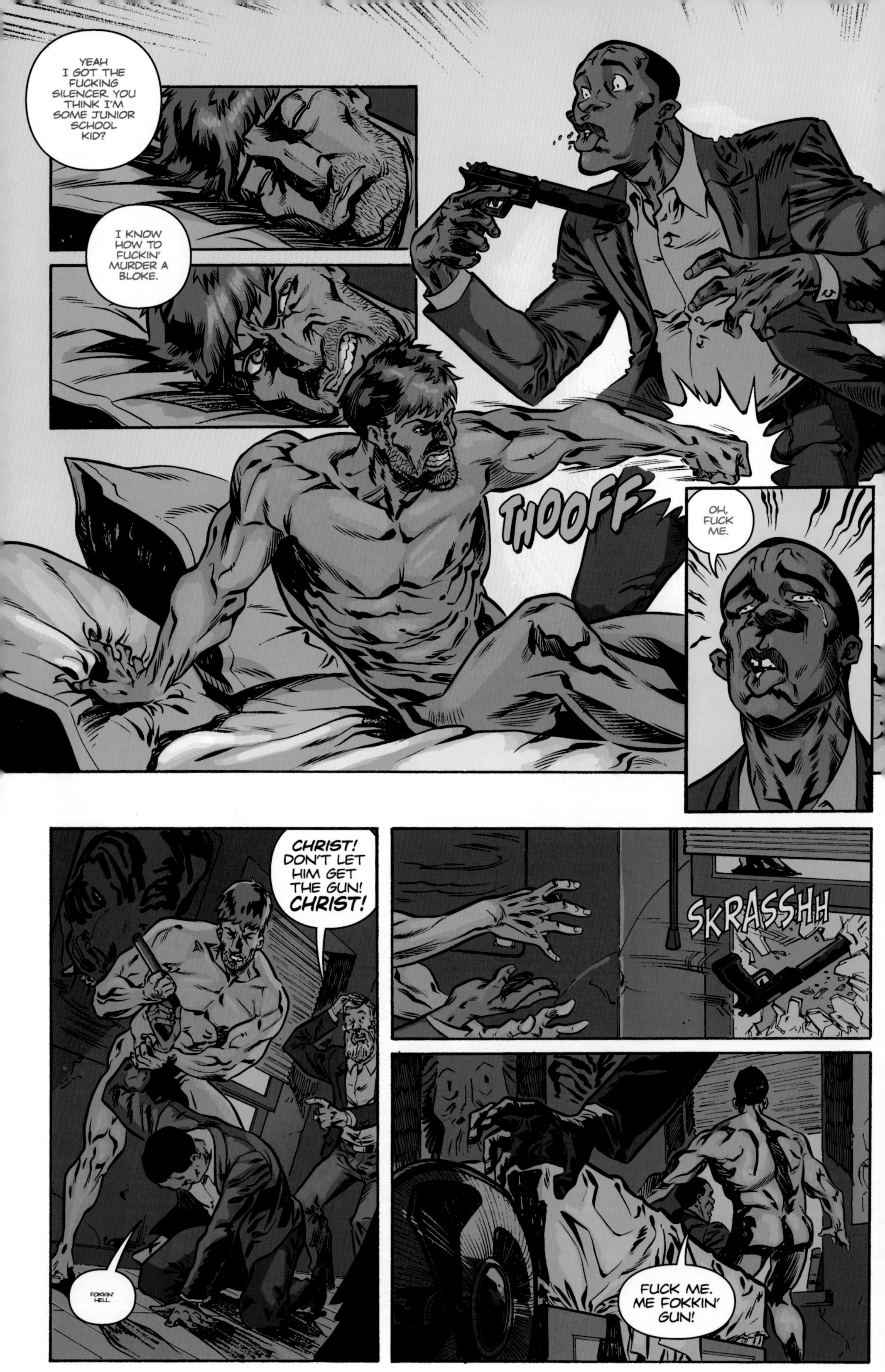
YEAH I GOT THE FUCKING SILENCER. YOU THINK I'M SOME JUNIOR SCHOOL KID?
I KNOW HOW TO FUCKIN' MURDER A BLOKE.
THOOFF
OH, FUCK ME.
CHRIST! DON'T LET HIM GET THE GUN! CHRIST!
FOKKIN' HELL.
SKRASSHH
FUCK ME. ME FOKKIN' GUN!

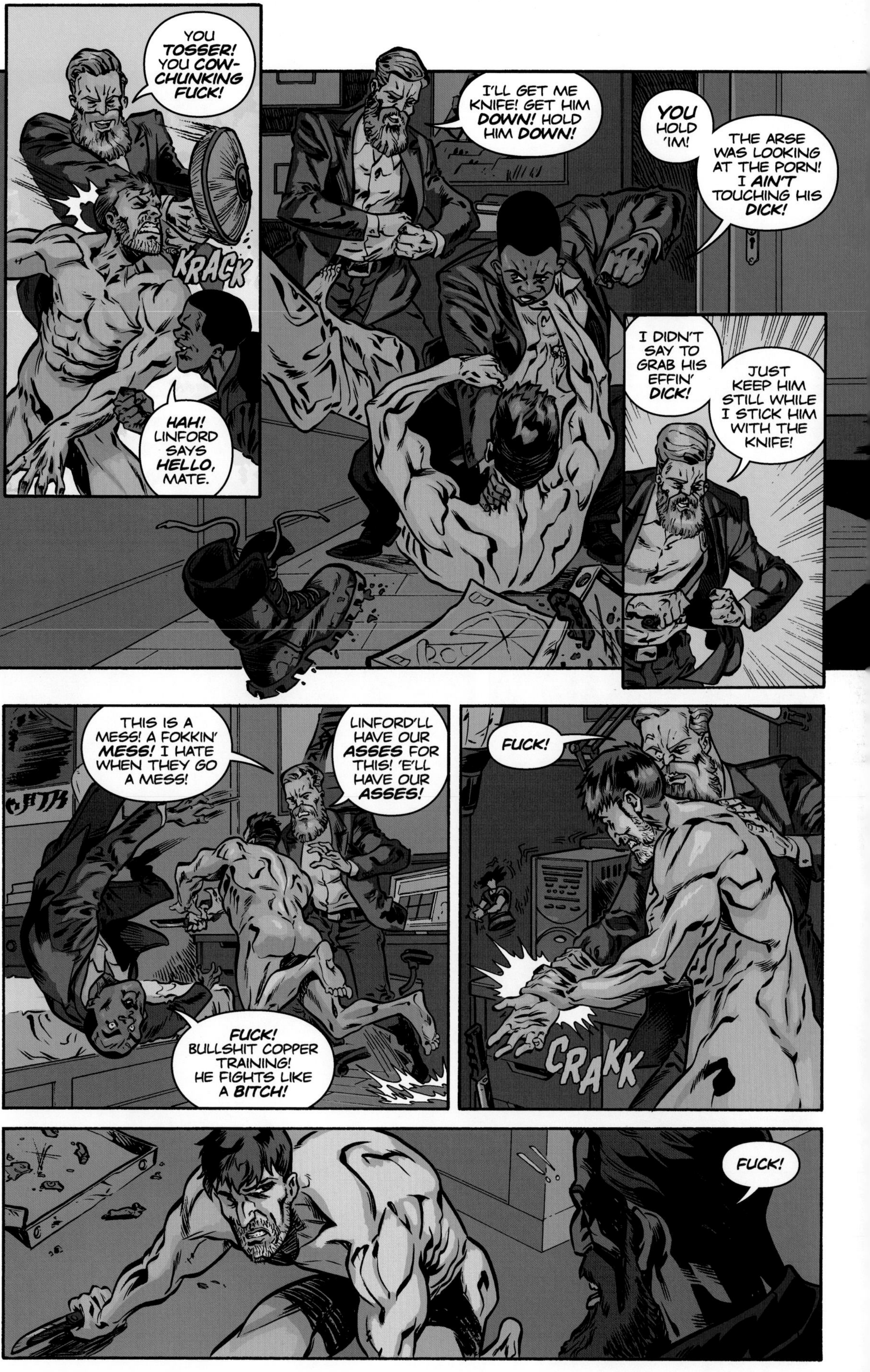
YOU TOSSER! YOU COW-CHUNKING FUCK!
KRACK
HAH! LINFORD SAYS HELLO, MATE.
I'LL GET ME KNIFE! GET HIM DOWN! HOLD HIM DOWN!
YOU HOLD 'IM!
THE ARSE WAS LOOKING AT THE PORN! I AIN'T TOUCHING HIS DICK!
I DIDN'T SAY TO GRAB HIS EFFIN' DICK!
JUST KEEP HIM STILL WHILE I STICK HIM WITH THE KNIFE!
THIS IS A MESS! A FOKKIN' MESS! I HATE WHEN THEY GO A MESS!
LINFORD'LL HAVE OUR ASSES FOR THIS! 'E'LL HAVE OUR ASSES!
FUCK! BULLSHIT COPPER TRAINING! HE FIGHTS LIKE A BITCH!
FUCK!
CRAKK
FUCK!

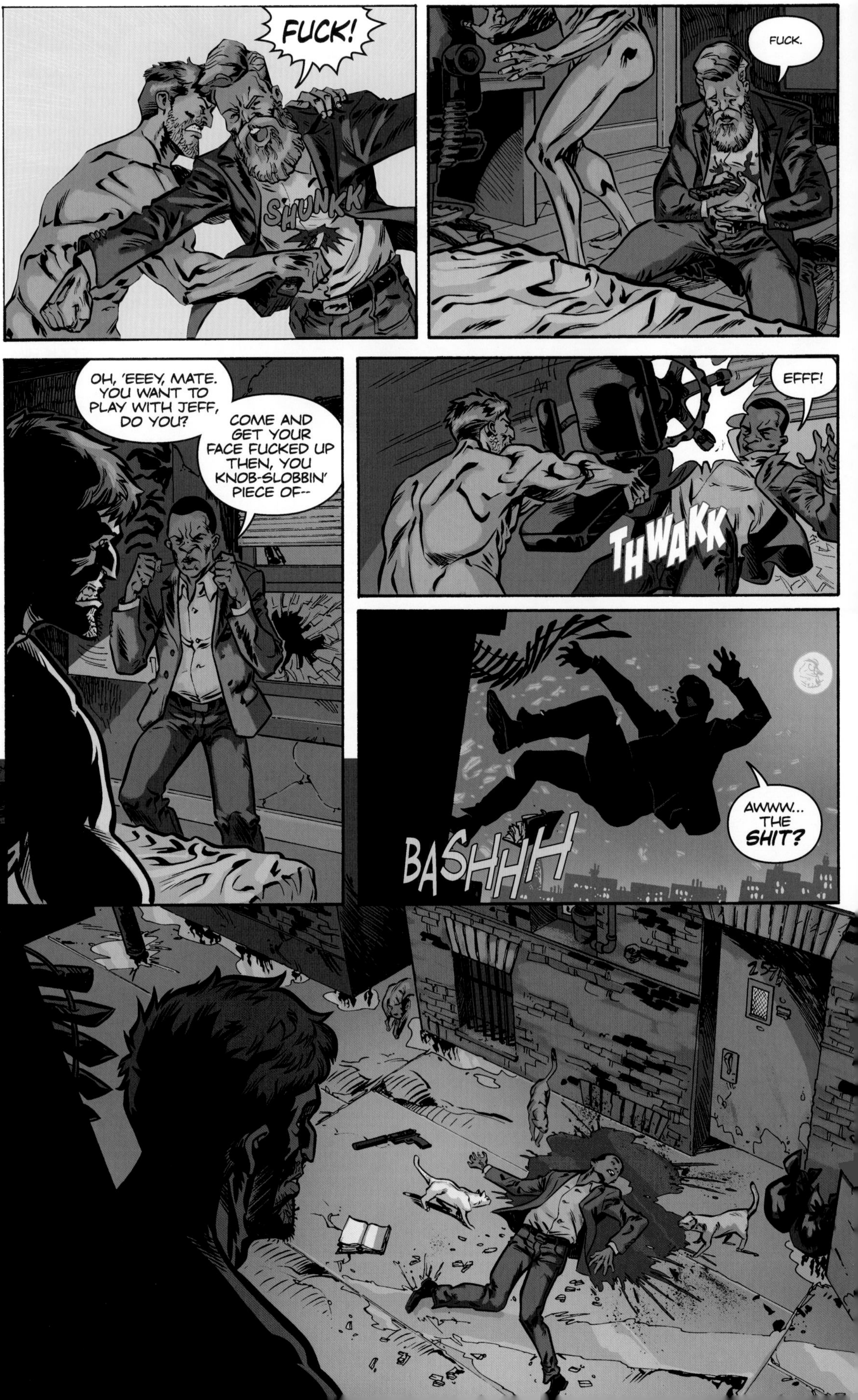
FUCK!
SHUNKK
FUCK.
OH, 'EEEY, MATE. YOU WANT TO PLAY WITH JEFF, DO YOU?
COME AND GET YOUR FACE FUCKED UP THEN, YOU KNOB-SLOBBIN' PIECE OF--
EFFF!
THWAKK
AWWW... THE SHIT?
BASHHH

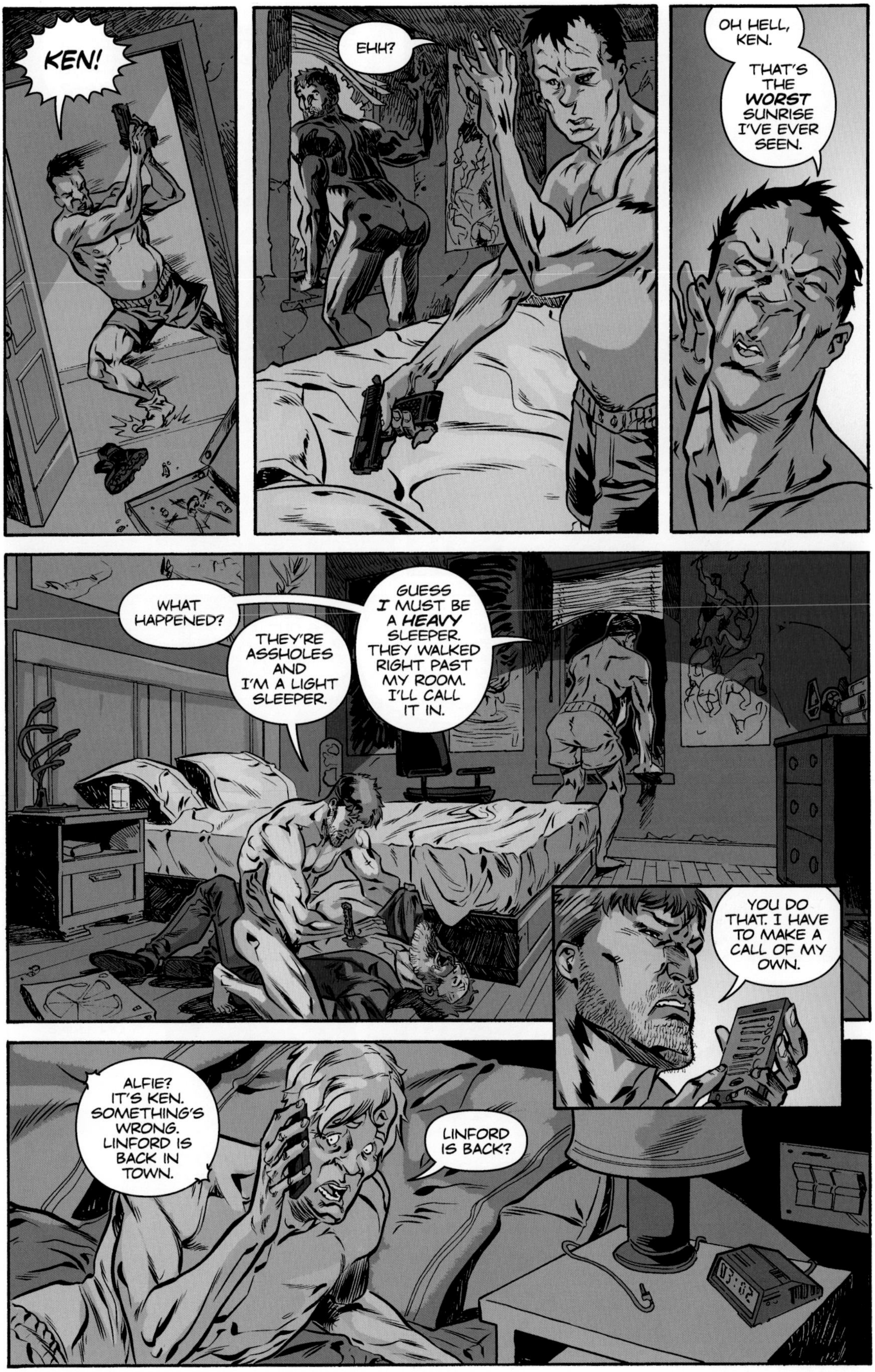
KEN!
EHH?
OH HELL, KEN.
THAT'S THE WORST SUNRISE I'VE EVER SEEN.
WHAT HAPPENED?
THEY'RE ASSHOLES AND I'M A LIGHT SLEEPER.
GUESS I MUST BE A HEAVY SLEEPER. THEY WALKED RIGHT PAST MY ROOM. I'LL CALL IT IN.
YOU DO THAT. I HAVE TO MAKE A CALL OF MY OWN.
ALFIE? IT'S KEN. SOMETHING'S WRONG. LINFORD IS BACK IN TOWN.
LINFORD IS BACK?

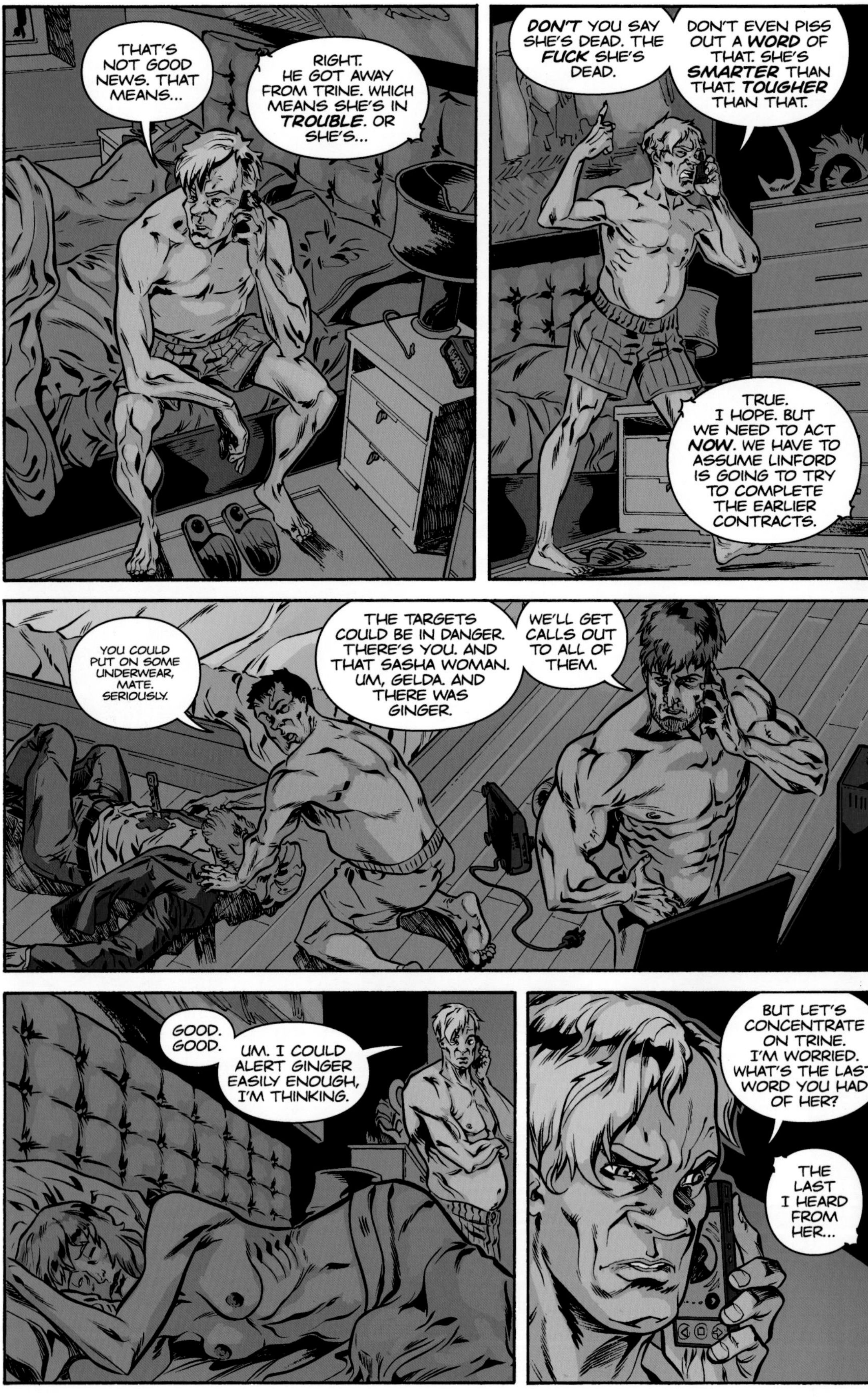
THAT'S NOT GOOD NEWS. THAT MEANS...
RIGHT. HE GOT AWAY FROM TRINE. WHICH MEANS SHE'S IN TROUBLE. OR SHE'S...
DON'T YOU SAY SHE'S DEAD. THE FUCK SHE'S DEAD.
DON'T EVEN PISS OUT A WORD OF THAT. SHE'S SMARTER THAN THAT. TOUGHER THAN THAT.
TRUE. I HOPE. BUT WE NEED TO ACT NOW. WE HAVE TO ASSUME LINFORD IS GOING TO TRY TO COMPLETE THE EARLIER CONTRACTS.
YOU COULD PUT ON SOME UNDERWEAR, MATE. SERIOUSLY.
THE TARGETS COULD BE IN DANGER. THERE'S YOU. AND THAT SASHA WOMAN. UM, GELDA. AND THERE WAS GINGER.
WE'LL GET CALLS OUT TO ALL OF THEM.
GOOD. GOOD.
UM. I COULD ALERT GINGER EASILY ENOUGH, I'M THINKING.
BUT LET'S CONCENTRATE ON TRINE. I'M WORRIED. WHAT'S THE LAST WORD YOU HAD OF HER?
THE LAST I HEARD FROM HER...

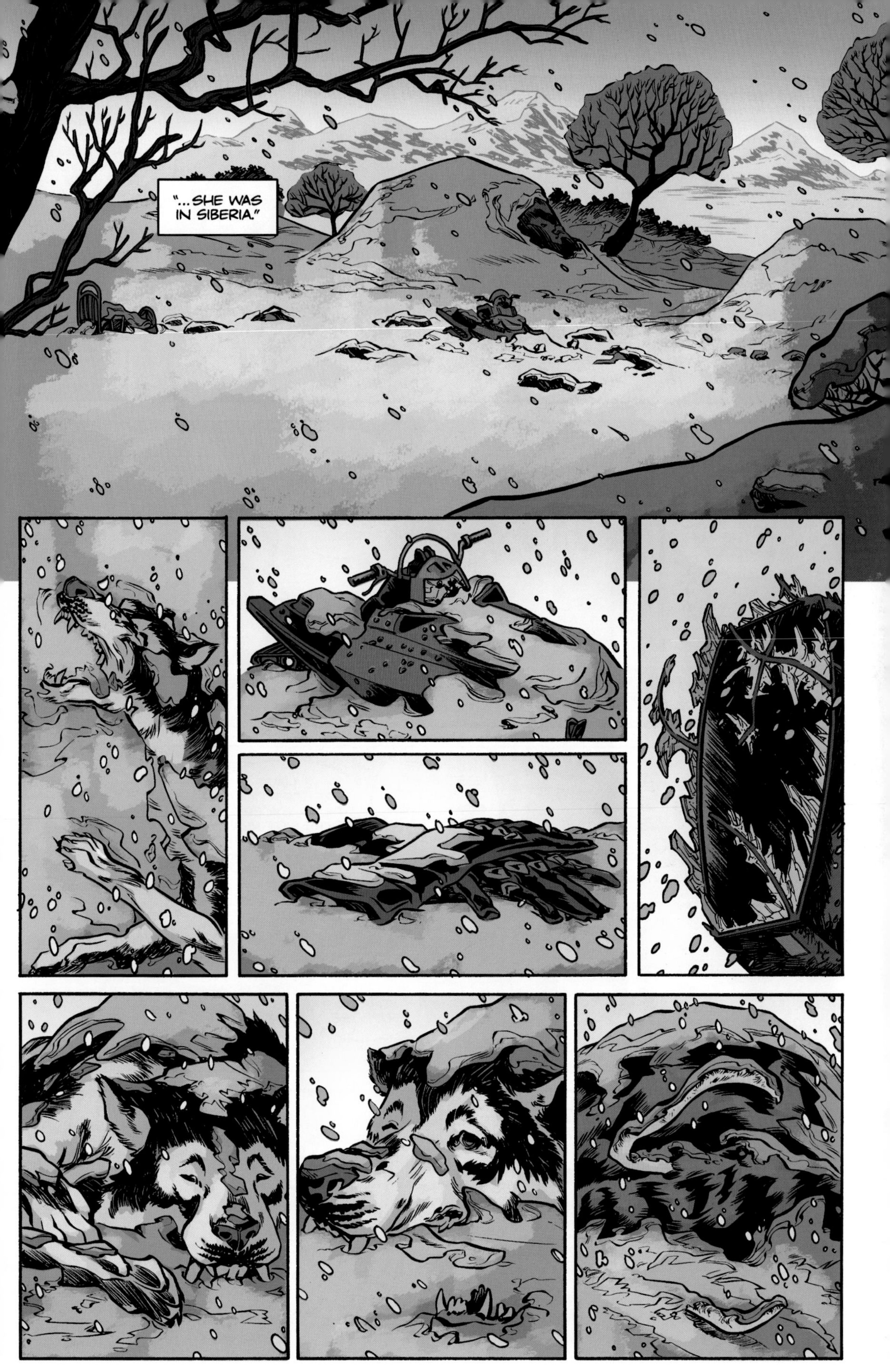
"...SHE WAS
IN SIBERIA."

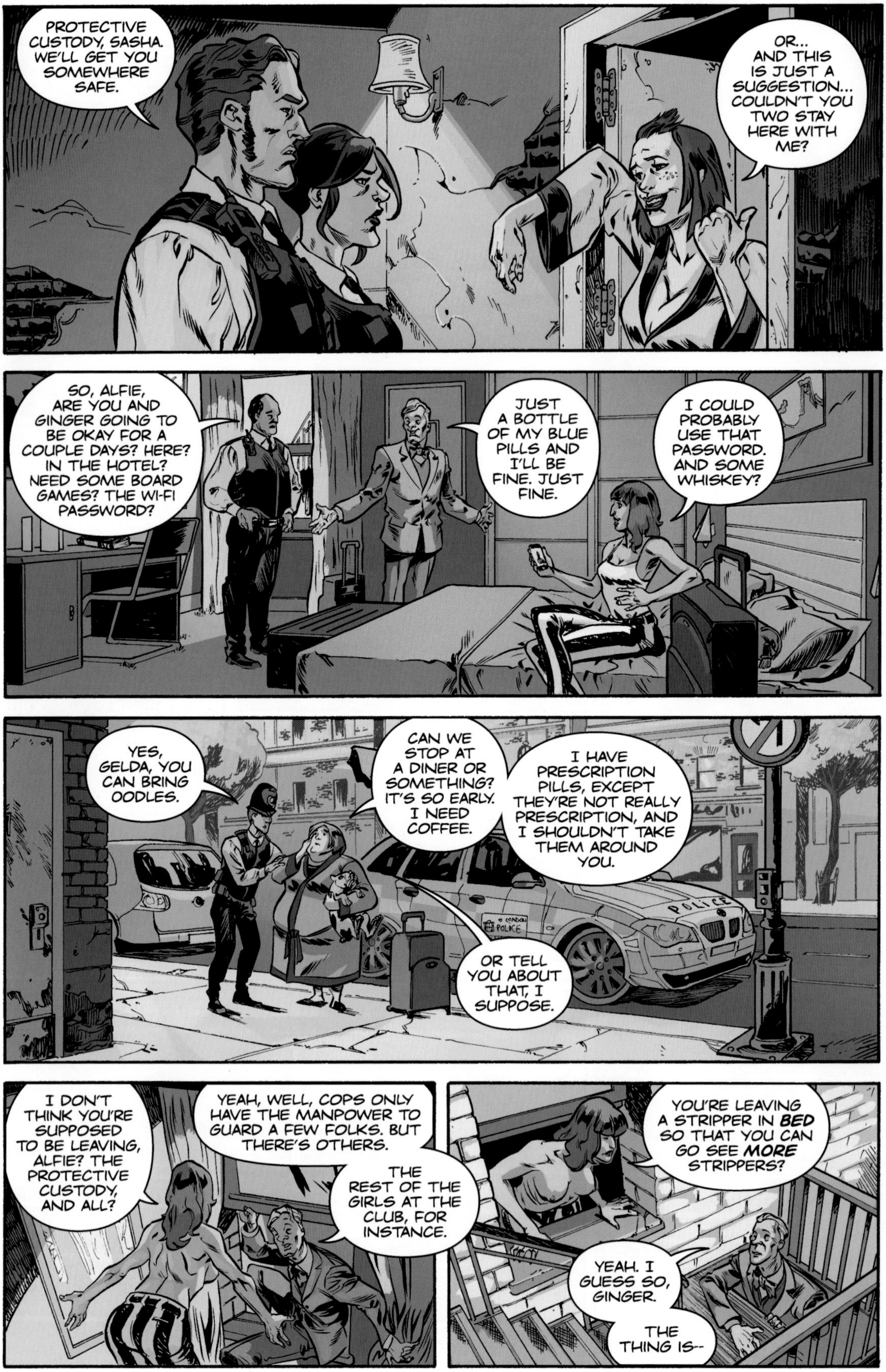
PROTECTIVE CUSTODY, SASHA. WE'LL GET YOU SOMEWHERE SAFE.
OR... AND THIS IS JUST A SUGGESTION... COULDN'T YOU TWO STAY HERE WITH ME?
SO, ALFIE, ARE YOU AND GINGER GOING TO BE OKAY FOR A COUPLE DAYS? HERE? IN THE HOTEL? NEED SOME BOARD GAMES? THE WI-FI PASSWORD?
JUST A BOTTLE OF MY BLUE PILLS AND I'LL BE FINE. JUST FINE.
I COULD PROBABLY USE THAT PASSWORD. AND SOME WHISKEY?
YES, GELDA, YOU CAN BRING OODLES.
CAN WE STOP AT A DINER OR SOMETHING? IT'S SO EARLY. I NEED COFFEE.
I HAVE PRESCRIPTION PILLS, EXCEPT THEY'RE NOT REALLY PRESCRIPTION, AND I SHOULDN'T TAKE THEM AROUND YOU.
OR TELL YOU ABOUT THAT, I SUPPOSE.
POLICE
I DON'T THINK YOU'RE SUPPOSED TO BE LEAVING, ALFIE? THE PROTECTIVE CUSTODY, AND ALL?
YEAH, WELL, COPS ONLY HAVE THE MANPOWER TO GUARD A FEW FOLKS. BUT THERE'S OTHERS.
THE REST OF THE GIRLS AT THE CLUB, FOR INSTANCE.
YOU'RE LEAVING A STRIPPER IN **BED** SO THAT YOU CAN GO SEE ***MORE*** STRIPPERS?
YEAH. I GUESS SO, GINGER.
THE THING IS--

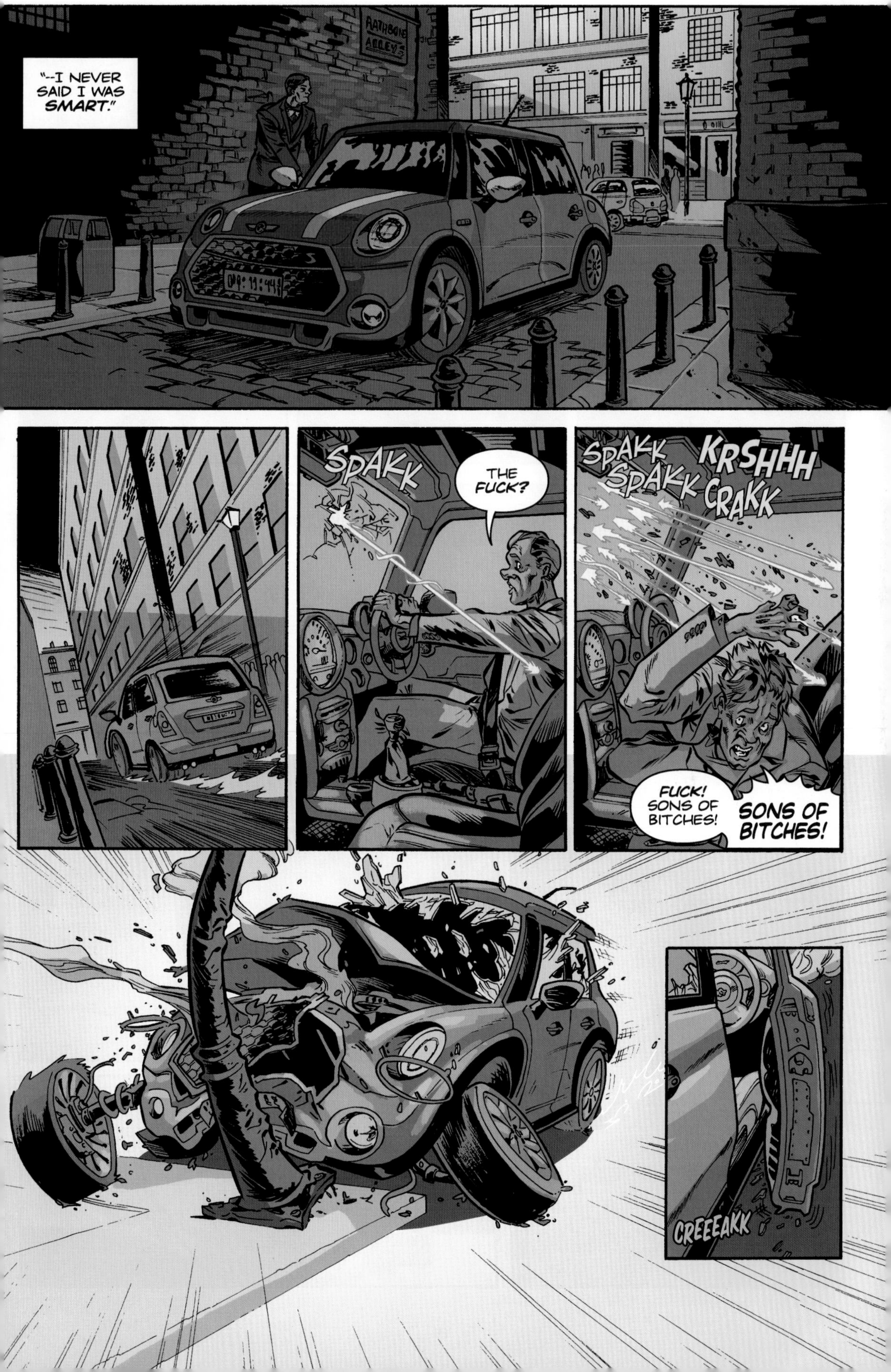
"--I NEVER SAID I WAS SMART."
RATHBONE ALLEY
SPAKK
THE FUCK?
SPAKK SPAKK KRSHHH CRAKK
FUCK! SONS OF BITCHES!
SONS OF BITCHES!
CREEEAKK

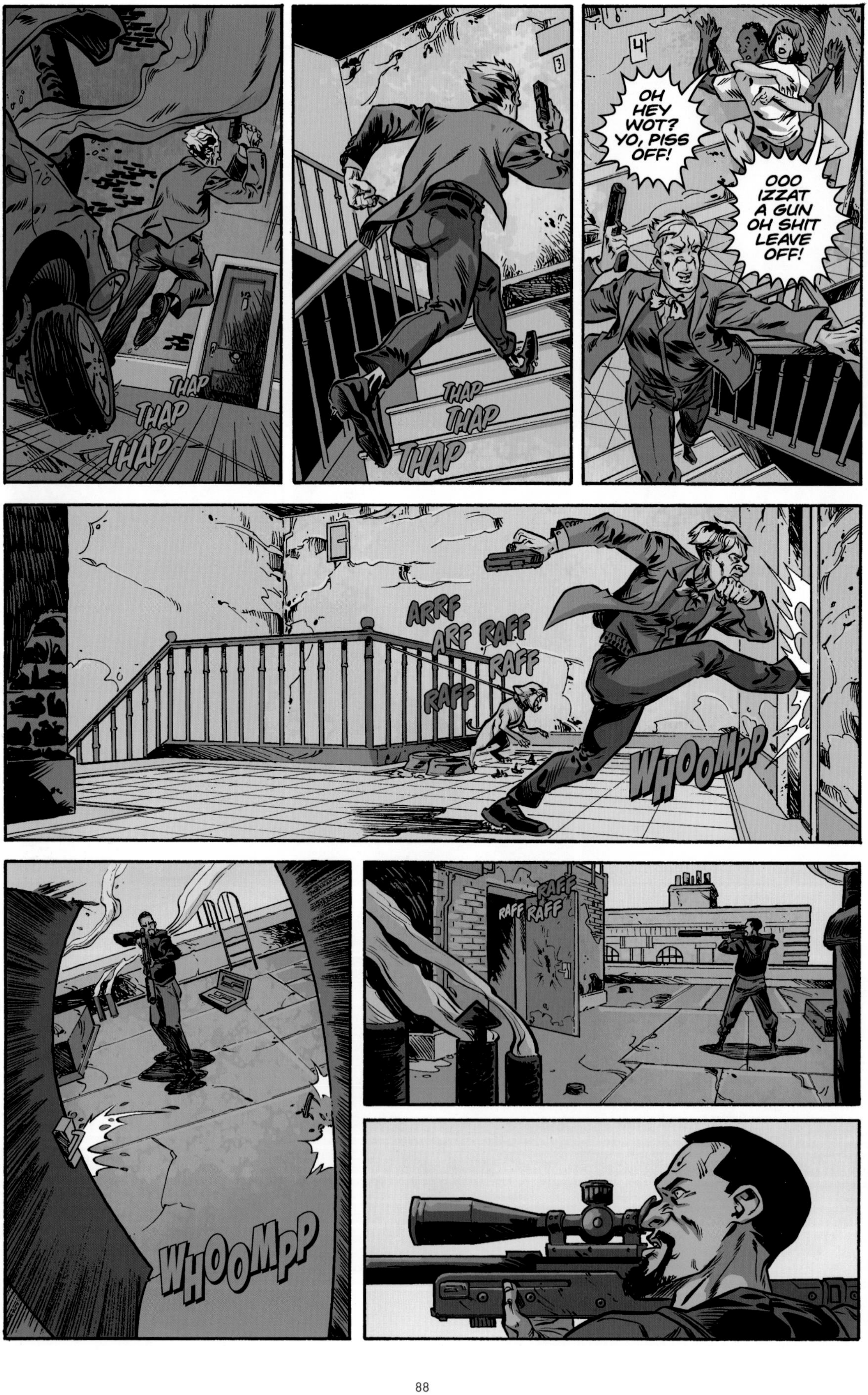
THAP
THAP
THAP
THAP
THAP
THAP
OH HEY WOT? YO, PISS OFF!
OOO IZZAT A GUN OH SHIT LEAVE OFF!
ARRF
ARF RAFF
RAFF
RAFF
WHOOMPP
WHOOMPP
RAFF
RAFF
RAFF

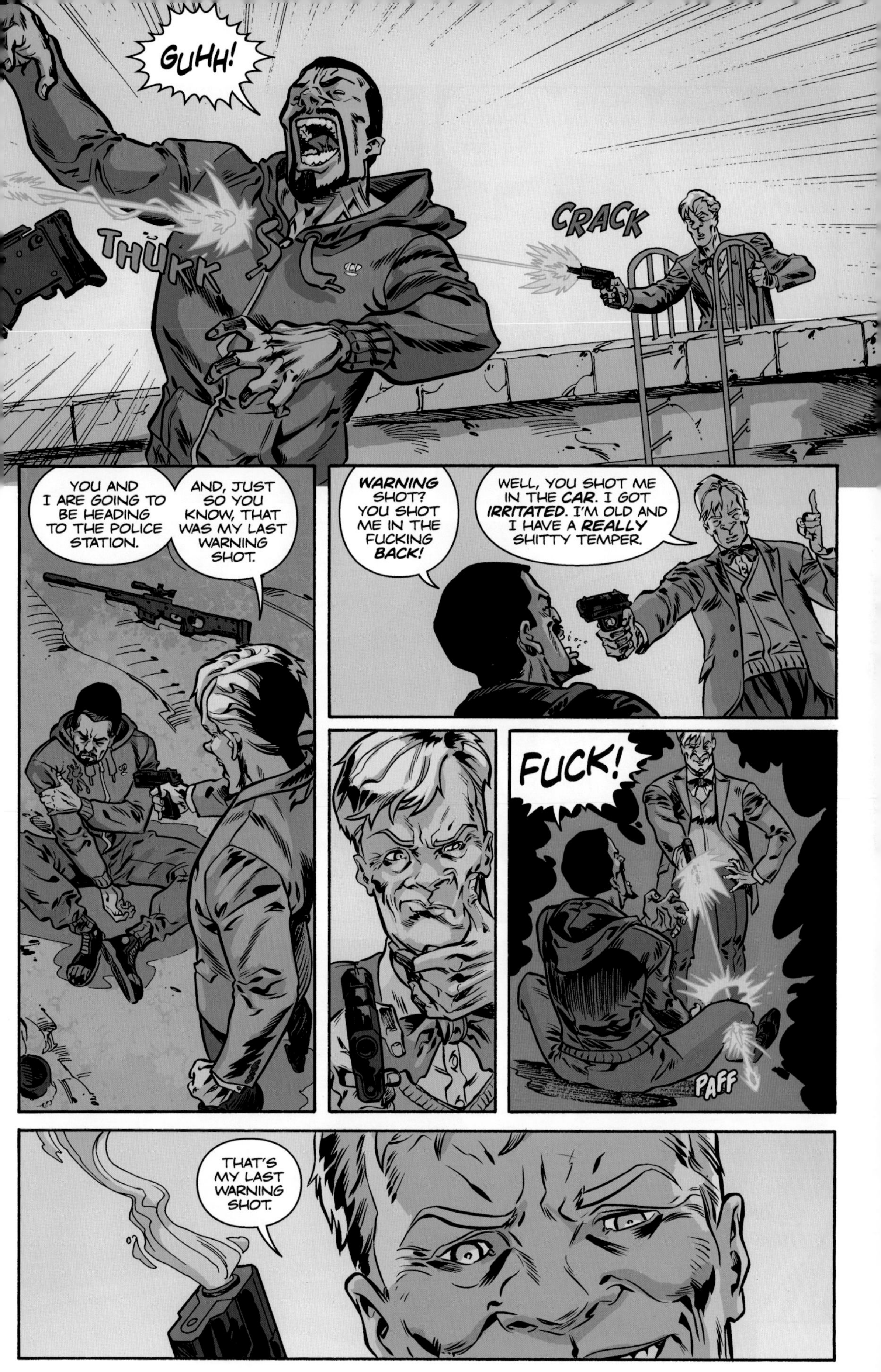
GUHH!
THUKK
CRACK
YOU AND I ARE GOING TO BE HEADING TO THE POLICE STATION.
AND, JUST SO YOU KNOW, THAT WAS MY LAST WARNING SHOT.
WARNING SHOT? YOU SHOT ME IN THE FUCKING BACK!
WELL, YOU SHOT ME IN THE CAR. I GOT IRRITATED. I'M OLD AND I HAVE A REALLY SHITTY TEMPER.
FUCK!
PAFF
THAT'S MY LAST WARNING SHOT.

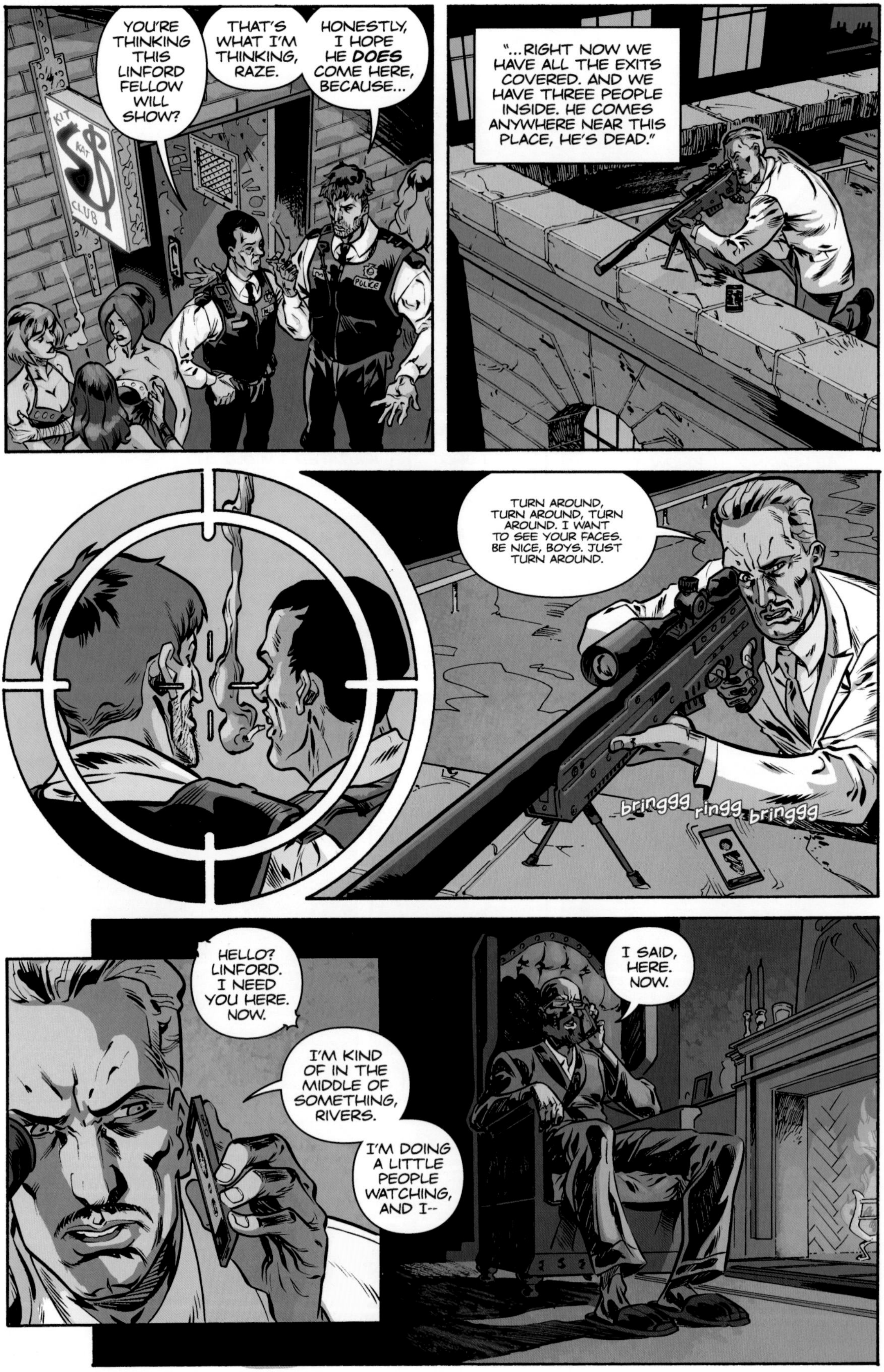
YOU'RE THINKING THIS LINFORD FELLOW WILL SHOW?
THAT'S WHAT I'M THINKING, RAZE.
HONESTLY, I HOPE HE **DOES** COME HERE, BECAUSE...
"...RIGHT NOW WE HAVE ALL THE EXITS COVERED. AND WE HAVE THREE PEOPLE INSIDE. HE COMES ANYWHERE NEAR THIS PLACE, HE'S DEAD."
TURN AROUND, TURN AROUND, TURN AROUND. I WANT TO SEE YOUR FACES. BE NICE, BOYS. JUST TURN AROUND.
bringgg ringg bringgg
HELLO? LINFORD. I NEED YOU HERE. NOW.
I'M KIND OF IN THE MIDDLE OF SOMETHING, RIVERS.
I'M DOING A LITTLE PEOPLE WATCHING, AND I--
I SAID, HERE. NOW.

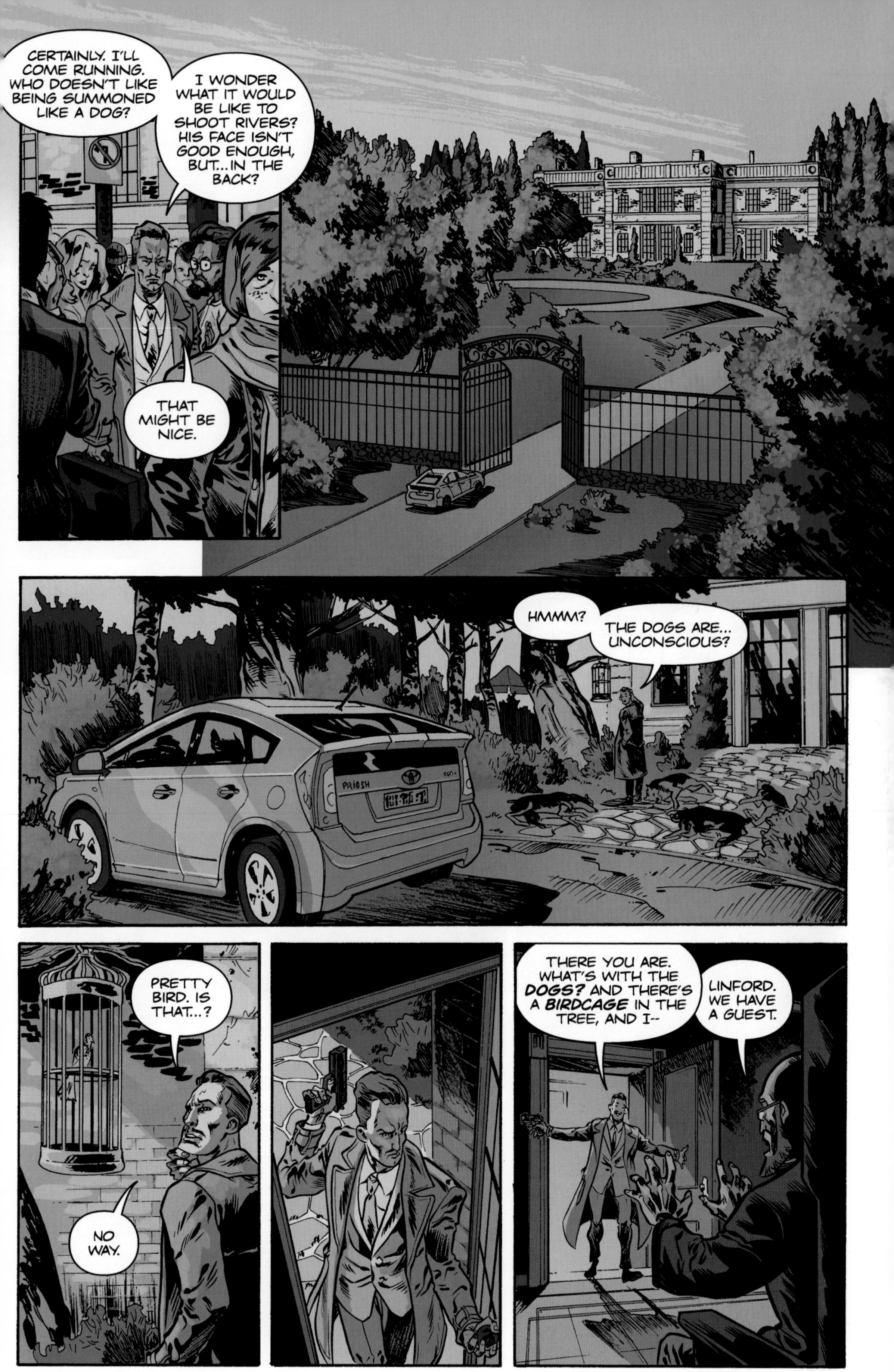
CERTAINLY. I'LL COME RUNNING. WHO DOESN'T LIKE BEING SUMMONED LIKE A DOG?
I WONDER WHAT IT WOULD BE LIKE TO SHOOT RIVERS? HIS FACE ISN'T GOOD ENOUGH, BUT...IN THE BACK?
THAT MIGHT BE NICE.
HMMM?
THE DOGS ARE... UNCONSCIOUS?
PRETTY BIRD. IS THAT...?
NO WAY.
THERE YOU ARE. WHAT'S WITH THE DOGS? AND THERE'S A BIRDCAGE IN THE TREE, AND I--
LINFORD. WE HAVE A GUEST.

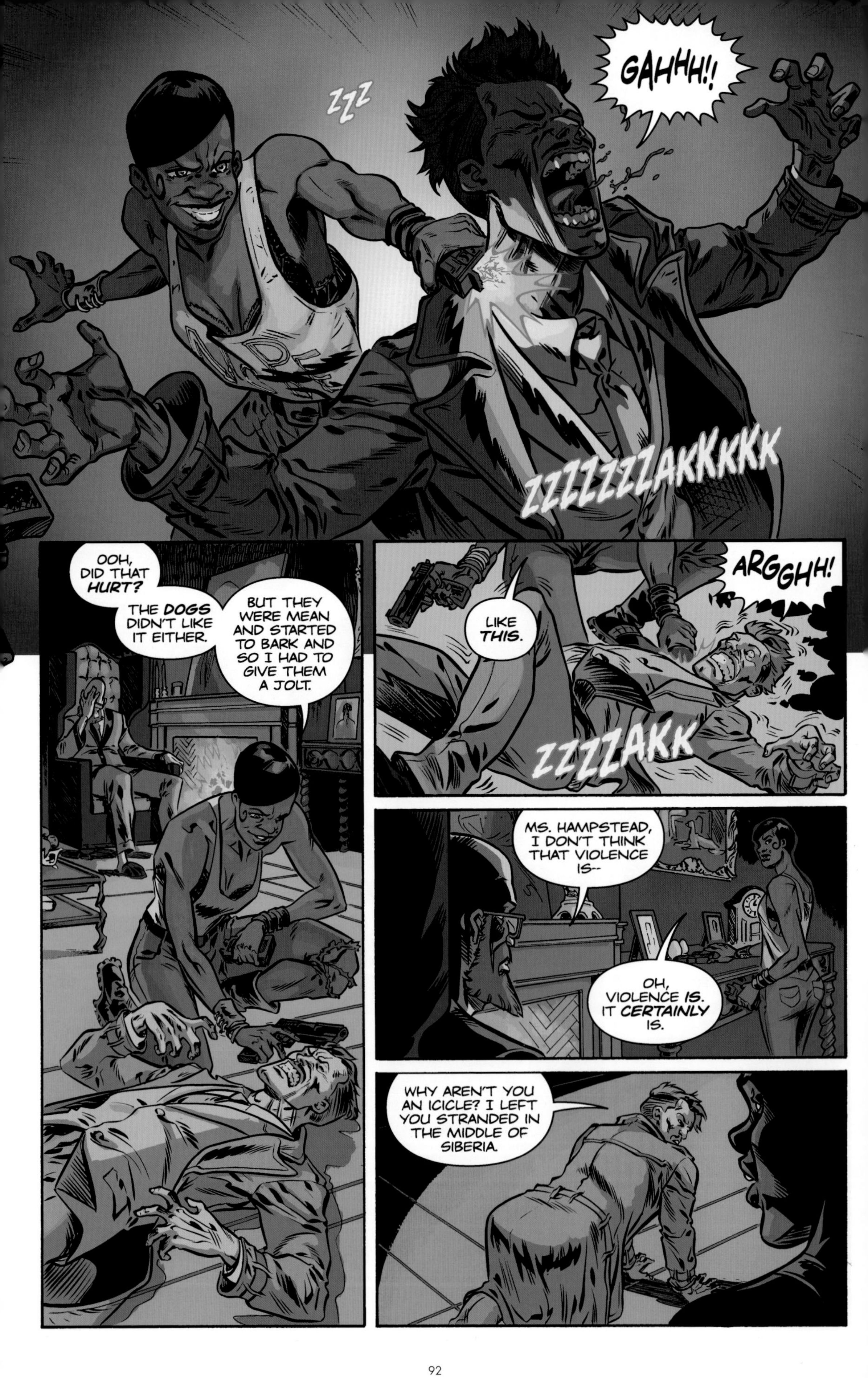
ZZZ
GAHHH!!
ZZZZZZZZAKKKKK
OOH, DID THAT HURT?
THE DOGS DIDN'T LIKE IT EITHER.
BUT THEY WERE MEAN AND STARTED TO BARK AND SO I HAD TO GIVE THEM A JOLT.
LIKE THIS.
ARGGHH!
ZZZZAKK
MS. HAMPSTEAD, I DON'T THINK THAT VIOLENCE IS--
OH, VIOLENCE IS. IT CERTAINLY IS.
WHY AREN'T YOU AN ICICLE? I LEFT YOU STRANDED IN THE MIDDLE OF SIBERIA.

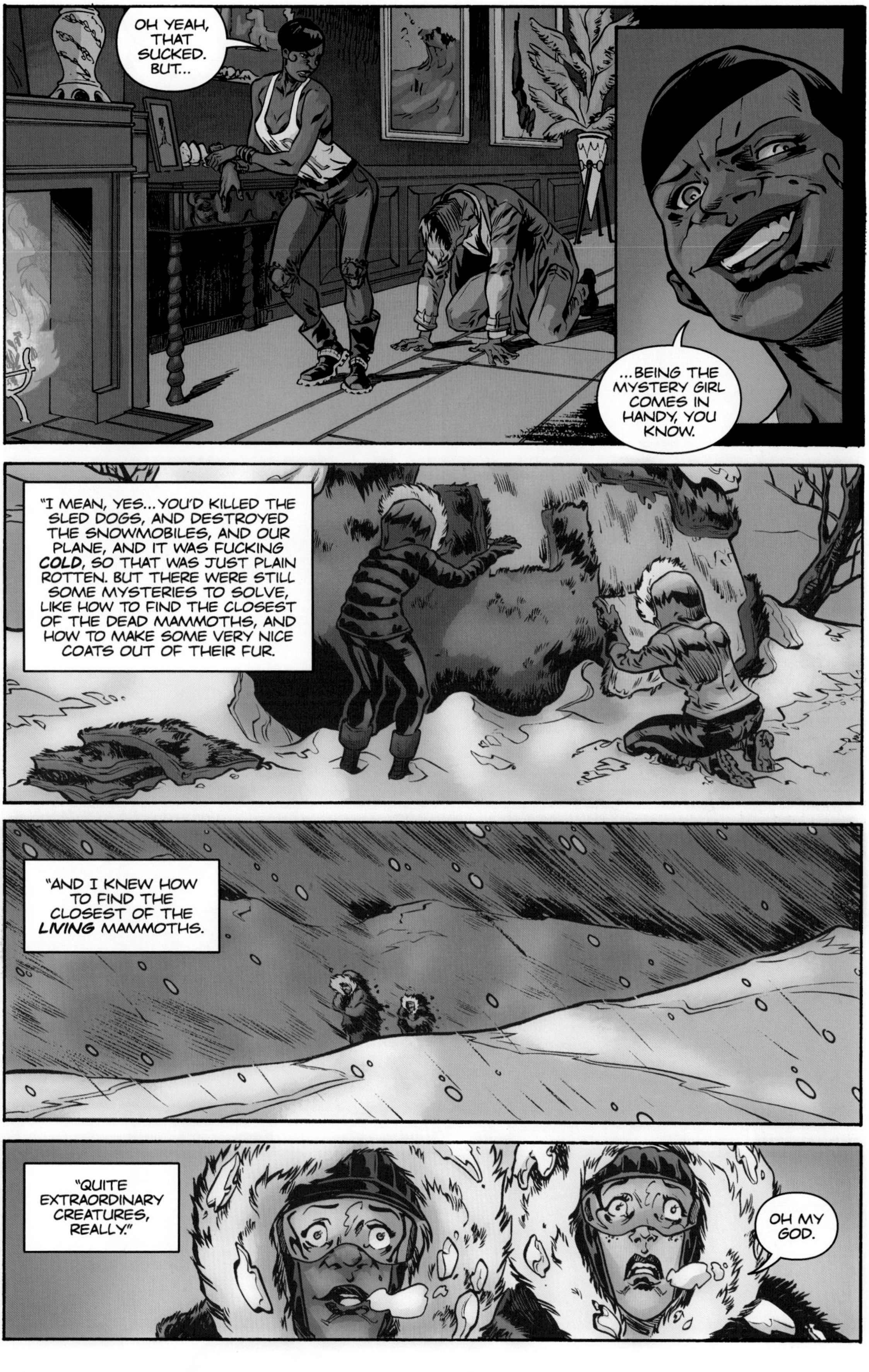
OH YEAH, THAT SUCKED. BUT...
...BEING THE MYSTERY GIRL COMES IN HANDY, YOU KNOW.
"I MEAN, YES... YOU'D KILLED THE SLED DOGS, AND DESTROYED THE SNOWMOBILES, AND OUR PLANE, AND IT WAS FUCKING COLD, SO THAT WAS JUST PLAIN ROTTEN. BUT THERE WERE STILL SOME MYSTERIES TO SOLVE, LIKE HOW TO FIND THE CLOSEST OF THE DEAD MAMMOTHS, AND HOW TO MAKE SOME VERY NICE COATS OUT OF THEIR FUR.
"AND I KNEW HOW TO FIND THE CLOSEST OF THE LIVING MAMMOTHS.
"QUITE EXTRAORDINARY CREATURES, REALLY."
OH MY GOD.

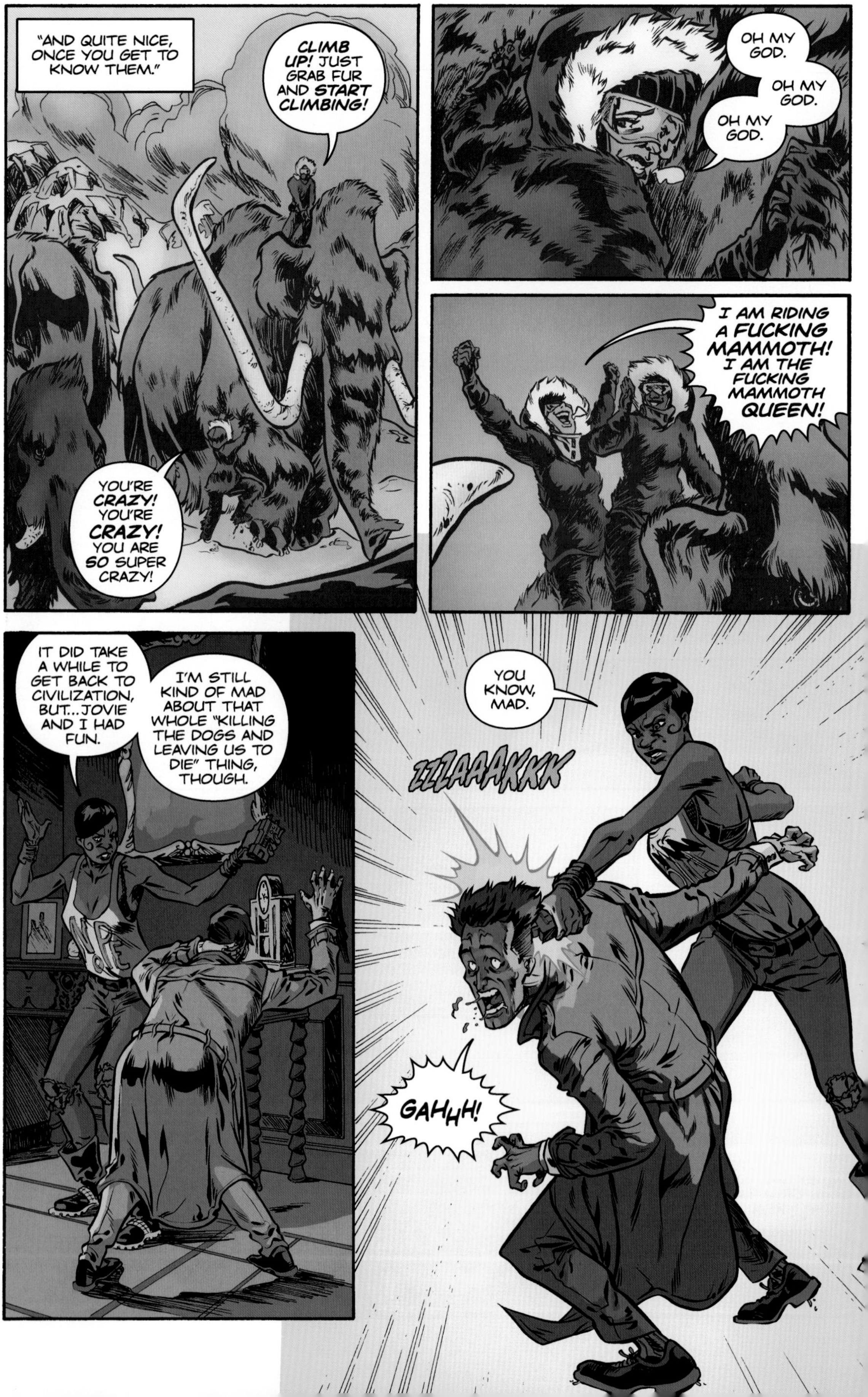
"AND QUITE NICE, ONCE YOU GET TO KNOW THEM."
CLIMB UP! JUST GRAB FUR AND START CLIMBING!
YOU'RE CRAZY! YOU'RE CRAZY! YOU ARE SO SUPER CRAZY!
OH MY GOD.
OH MY GOD.
OH MY GOD.
I AM RIDING A FUCKING MAMMOTH! I AM THE FUCKING MAMMOTH QUEEN!
IT DID TAKE A WHILE TO GET BACK TO CIVILIZATION, BUT...JOVIE AND I HAD FUN.
I'M STILL KIND OF MAD ABOUT THAT WHOLE "KILLING THE DOGS AND LEAVING US TO DIE" THING, THOUGH.
YOU KNOW, MAD.
ZZZAAAKKK
GAHHH!

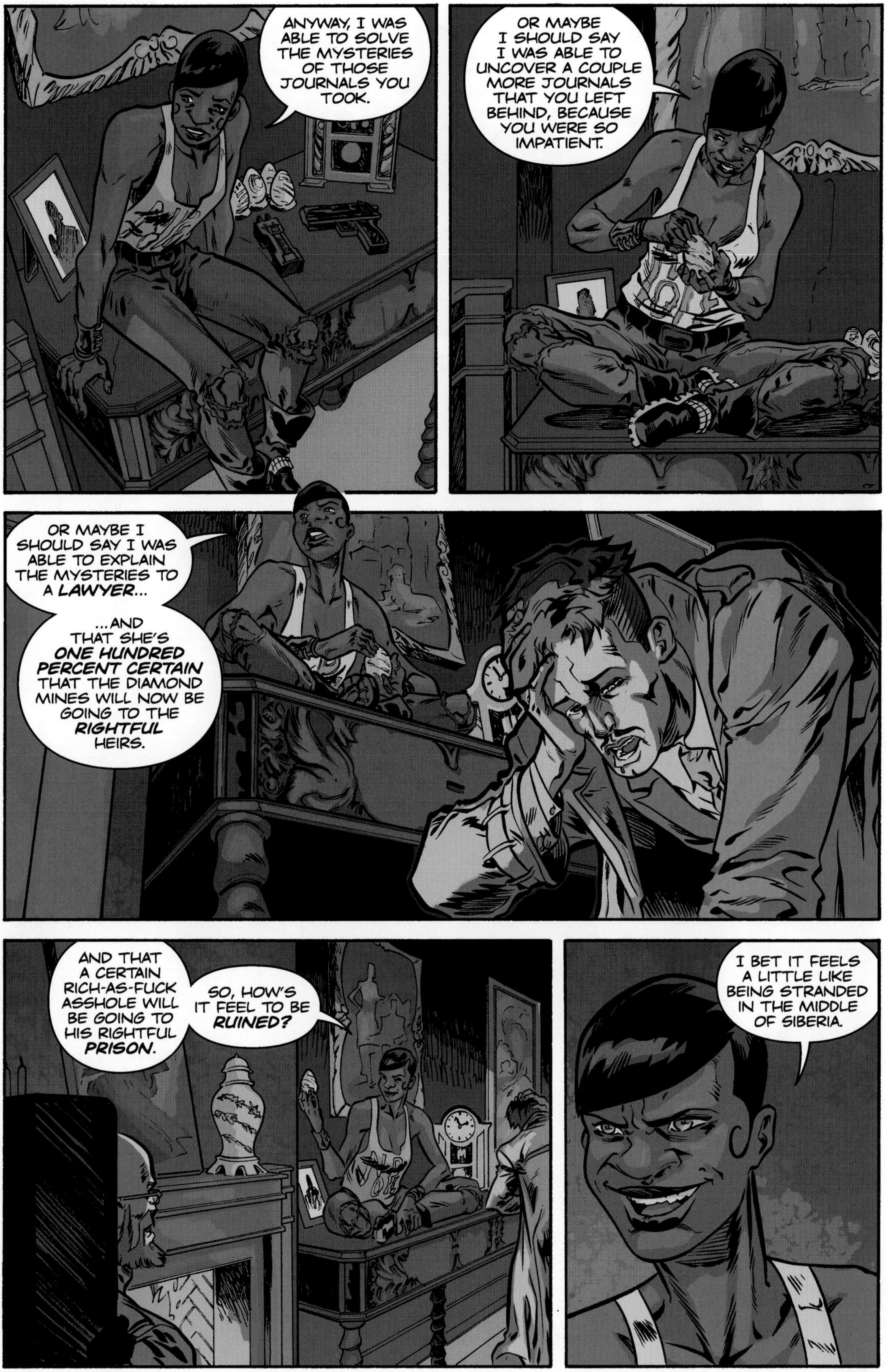
ANYWAY, I WAS ABLE TO SOLVE THE MYSTERIES OF THOSE JOURNALS YOU TOOK.
OR MAYBE I SHOULD SAY I WAS ABLE TO UNCOVER A COUPLE MORE JOURNALS THAT YOU LEFT BEHIND, BECAUSE YOU WERE SO IMPATIENT.
OR MAYBE I SHOULD SAY I WAS ABLE TO EXPLAIN THE MYSTERIES TO A LAWYER...
...AND THAT SHE'S ONE HUNDRED PERCENT CERTAIN THAT THE DIAMOND MINES WILL NOW BE GOING TO THE RIGHTFUL HEIRS.
AND THAT A CERTAIN RICH-AS-FUCK ASSHOLE WILL BE GOING TO HIS RIGHTFUL PRISON.
SO, HOW'S IT FEEL TO BE RUINED?
I BET IT FEELS A LITTLE LIKE BEING STRANDED IN THE MIDDLE OF SIBERIA.

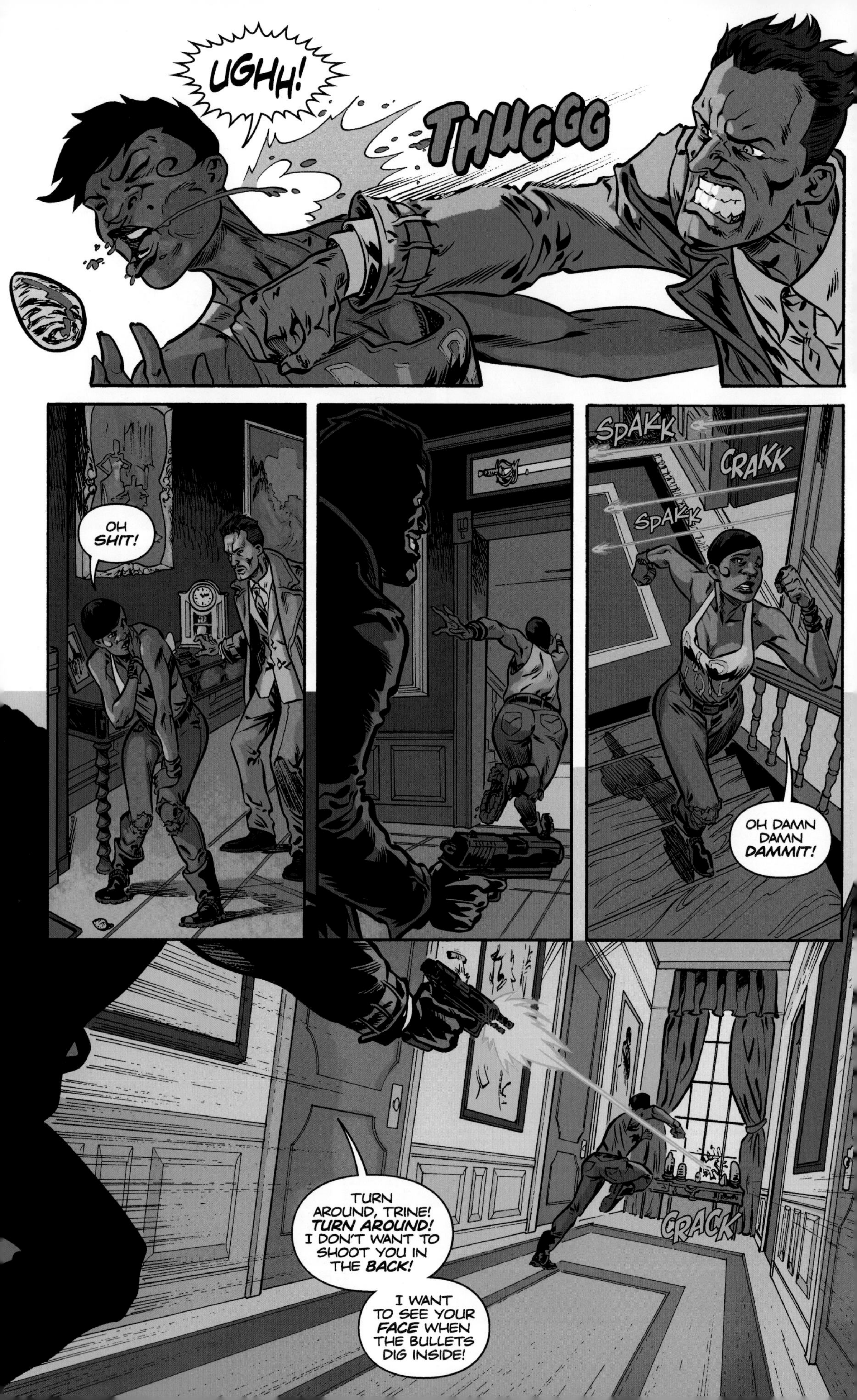
UGHH!
THUGGG
OH SHIT!
SPAKK
CRAKK
SPAKK
OH DAMN DAMN DAMMIT!
TURN AROUND, TRINE! TURN AROUND! I DON'T WANT TO SHOOT YOU IN THE BACK!
I WANT TO SEE YOUR FACE WHEN THE BULLETS DIG INSIDE!
CRACK

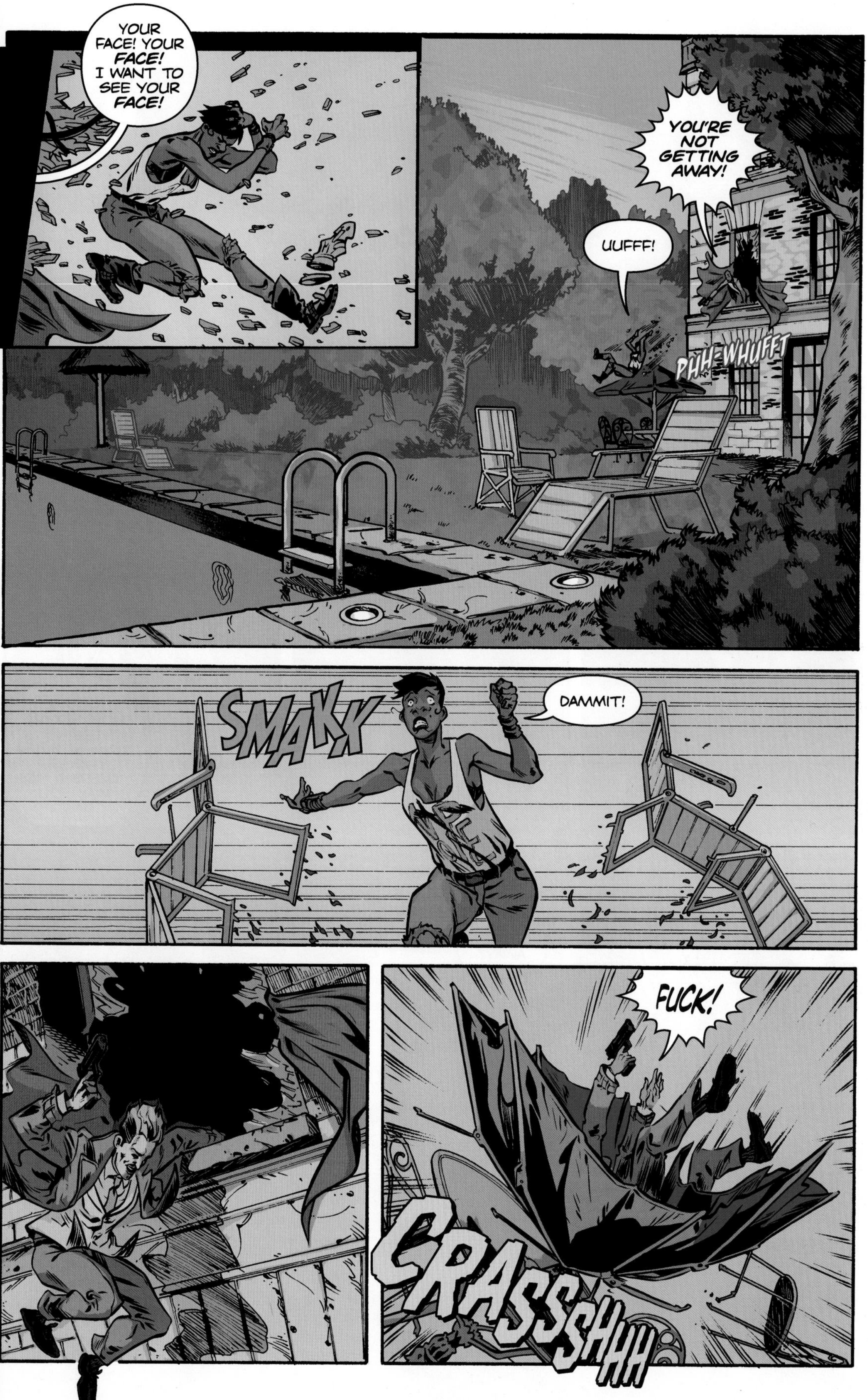
YOUR FACE! YOUR FACE! I WANT TO SEE YOUR FACE!
YOU'RE NOT GETTING AWAY!
UUFFF!
PHH-WHUFFT
SMAKK
DAMMIT!
FUCK!
CRASSSHHH

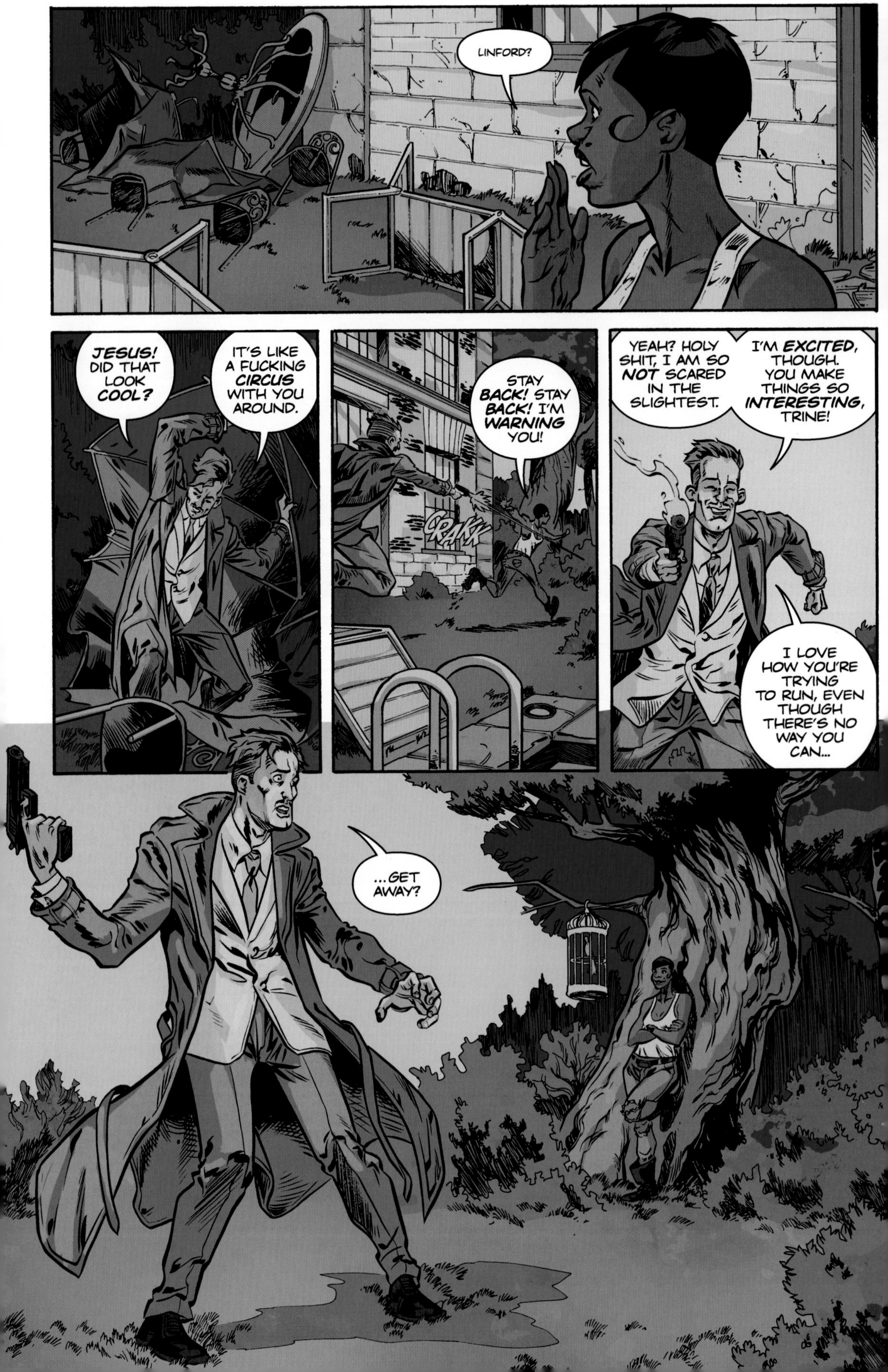
LINFORD?
JESUS! DID THAT LOOK COOL?
IT'S LIKE A FUCKING CIRCUS WITH YOU AROUND.
STAY BACK! STAY BACK! I'M WARNING YOU!
CRAKK
YEAH? HOLY SHIT, I AM SO NOT SCARED IN THE SLIGHTEST.
I'M EXCITED, THOUGH. YOU MAKE THINGS SO INTERESTING, TRINE!
I LOVE HOW YOU'RE TRYING TO RUN, EVEN THOUGH THERE'S NO WAY YOU CAN...
...GET AWAY?

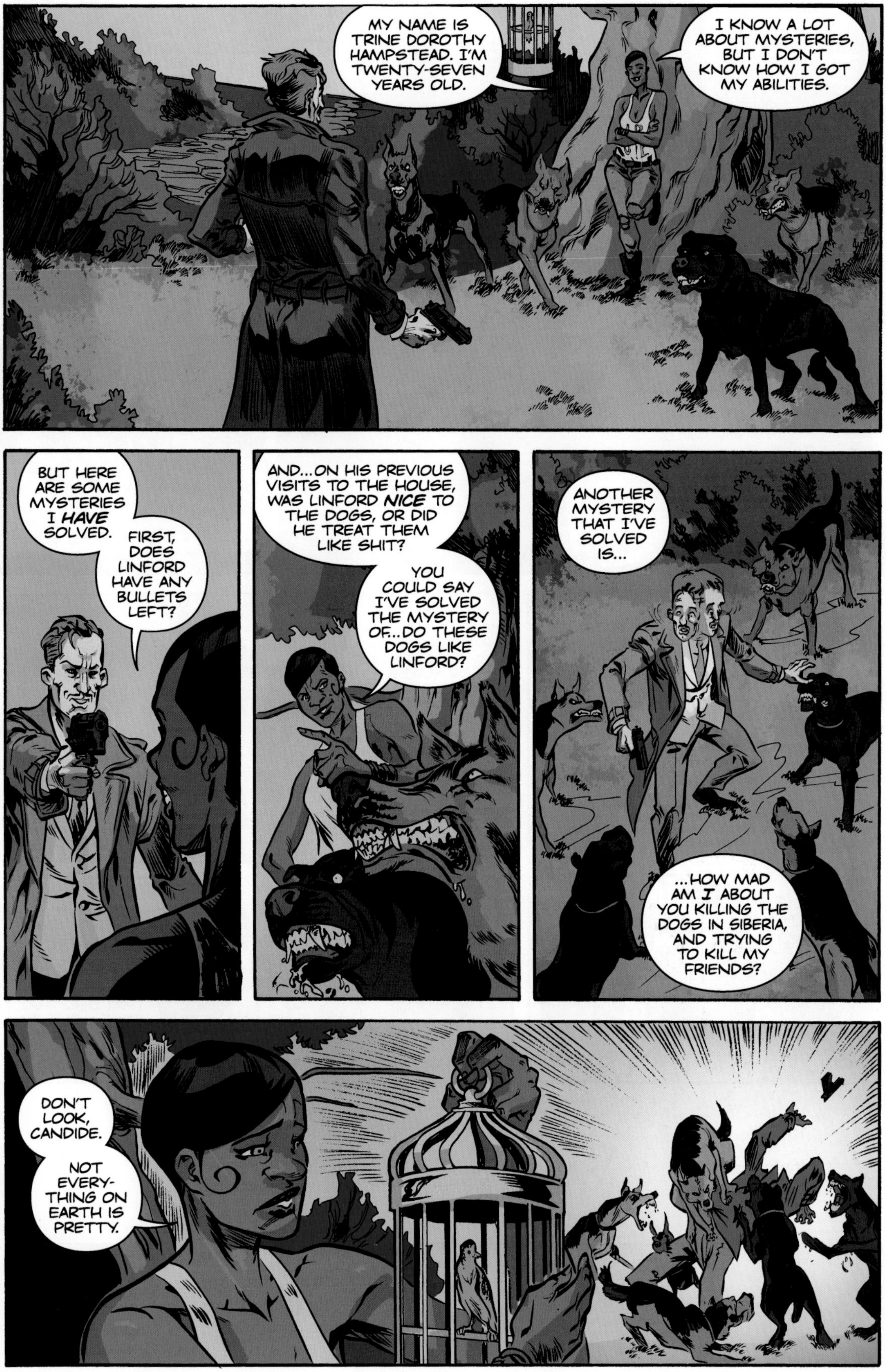

MY NAME IS TRINE DOROTHY HAMPSTEAD. I'M TWENTY-SEVEN YEARS OLD.
I KNOW A LOT ABOUT MYSTERIES, BUT I DON'T KNOW HOW I GOT MY ABILITIES.
BUT HERE ARE SOME MYSTERIES I *HAVE* SOLVED.
FIRST, DOES LINFORD HAVE ANY BULLETS LEFT?
AND...ON HIS PREVIOUS VISITS TO THE HOUSE, WAS LINFORD *NICE* TO THE DOGS, OR DID HE TREAT THEM LIKE SHIT?
YOU COULD SAY I'VE SOLVED THE MYSTERY OF...DO THESE DOGS LIKE LINFORD?
ANOTHER MYSTERY THAT I'VE SOLVED IS...
...HOW MAD AM *I* ABOUT YOU KILLING THE DOGS IN SIBERIA, AND TRYING TO KILL MY FRIENDS?
DON'T LOOK, CANDIDE.
NOT EVERY-THING ON EARTH IS PRETTY.

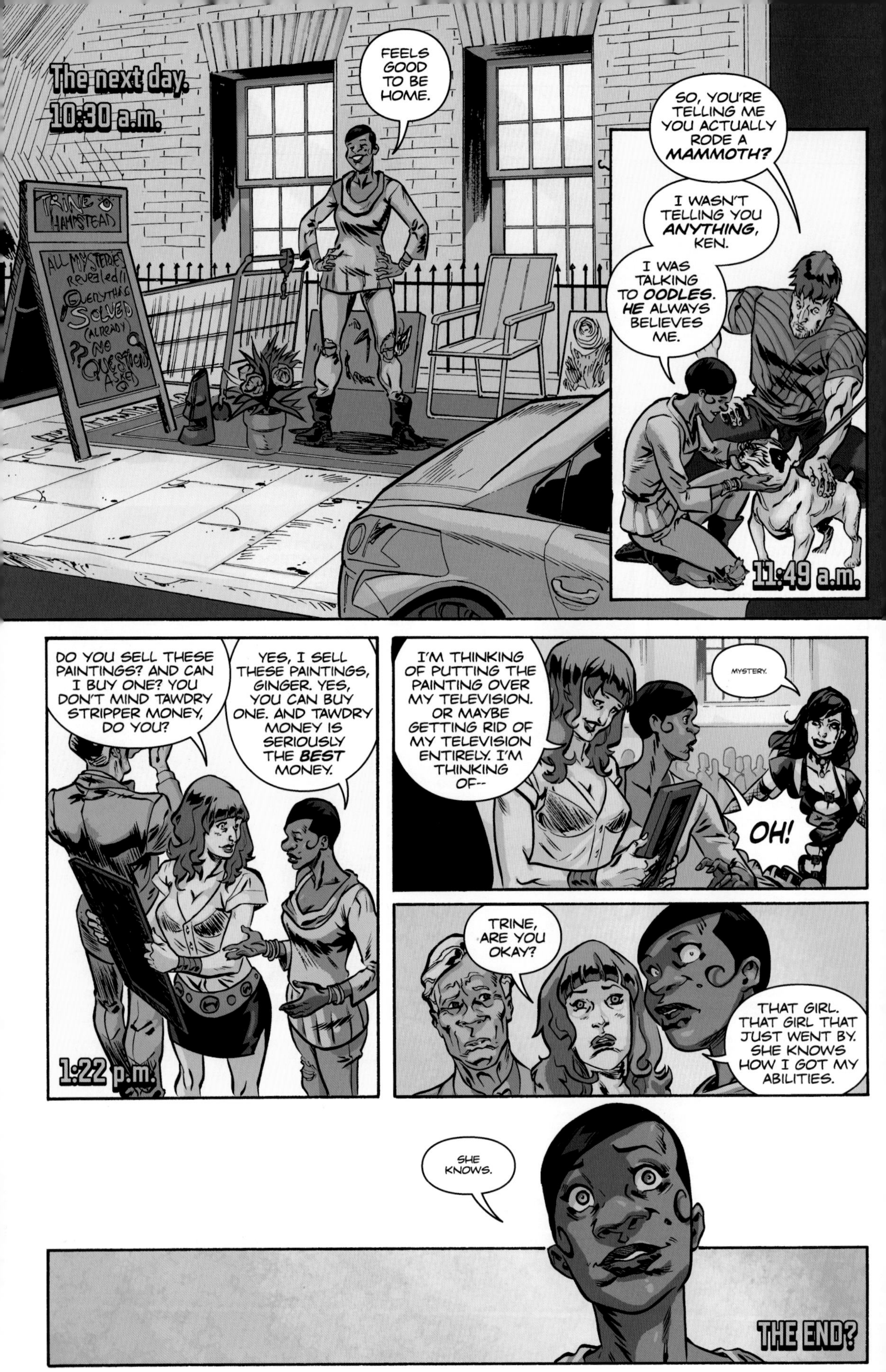
The next day.
10:30 a.m.
FEELS GOOD TO BE HOME.
TRINE HAMPSTEAD
ALL MYSTERIES revealed!! EVERYTHING SOLVED (ALREADY) NO QUESTIONS ASKED
SO, YOU'RE TELLING ME YOU ACTUALLY RODE A MAMMOTH?
I WASN'T TELLING YOU ANYTHING, KEN.
I WAS TALKING TO OODLES. HE ALWAYS BELIEVES ME.
11:49 a.m.
DO YOU SELL THESE PAINTINGS? AND CAN I BUY ONE? YOU DON'T MIND TAWDRY STRIPPER MONEY, DO YOU?
YES, I SELL THESE PAINTINGS, GINGER. YES, YOU CAN BUY ONE. AND TAWDRY MONEY IS SERIOUSLY THE BEST MONEY.
1:22 p.m.
I'M THINKING OF PUTTING THE PAINTING OVER MY TELEVISION. OR MAYBE GETTING RID OF MY TELEVISION ENTIRELY. I'M THINKING OF--
MYSTERY.
OH!
TRINE, ARE YOU OKAY?
THAT GIRL. THAT GIRL THAT JUST WENT BY. SHE KNOWS HOW I GOT MY ABILITIES.
SHE KNOWS.
THE END?

SKETCHBOOK

Notes by Paul Tobin and Alberto J. Alburquerque

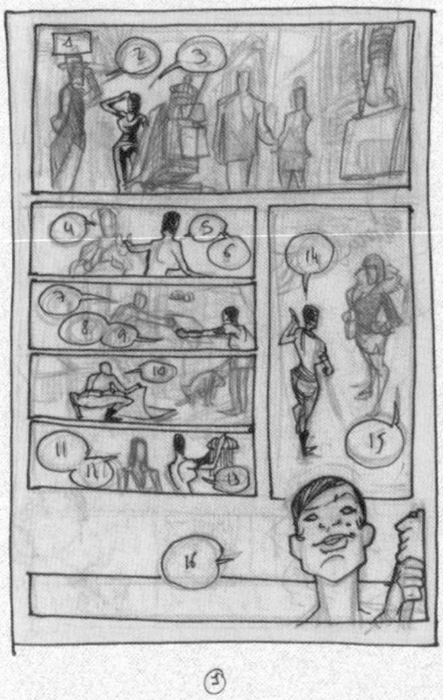

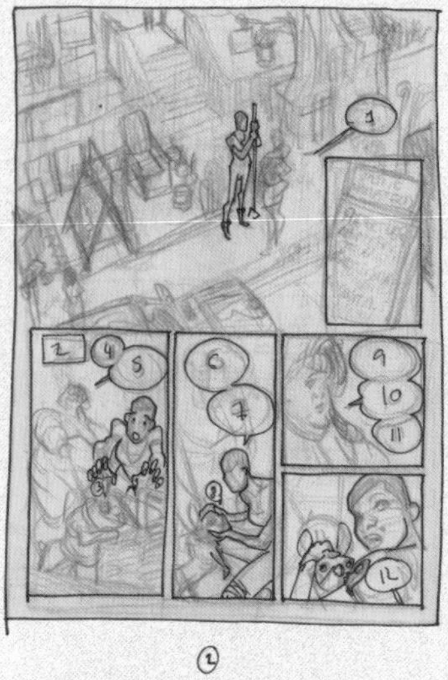

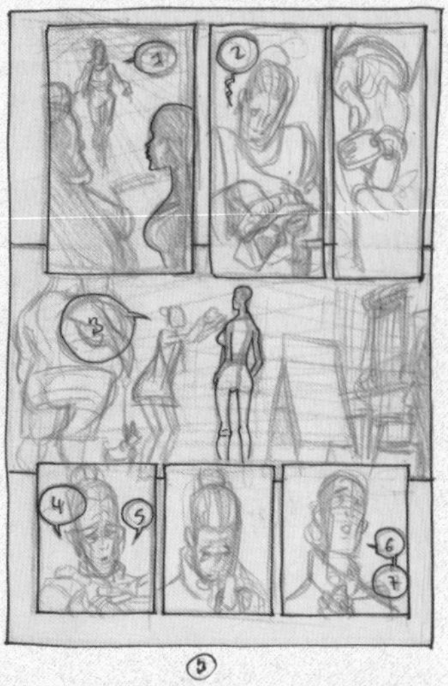

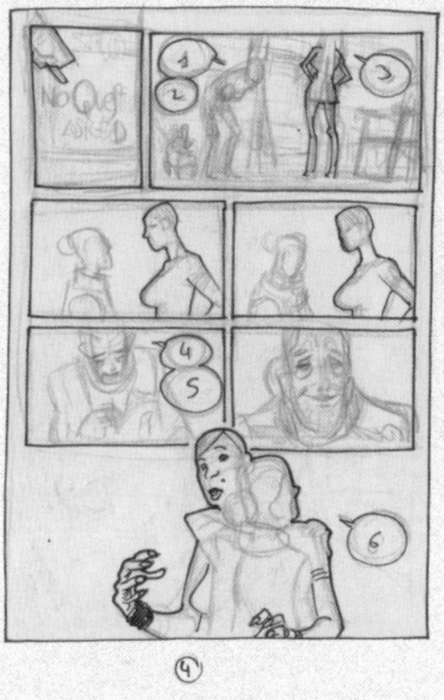

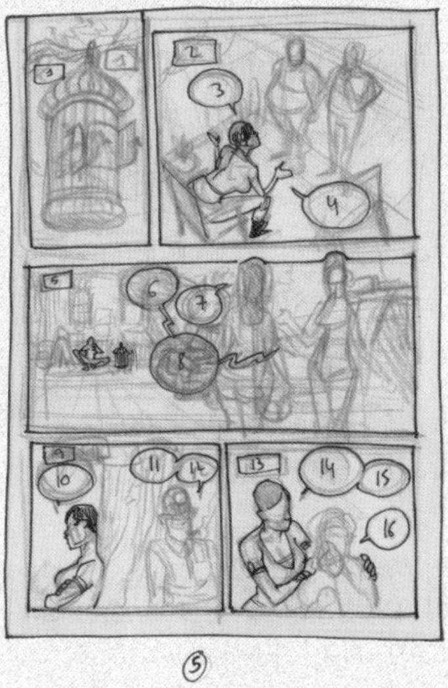

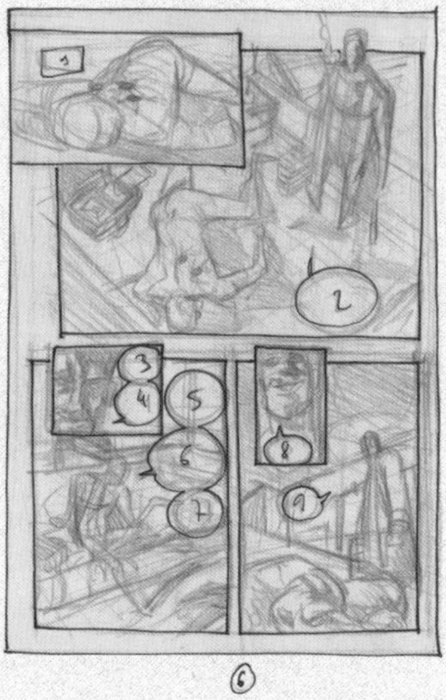

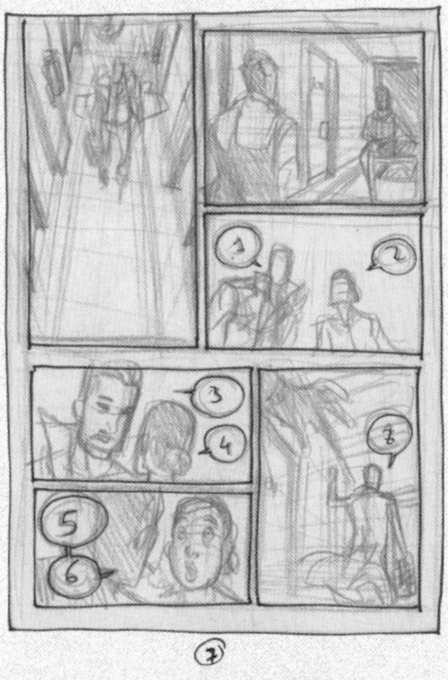

Alberto: Paul's scripts are very clear, but for me layouts are the first step before starting to draw the final pages. I like to plan everything there, including balloons. Don't get me wrong, I trust Marshall a hundred percent, but placing the balloons helps me organize my drawings and Paul's dialogue better.

Paul: As a writer, I love how Alberto plans where all the word balloons will go. It helps us coordinate the flow of the story and maintain the pacing that I'm going for. Bravo, Alberto! You are a creative workhorse!

P: **At this small size, you can easily grasp how many times Alberto must have gnashed his teeth while reading yet another crowd scene in the script.**

A: **Crowd scenes and scenes with a lot of dialogue are really hard to plan. Placing the characters in the right positions without losing coherence is key, and I try to make the layouts as understandable as possible. Actually, I love drawing crowd scenes, but please, don't tell Paul . . .**

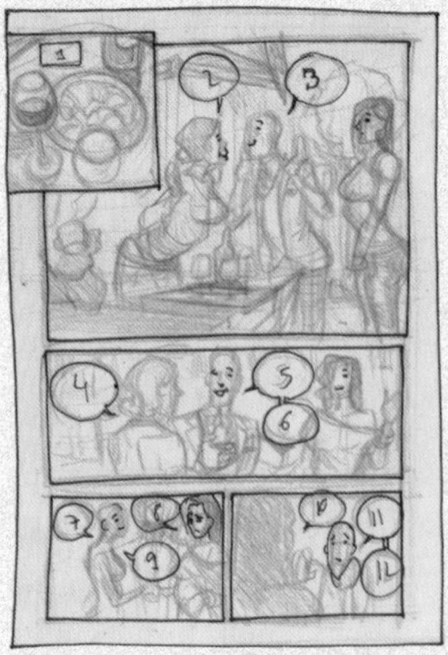

8

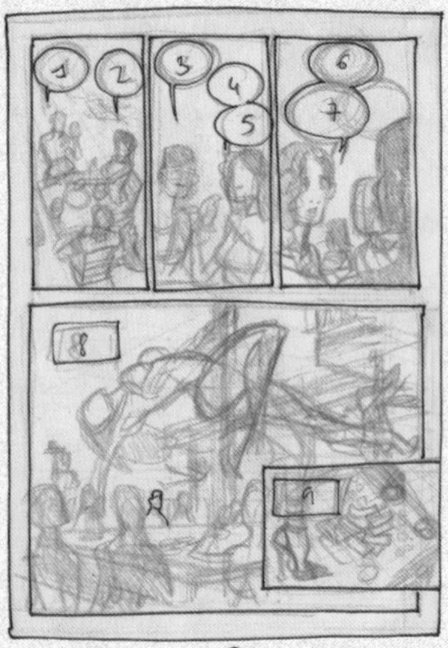

9

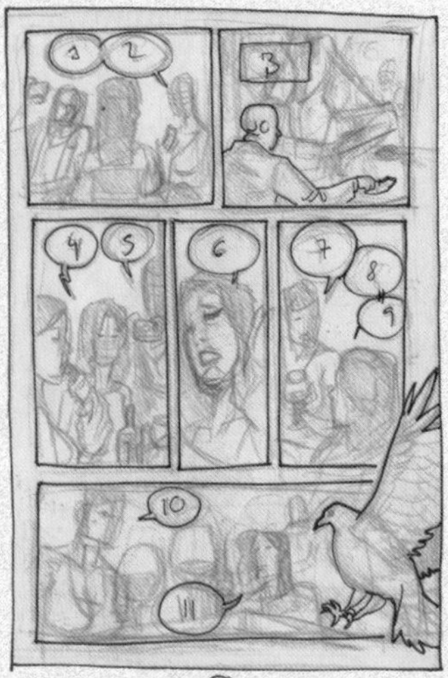

10

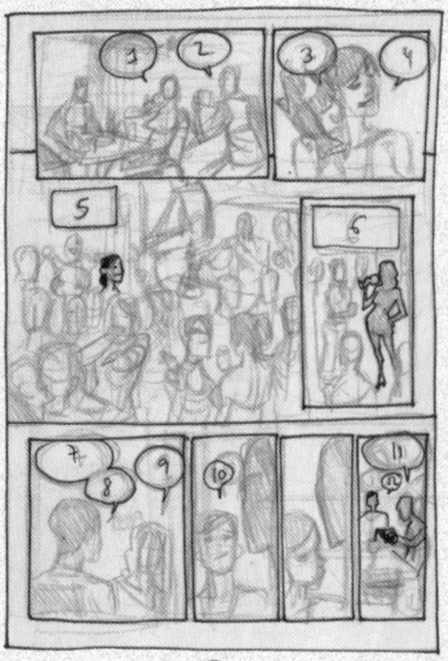

11

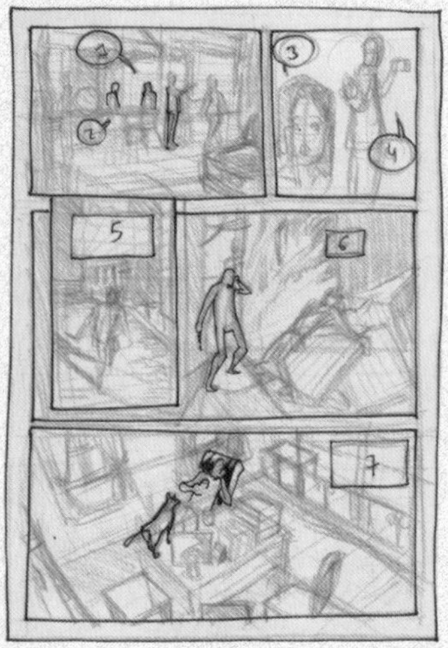

12

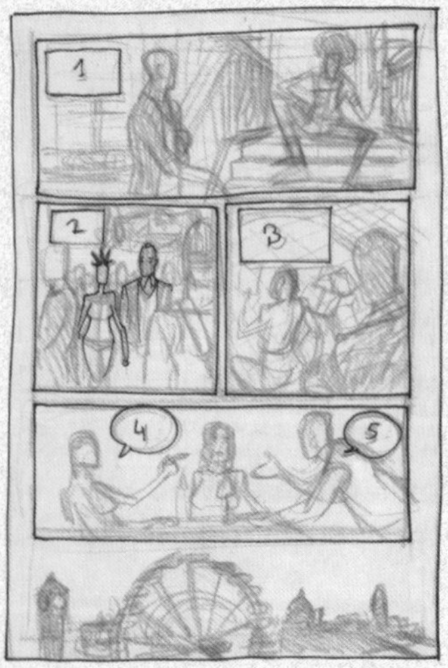

13

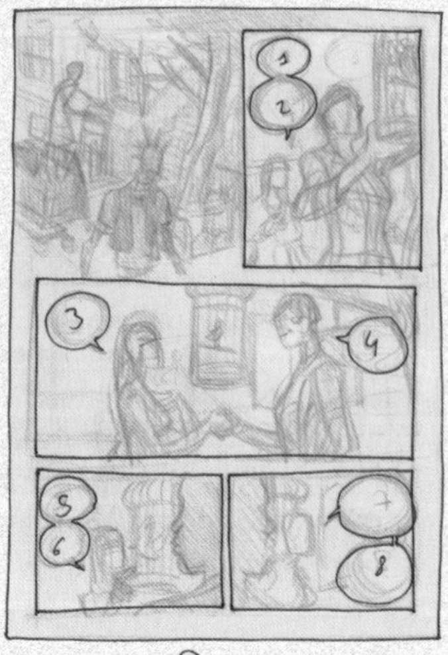

14

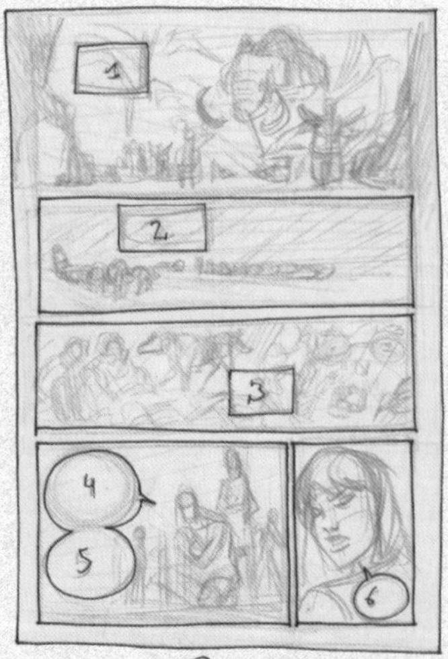

15

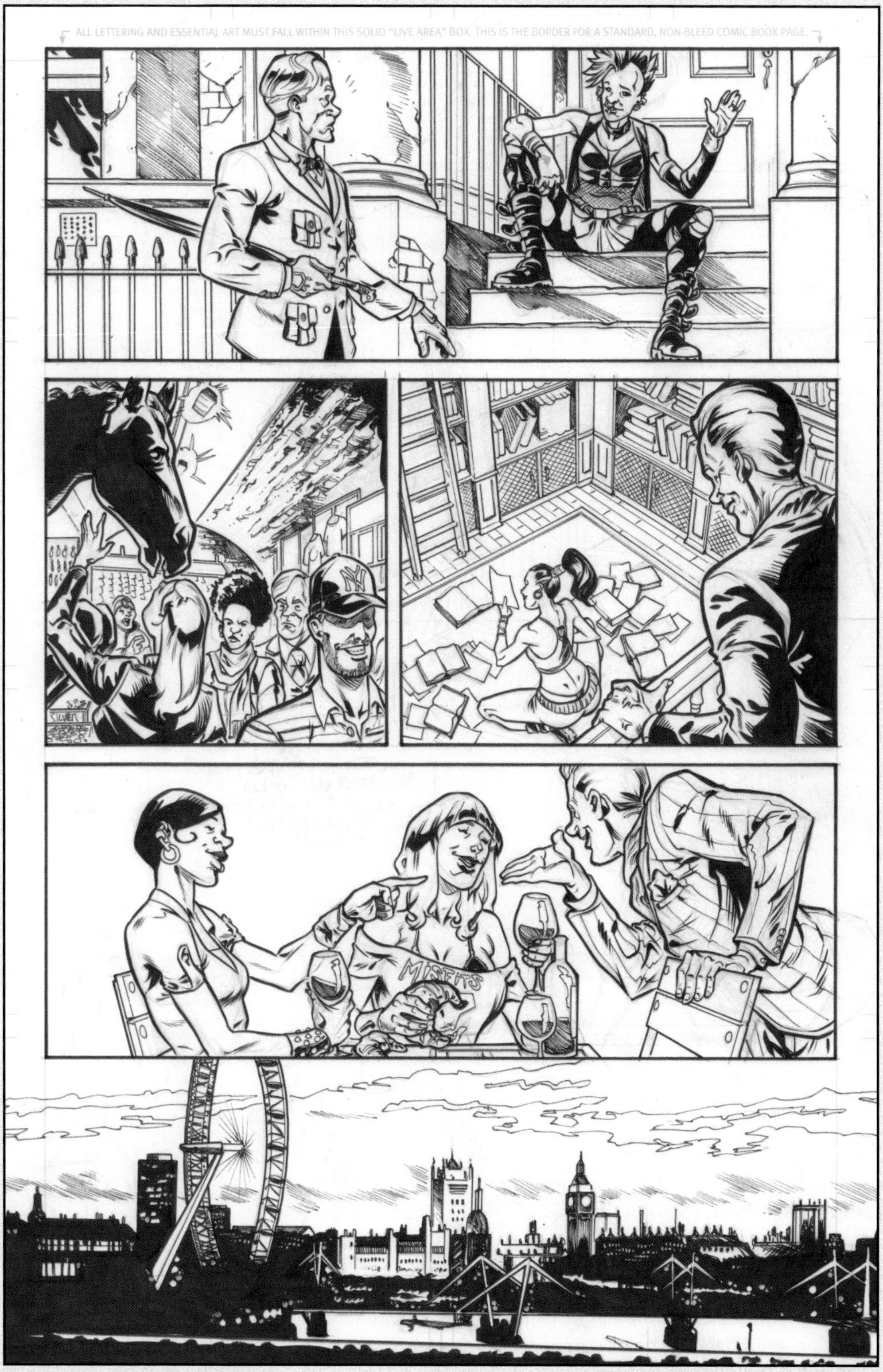
ALL LETTERING AND ESSENTIAL ART MUST FALL WITHIN THIS SOLID "LIVE AREA" BOX. THIS IS THE BORDER FOR A STANDARD, NON-BLEED COMIC BOOK PAGE.
NY
MISFITS

P: This is one of my favorite pages because Alberto shows Trine in so many different incarnations over time. It's a good way of showing that she's always changing, striving, and moving in many directions.

A: One of Paul's concerns when starting the project was to show the characters' different personalities and emotions. People change with time and go through different phases. So does Trine, as we can see here. I had a lot of fun drawing that Afro and her goth period!

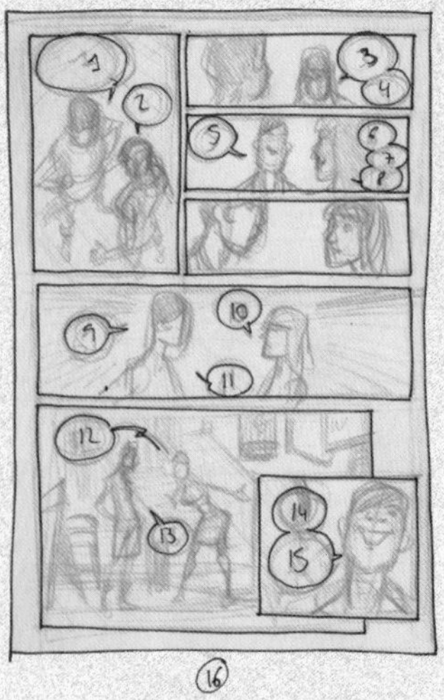

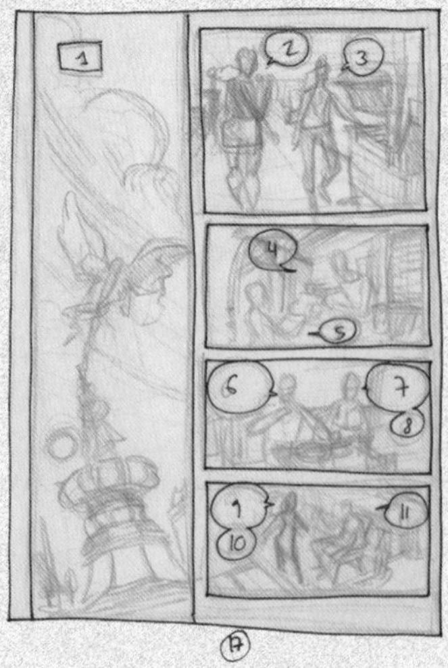

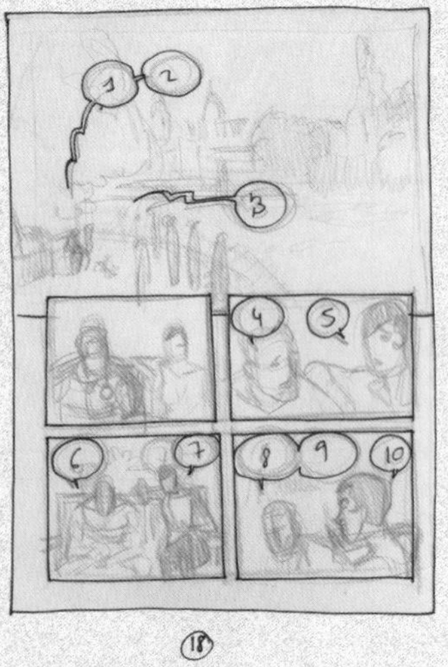

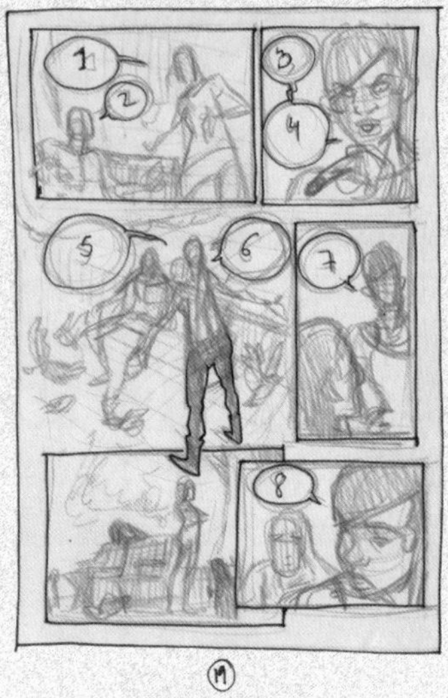

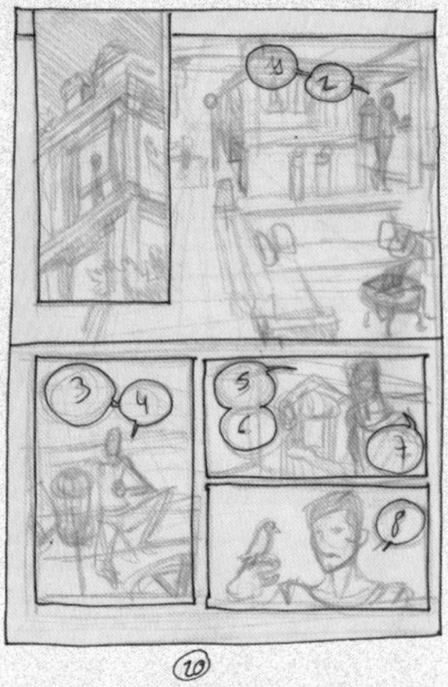

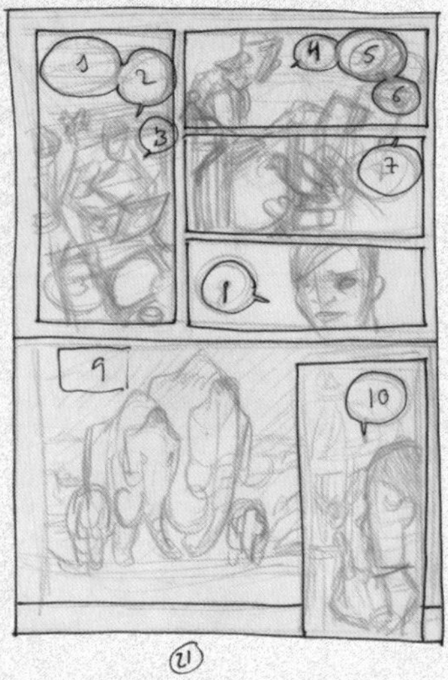

P: **See, Alberto? It's not *always* crowd scenes. Sometimes it's sweeping architectural views of the city!**

A: **Sometimes I try to cheat on those views of the city . . . I know writers love huge, open shots, but from time to time, a small detail (like the Piccadilly Circus statue) helps convey all the meaning needed in an establishing shot. I compensate later on in crowd scenes like the one at Victoria Station.**

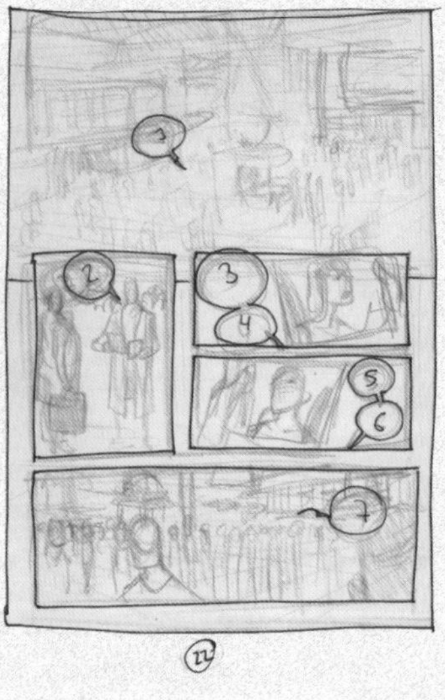

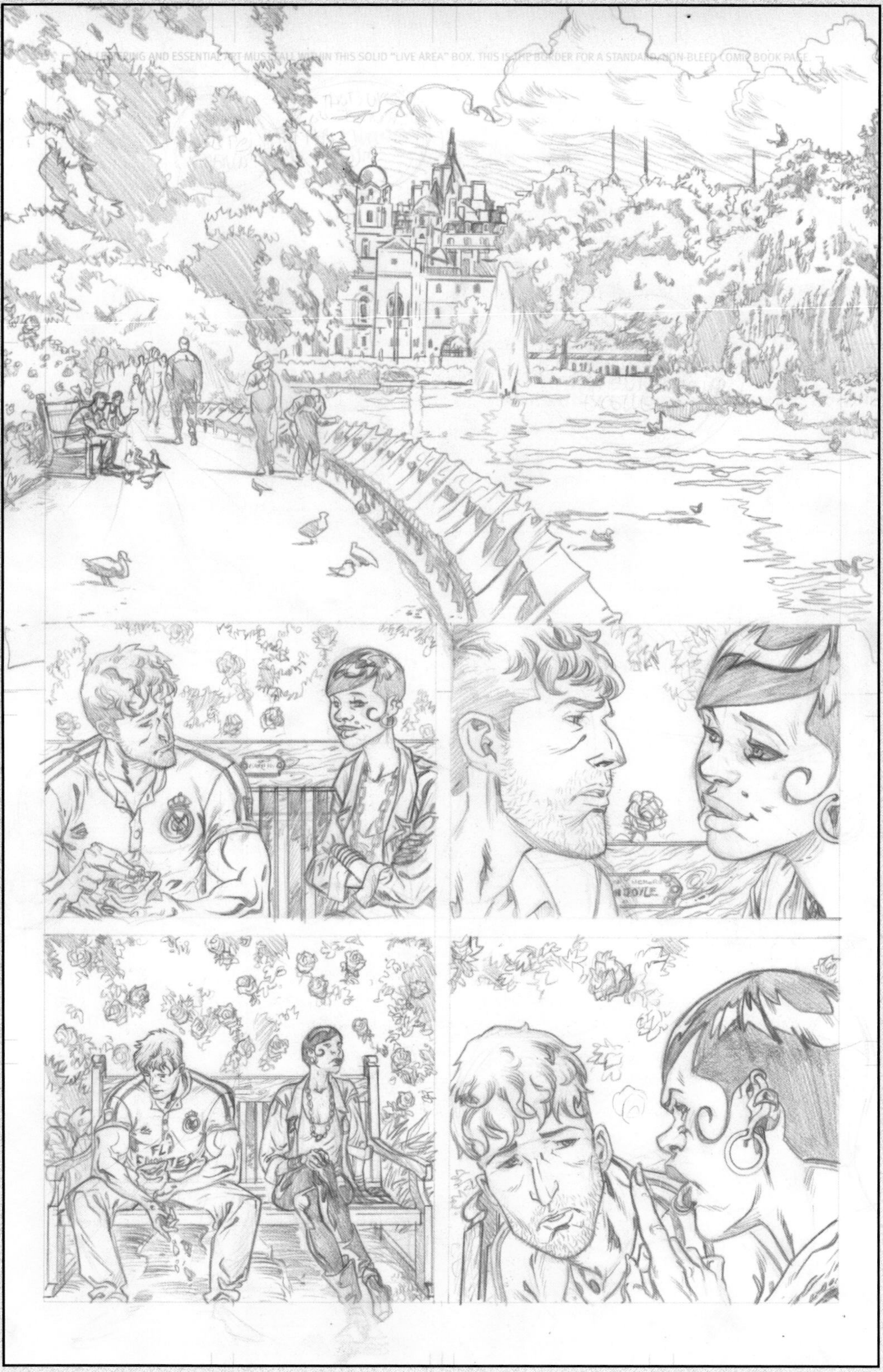

P: **Love the two emotional states portrayed here. Anguished but trying, as opposed to blithe but caring.**

A: **Portraying acting is one of the most difficult things to get right in a comic book. Paul writes feelings like no other, and that makes my job much tougher but more enjoyable at the same time. Love drawing roses in a hedge, too!**

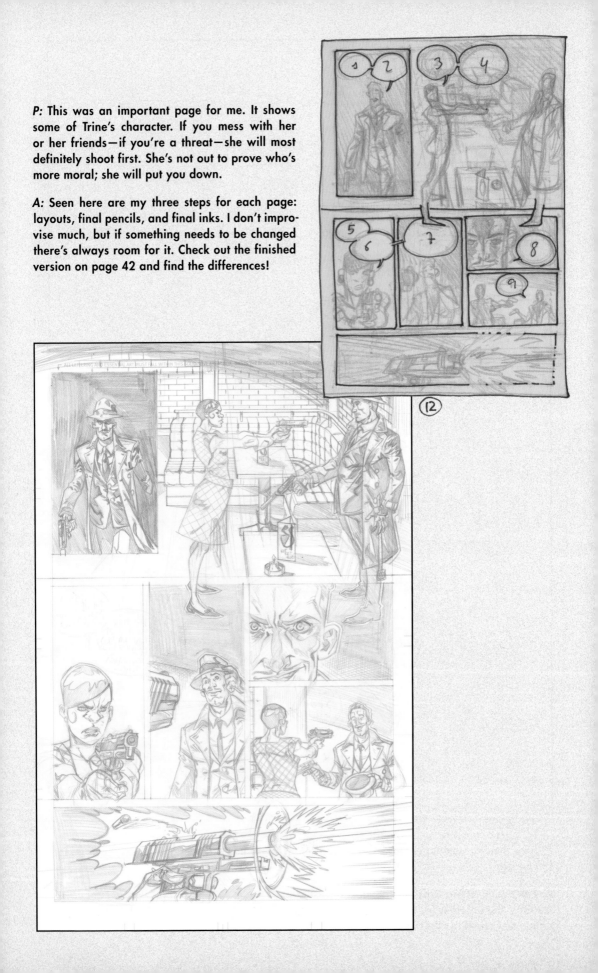

P: This was an important page for me. It shows some of Trine's character. If you mess with her or her friends—if you're a threat—she will most definitely shoot first. She's not out to prove who's more moral; she will put you down.

A: Seen here are my three steps for each page: layouts, final pencils, and final inks. I don't improvise much, but if something needs to be changed there's always room for it. Check out the finished version on page 42 and find the differences!

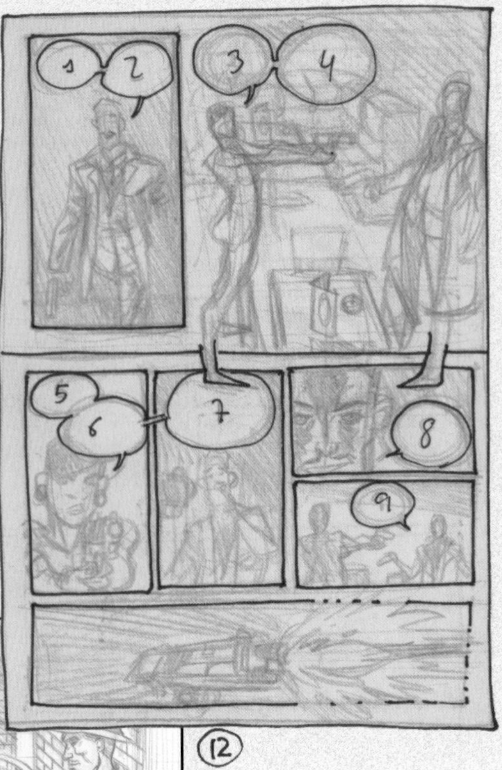
1
2
3
4
5
6
7
8
9
12

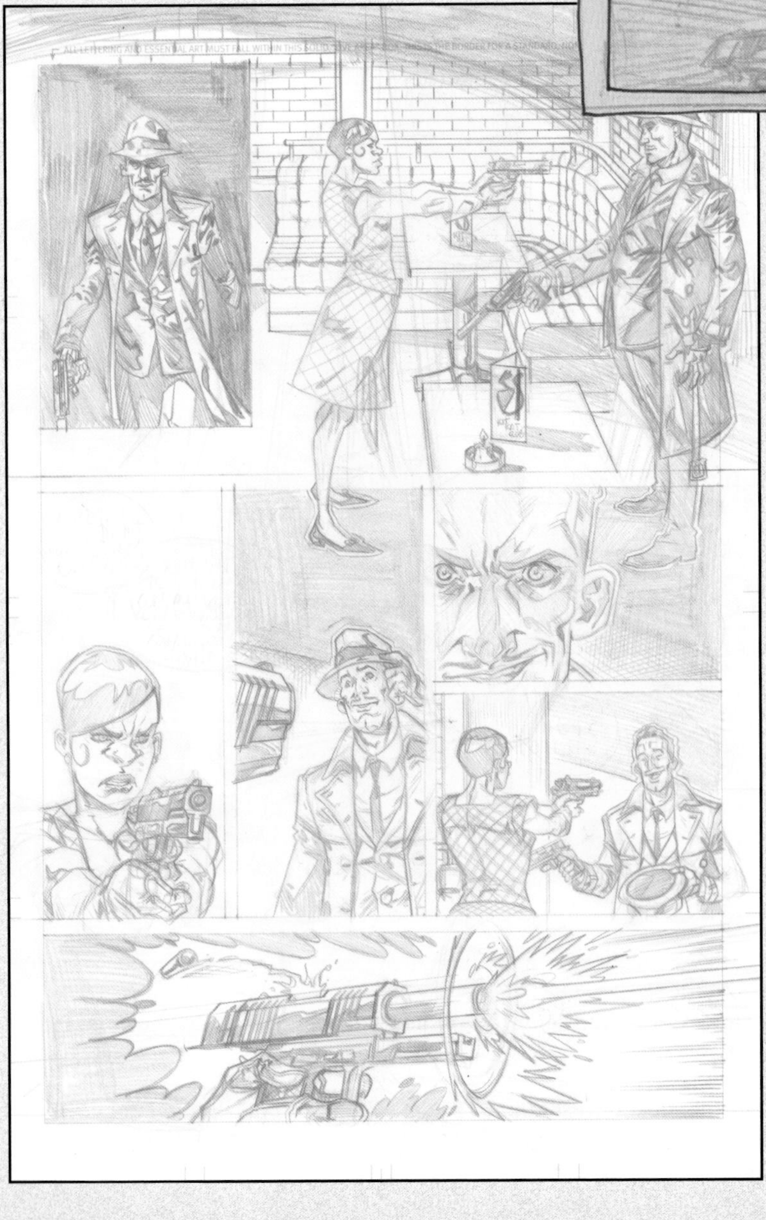

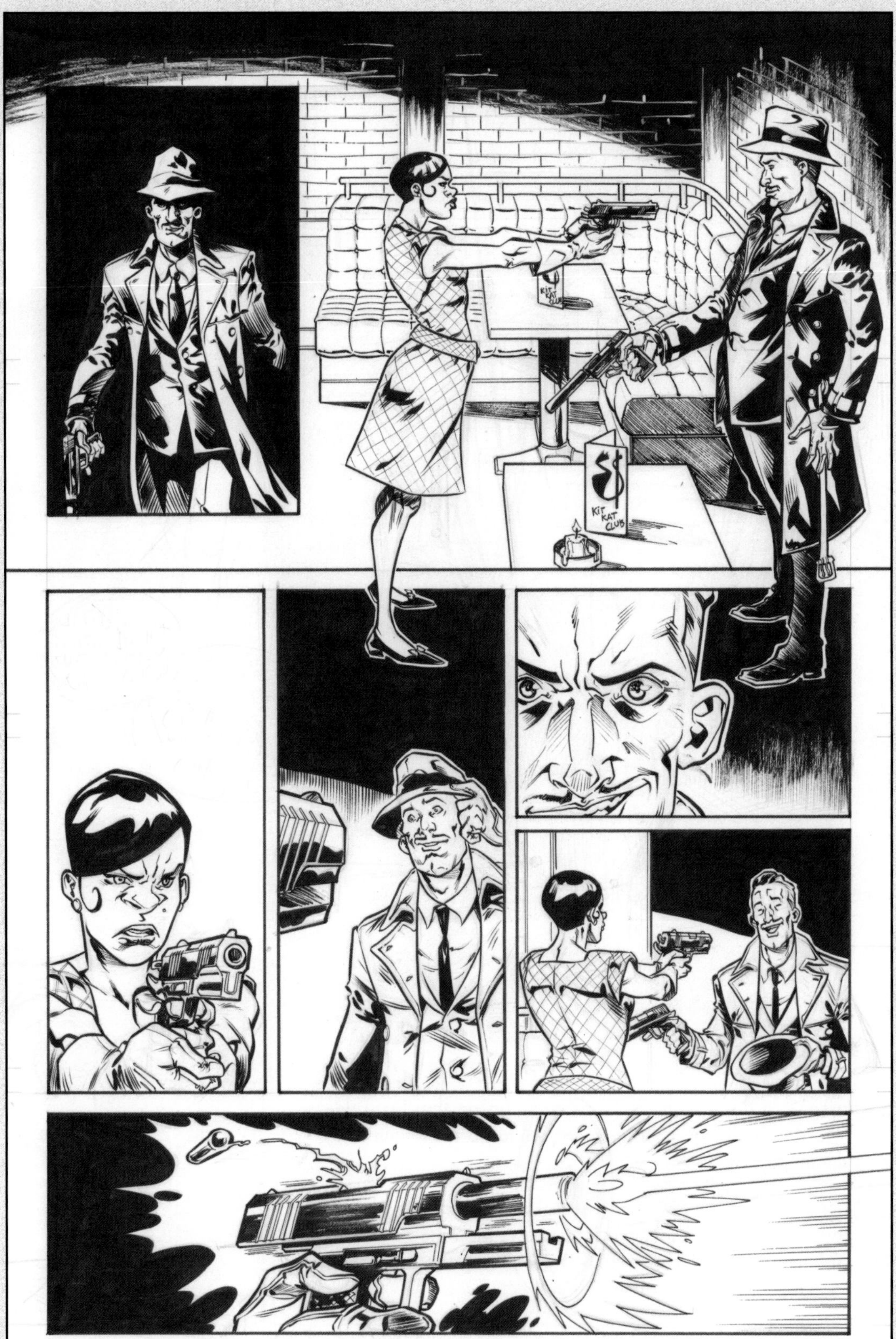
KIT KAT CLUB

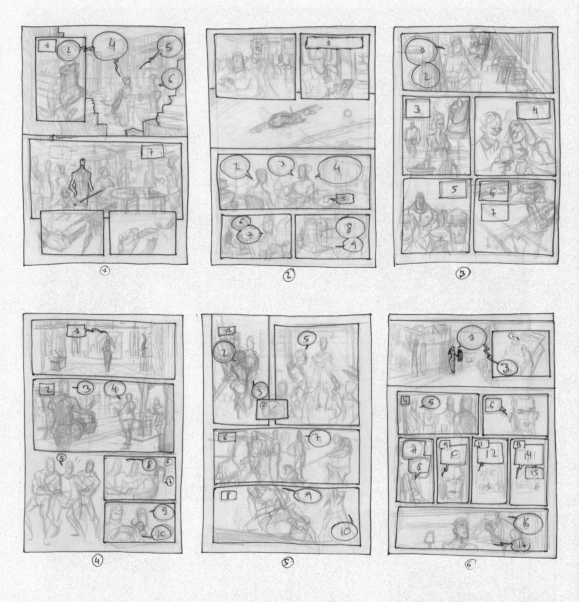

P: Ha! Look at those word balloons stack up on that last page. I like words. It's always a balance for me to do maximum story with minimum words.

A: Planning action scenes is awesome! They're really hard to choreograph, but for me, it's much harder to plan the quiet ones. That balance that Paul tries to find is something that I try to reflect . . . Hope I get it from time to time!

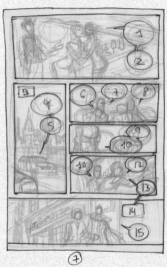

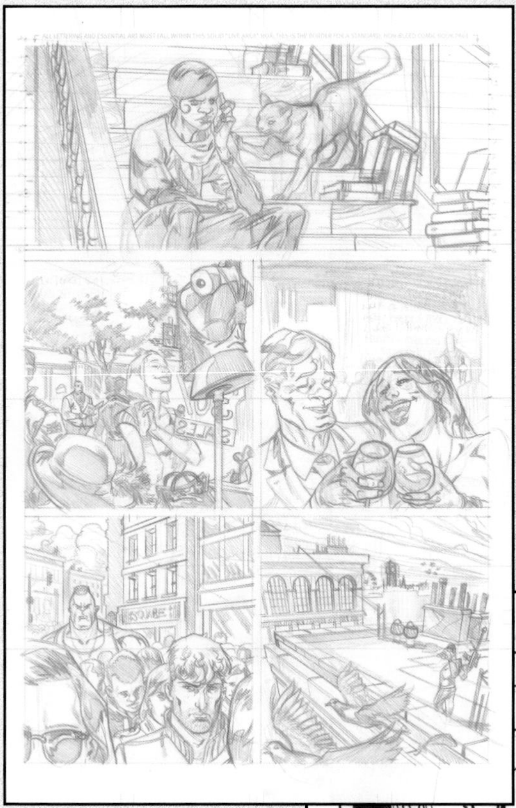
SALES
SQUARE

P: Because I want maximum story, I do tend to use time slips in comic stories. They're a valuable space-saving and story-maximizing tool.

A: Those changes of scenery are great for me. They keep me alert and never bored with drawing the same characters and spaces all the time.

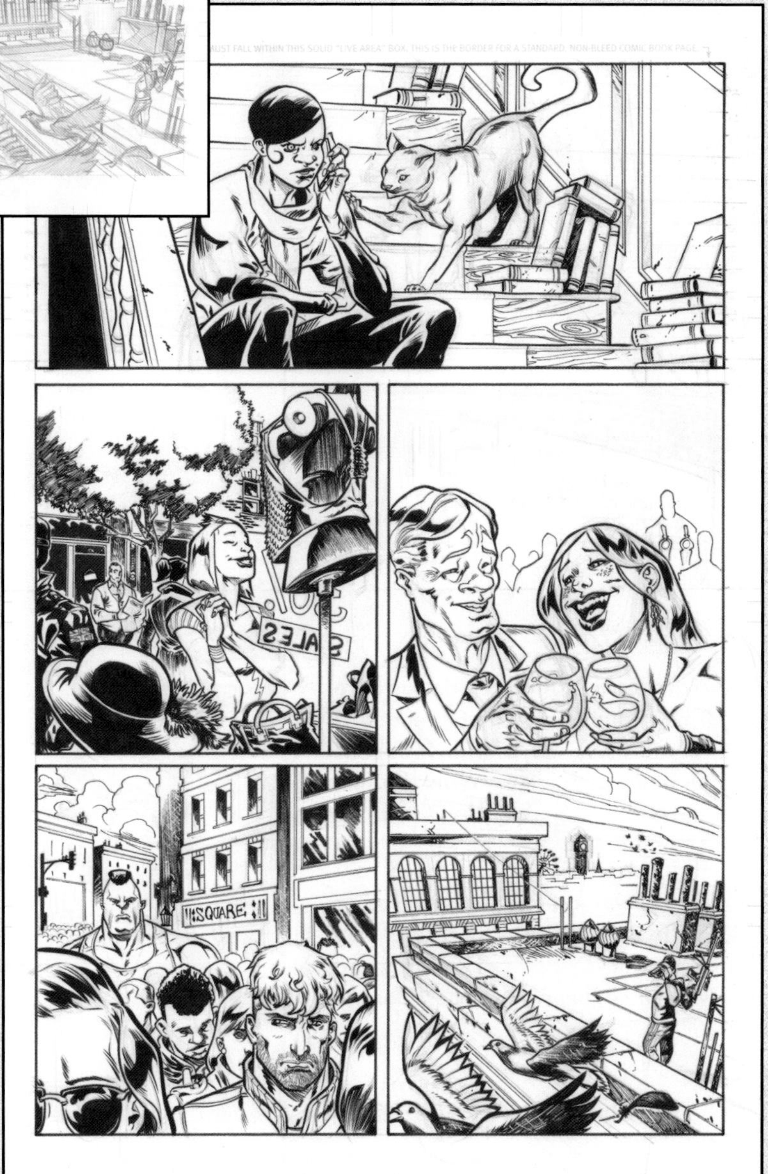
MUST FALL WITHIN THIS SOLID "LIVE AREA" BOX. THIS IS THE BORDER FOR A STANDARD, NON-BLEED COMIC BOOK PAGE.
SALES
SQUARE

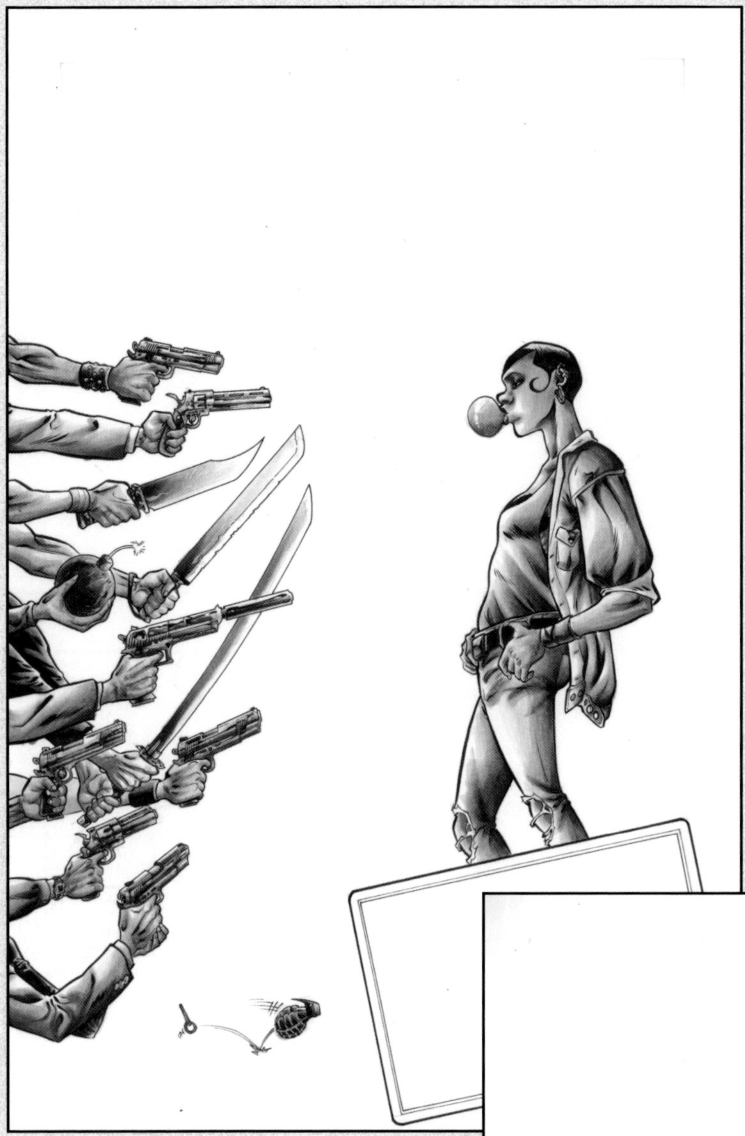

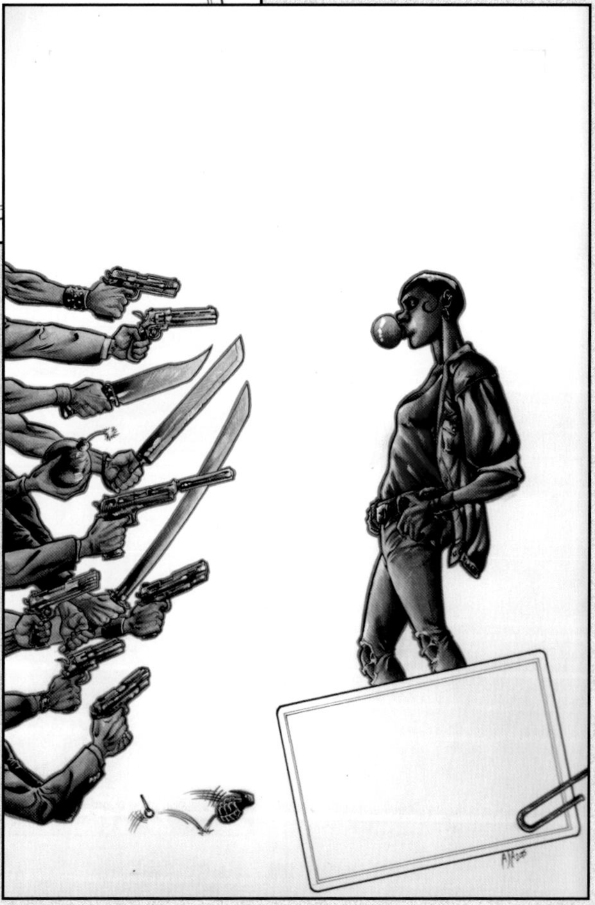

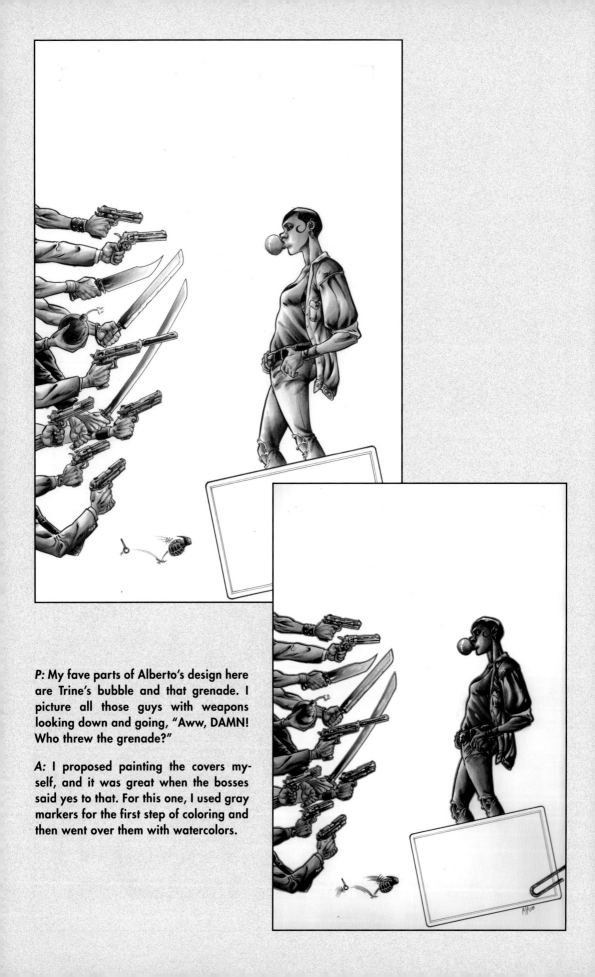

P: My fave parts of Alberto's design here are Trine's bubble and that grenade. I picture all those guys with weapons looking down and going, "Aww, DAMN! Who threw the grenade?"

A: I proposed painting the covers myself, and it was great when the bosses said yes to that. For this one, I used gray markers for the first step of coloring and then went over them with watercolors.

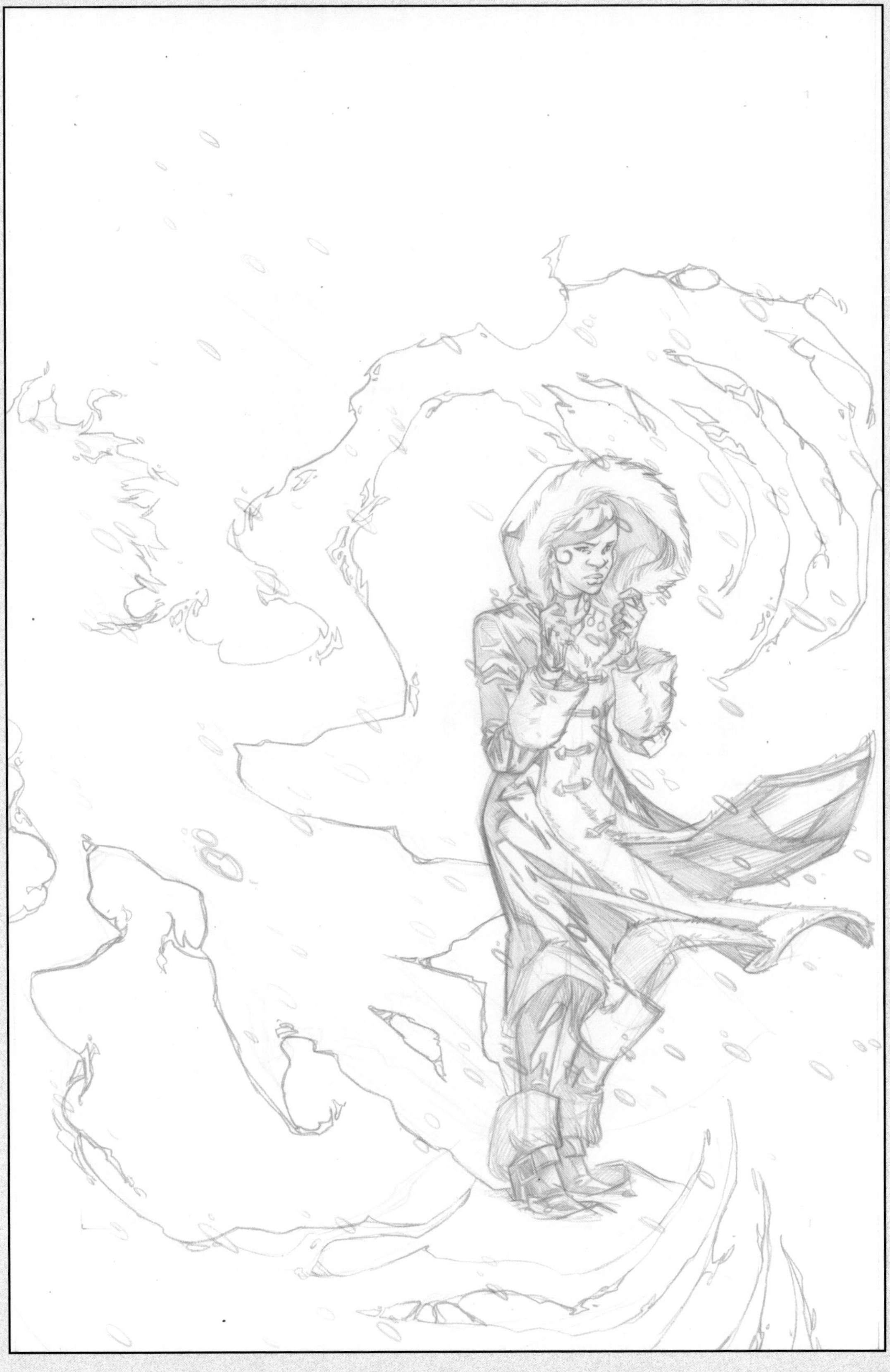

P: **Really happy with how Alberto captured the feeling of being cold here.**

A: **This cover was hard to do because I wanted to reflect a feeling of solitude and coldness and, at the same time, make it menacing for Trine. Red shadows are always menacing, I think!**

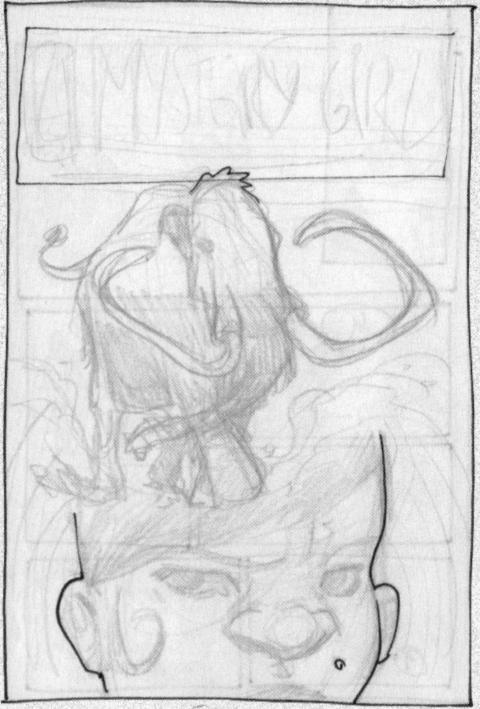

C#3-1

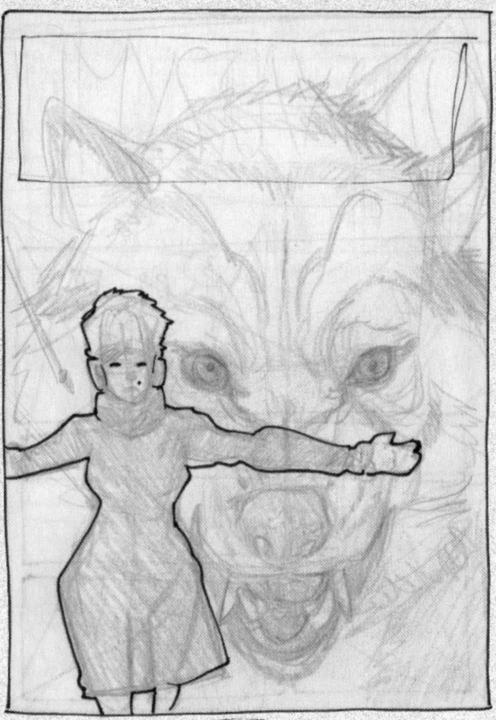

C#3-2

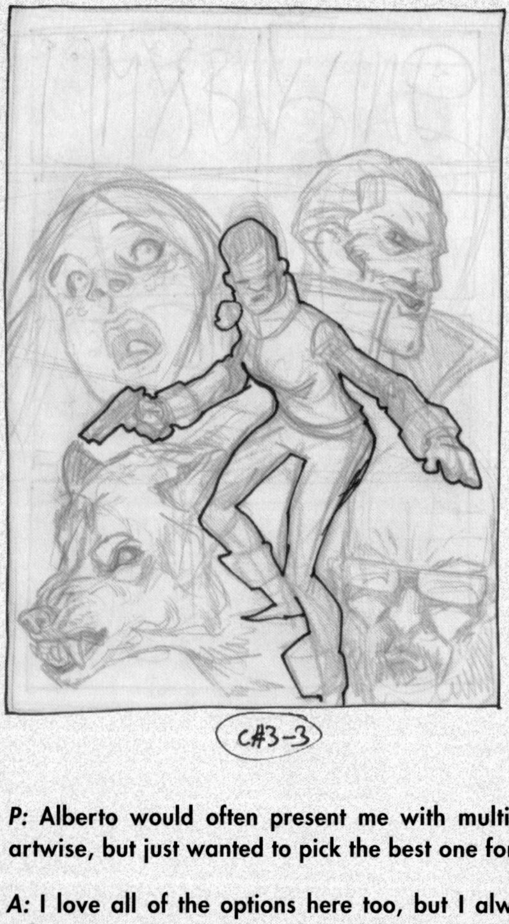

C#3-3

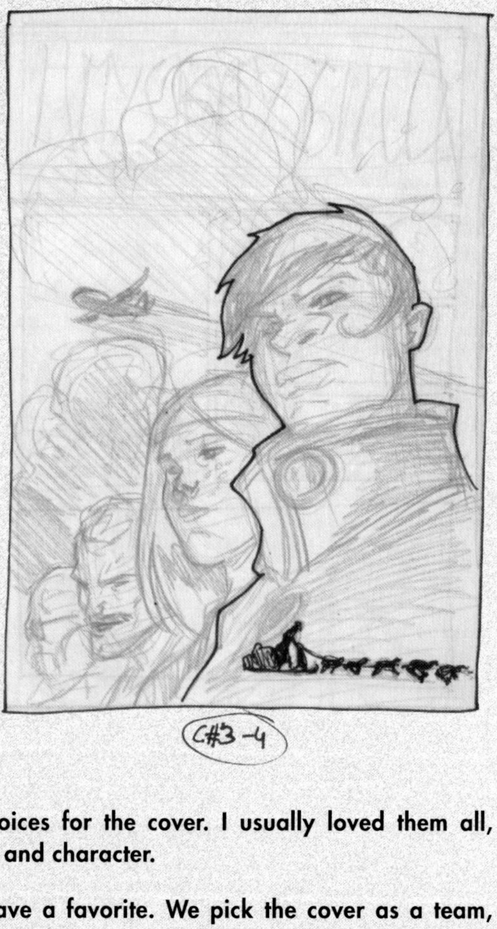

C#3-4

P: **Alberto would often present me with multiple choices for the cover. I usually loved them all, artwise, but just wanted to pick the best one for story and character.**

A: **I love all of the options here too, but I always have a favorite. We pick the cover as a team, taking into account everyone's ideas, but I tend to trust the opinions of Paul and the editors over my own . . . They're always right! Ha ha.**

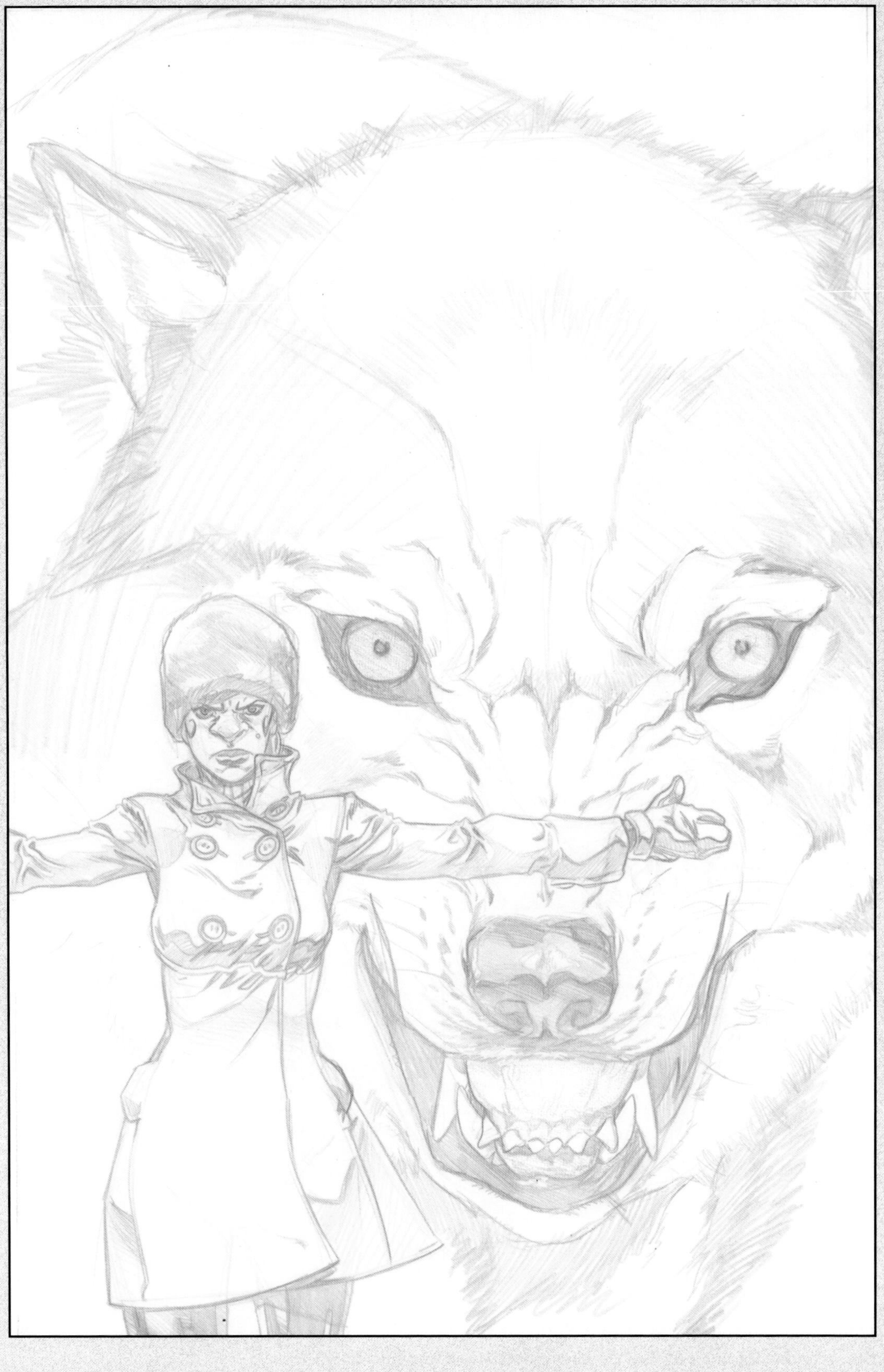

P: **To me, Trine is a fierce character. And a predator. Love how Alberto captured that in her expression.**

A: **This is my favorite cover of the series. I love drawing animals! Also, the symbolic value of the cover is palpable. Trine's wild side is reflected here in the wolf's eyes . . . Well, also in hers!**

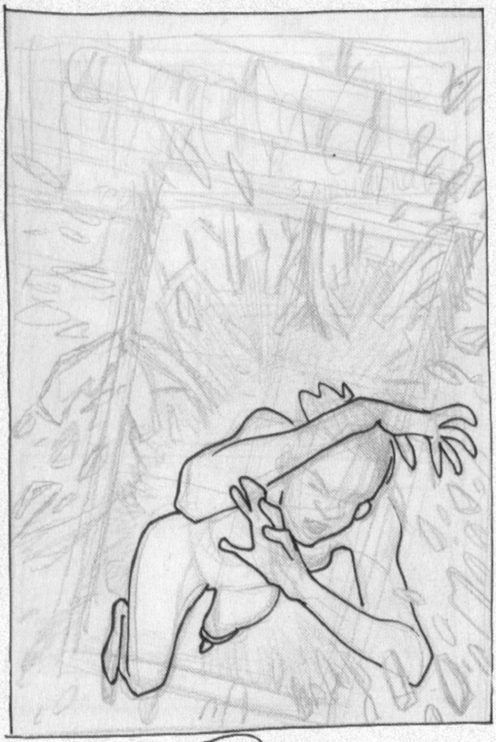

C#4-1

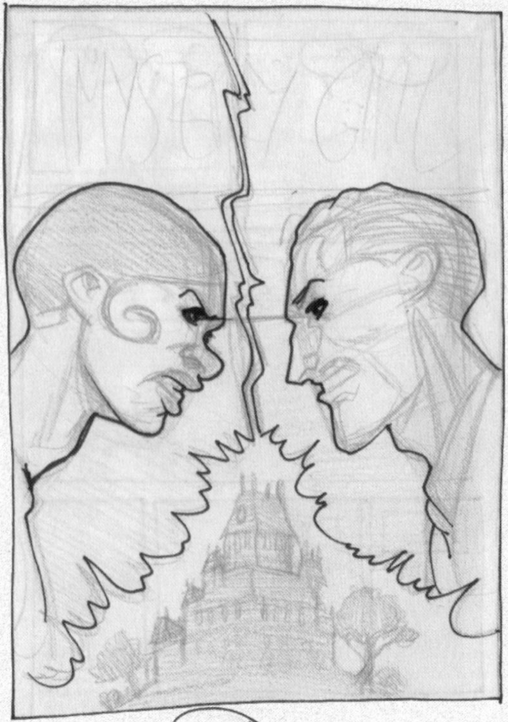

C#4-2

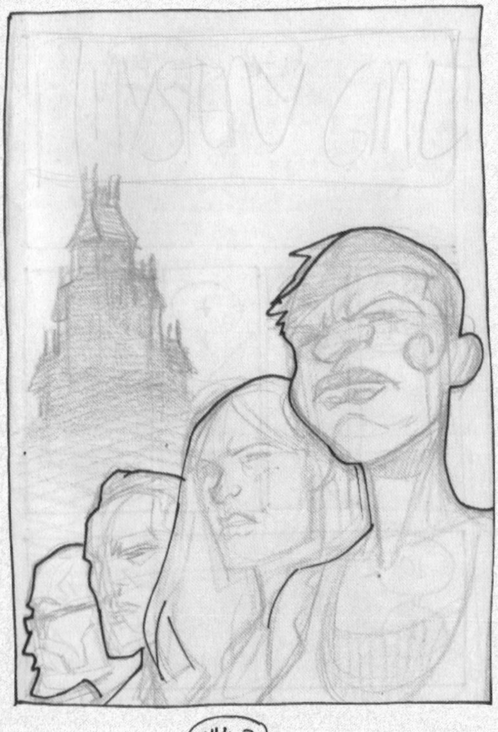

C#4-3

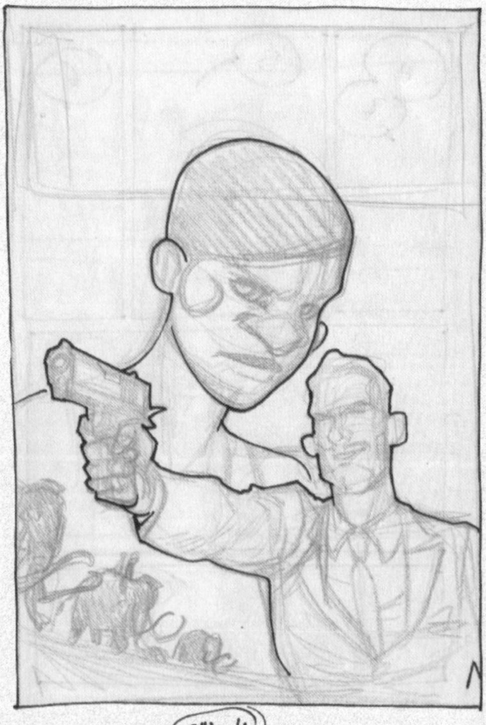

C#4-4

P: **More cover choices. We went with the window cover, simply because it best conveyed action and desperation. You look at that cover and know shit is going *down*.**

A: **The cover is probably one of the most difficult things to draw in a comic book. We have to find the right one so people will be attracted to it. I just try to have as much fun as possible with them, and Paul makes it easy with his suggestions.**

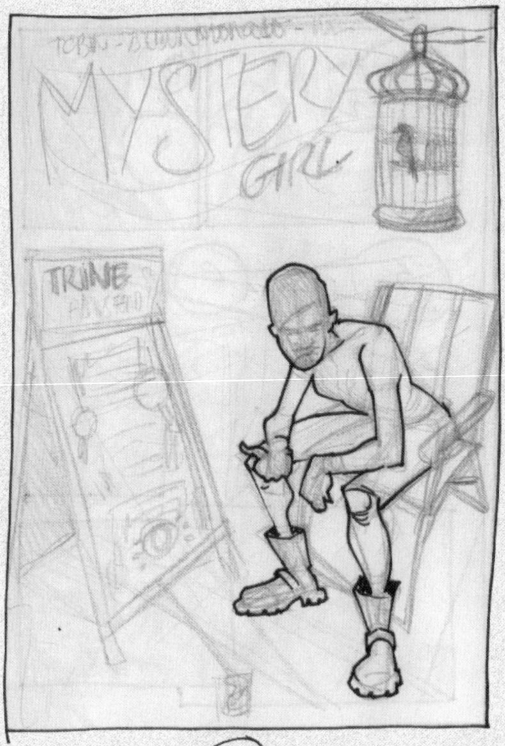
MYSTERY
GIRL
TRINE

C1-1

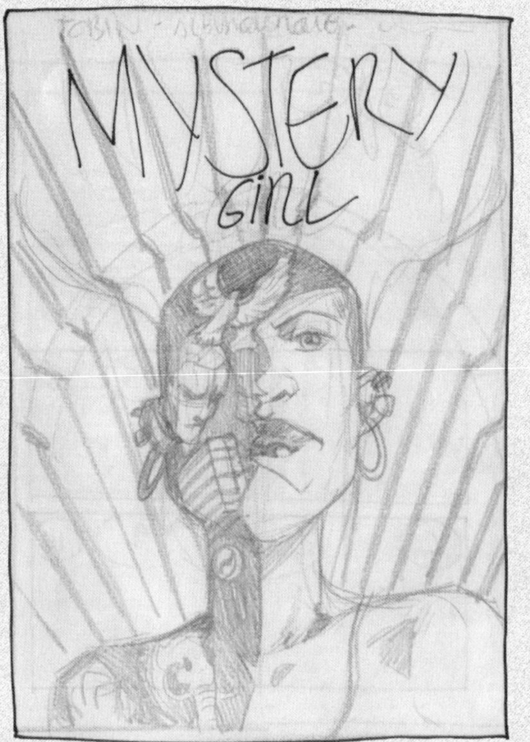
MYSTERY
GIRL

C1-2

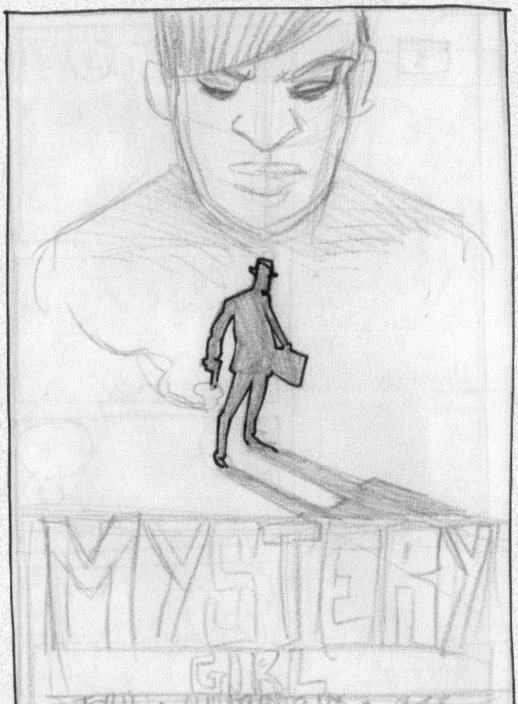
MYSTERY
GIRL

C1-3

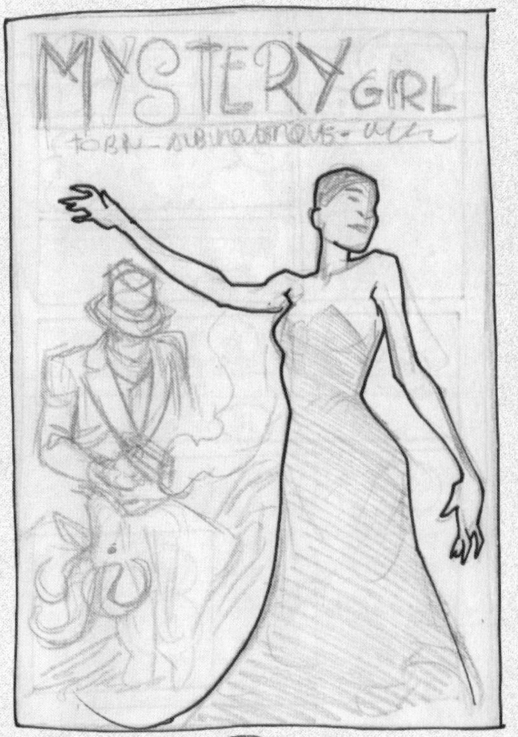
MYSTERY GIRL

C1-4

P: **Early designs for the first cover. I wanted to get a sense of who Trine was—Trine the street detective—so we went with the one of her actually on the street.**

A: **This first cover wasn't used. It was an establishing shot of Trine's "office" and I loved painting it, but we decided to go in a different direction in the end.**

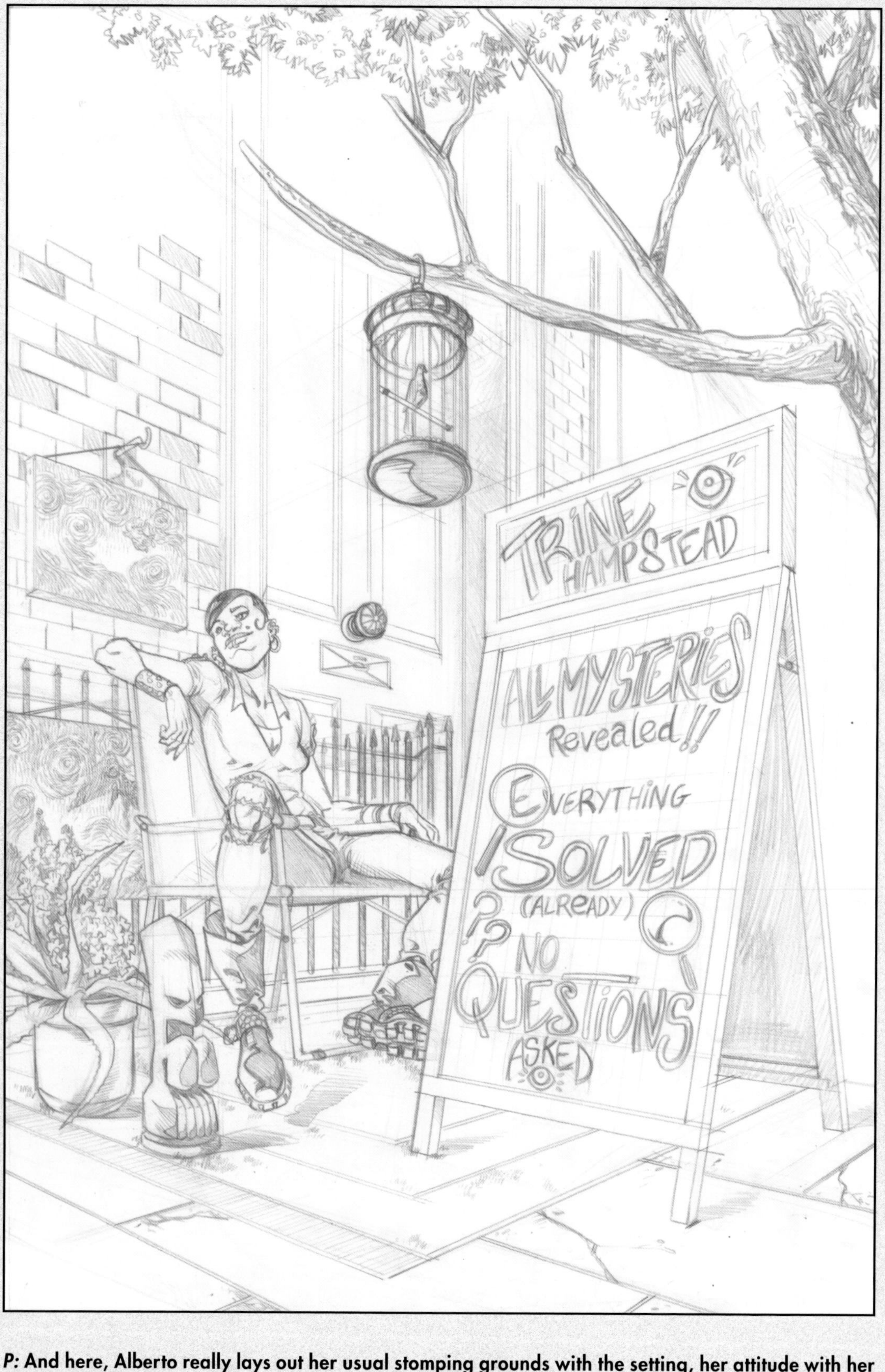
TRINE HAMPSTEAD
ALL MYSTERIES Revealed!!
EVERYTHING
SOLVED
(ALREADY)
NO
QUESTIONS
ASKED

P: **And here, Alberto really lays out her usual stomping grounds with the setting, her attitude with her casual position, and much of the story's premise with her sign.**

A: **Paul made Trine's personality clear, and I tried to reflect it in every shot. This cover may be the best example. Trine's cool all the time, and I always enjoy drawing that attitude.**

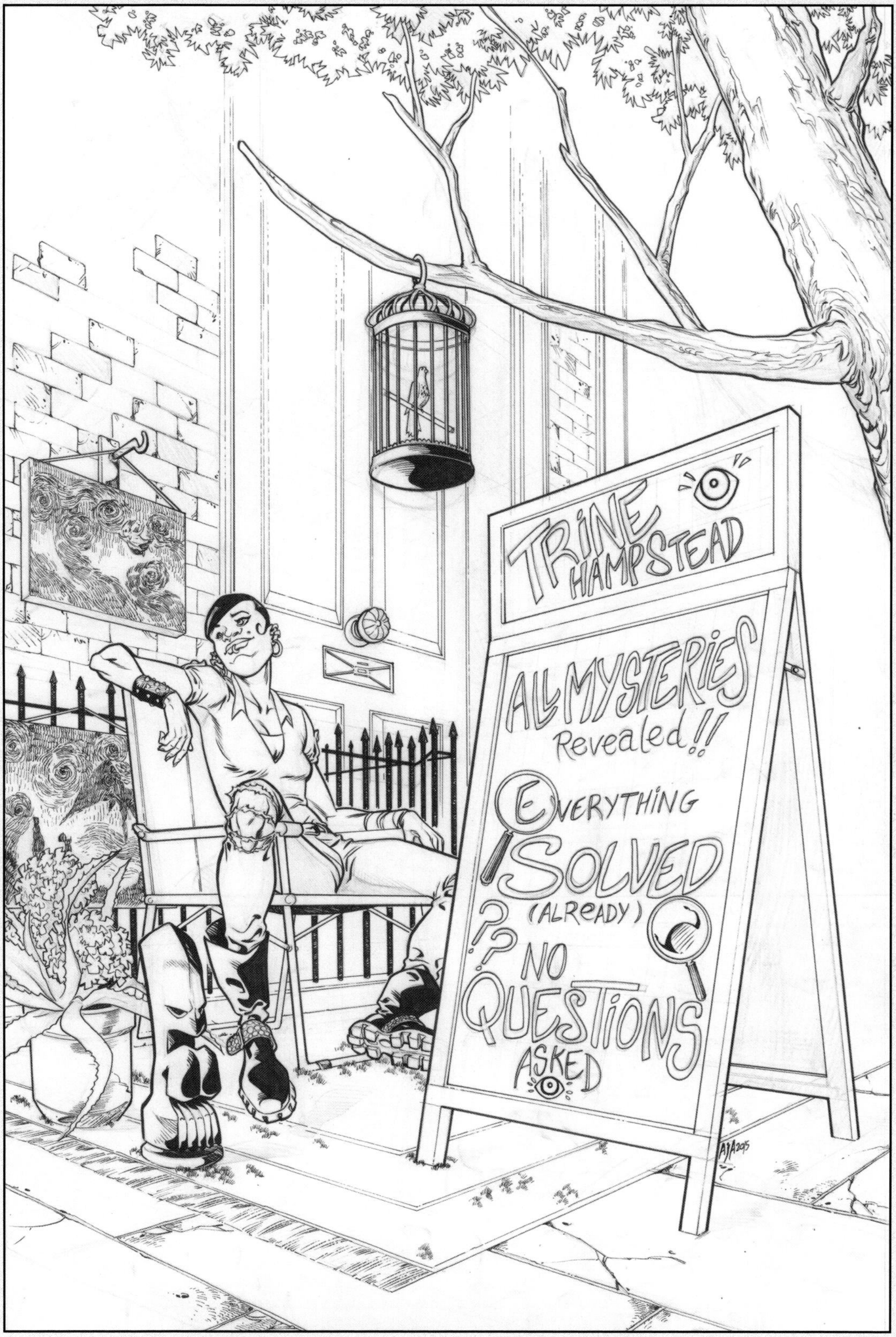
TRINE HAMPSTEAD
ALL MYSTERIES
Revealed!!
EVERYTHING
SOLVED
(ALREADY)
NO
QUESTIONS
ASKED

P: **Finished in the inks. This is still my favorite view of Trine.**

A: **I went for a lot of detail in the inks (well, also in the pencils) and had a lot of fun with different textures and techniques. However, by the end of the series, I had decided to skip the inks for the final covers, giving them a more painterly look.**

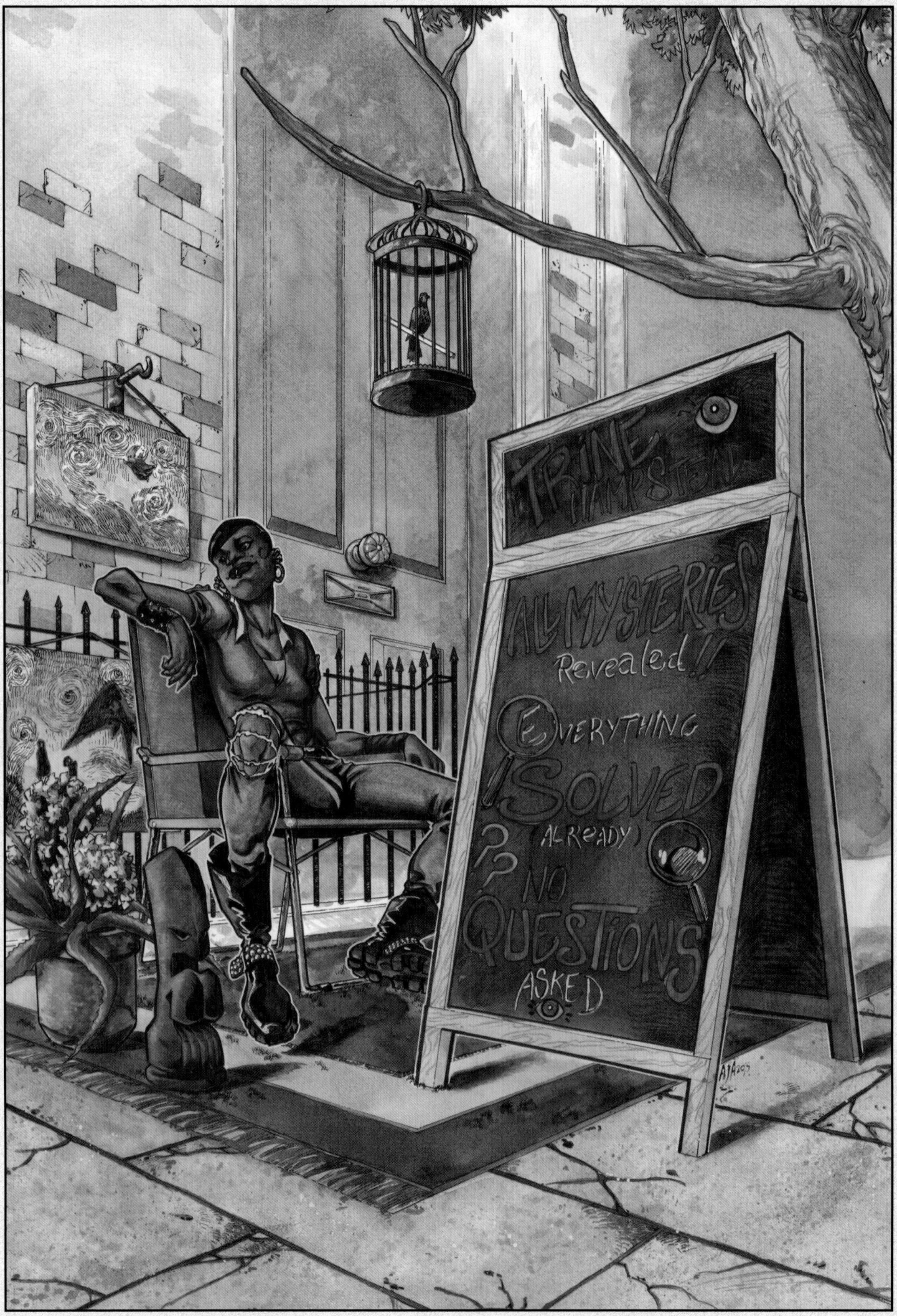
TRINE HAMPSTEN
ALL MYSTERIES Revealed!!
EVERYTHING SOLVED (ALREADY)
?? NO QUESTIONS ASKED

P: Unfortunately, the powers that be didn't like it, so we were forced to change the first issue's cover. In the end, I really do like the cover we went with for #1, but I miss this cover, too.

A: Looking at the first painted cover I did, I see now some things to make better. Maybe the bosses saw that then, and that's why they decided to try a different thing. As I said, I trust them, so we went for it, but this one will always be my first . . .

ALSO BY PAUL TOBIN

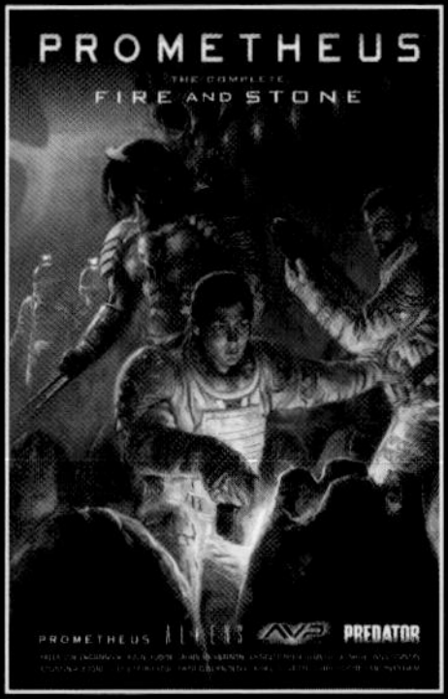
PROMETHEUS
THE COMPLETE
FIRE AND STONE
PREDATOR

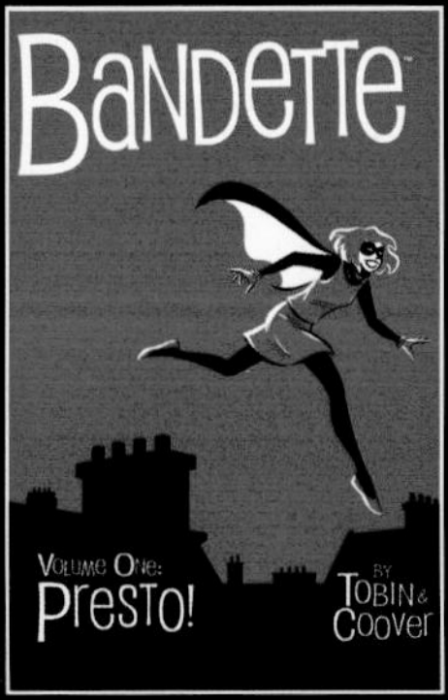
Bandette
Volume One:
Presto!
By
Tobin & Coover

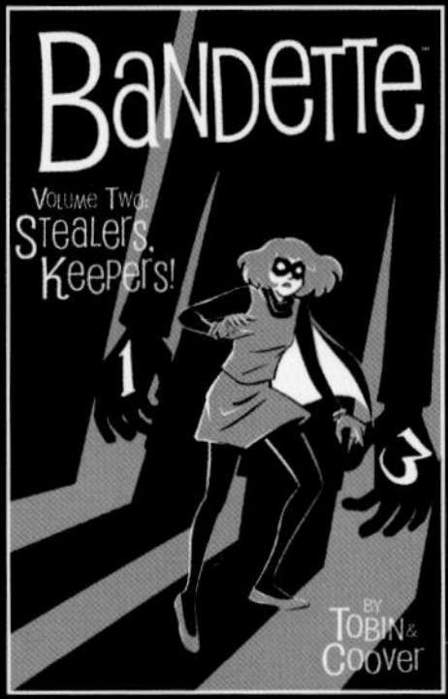
Bandette
Volume Two:
Stealers, Keepers!
By
Tobin & Coover

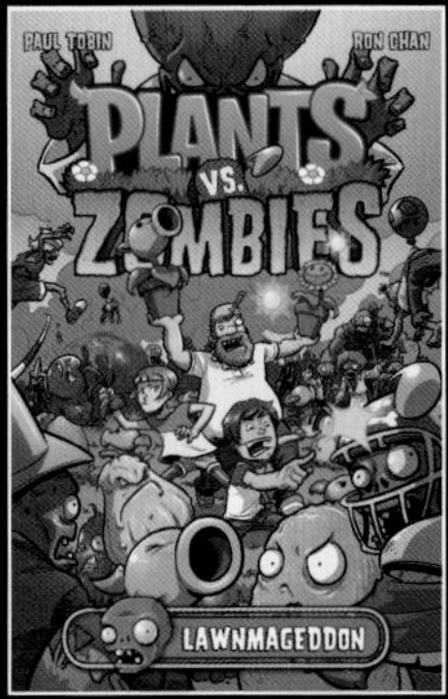
PAUL TOBIN
RON CHAN
PLANTS VS. ZOMBIES
LAWNMAGEDDON

MYSTERY GIRL VOLUME 1
Written by Paul Tobin, art by Alberto J. Alburquerque
ISBN 978-1-61655-959-5 | $12.99

COLDER VOLUME 1
Written by Paul Tobin, art by Juan Ferreyra
ISBN 978-1-61655-136-0 | $17.99

COLDER VOLUME 2: THE BAD SEED
Written by Paul Tobin, art by Juan Ferreyra
ISBN 978-1-61655-647-1 | $17.99

COLDER VOLUME 3: TOSS THE BONES
Written by Paul Tobin, art by Juan Ferreyra
ISBN 978-1-61655-776-8 | $17.99

BANDETTE VOLUME 1: PRESTO!
Written by Paul Tobin, art by Colleen Coover
ISBN 978-1-61655-279-4 | $14.99

BANDETTE VOLUME 2: STEALERS, KEEPERS!
Written by Paul Tobin, art by Colleen Coover, Jonathan Hill, and others
ISBN 978-1-61655-668-6 | $14.99

PLANTS VS. ZOMBIES: LAWNMAGEDDON
Written by Paul Tobin, art by Ron Chan
ISBN 978-1-61655-192-6 | $9.99

PLANTS VS. ZOMBIES: TIMEPOCALYPSE
Written by Paul Tobin, art by Ron Chan
ISBN 978-1-61655-621-1 | $9.99

PLANTS VS. ZOMBIES: BULLY FOR YOU
Written by Paul Tobin, art by Ron Chan
ISBN 978-1-61655-889-5 | $9.99

PLANTS VS. ZOMBIES: GROWN SWEET HOME
Written by Paul Tobin, art by Andie Tong, Karim Freha, Nneka Myers, and others
ISBN 978-1-61655-971-71 | $9.99

PROMETHEUS: THE COMPLETE FIRE AND STONE
Written by Kelly Sue DeConnick, Paul Tobin, and others
Art by Juan Ferreyra, Patric Reynolds, Ariel Olivetti, and others
ISBN 978-1-61655-772-0 | $49.99

THE WITCHER VOLUME 1: HOUSE OF GLASS
Written by Paul Tobin, art by Joe Querio
ISBN 978-1-61655-474-3 | $17.99

THE WITCHER VOLUME 2: FOX CHILDREN
Written by Paul Tobin, art by Joe Querio
ISBN 978-1-61655-793-5 | $17.99

FALLING SKIES VOLUME 1
Written by Paul Tobin, art by Juan Ferreyra
ISBN 978-1-59582-737-1 | $9.99

FALLING SKIES VOLUME 2: THE BATTLE OF FITCHBURG
Written by Paul Tobin, Mark Verheiden, and Danilo Beyruth
Art by Danilo Beyruth, Juan Ferreyra, and Patric Reynolds
ISBN 978-1-61655-014-1 | $9.99

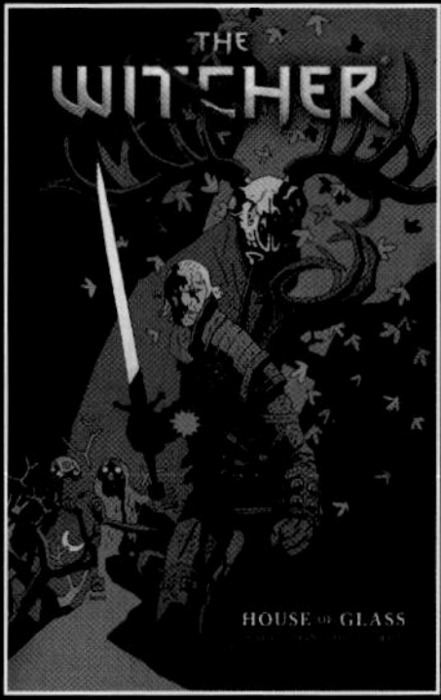
THE WITCHER
HOUSE OF GLASS

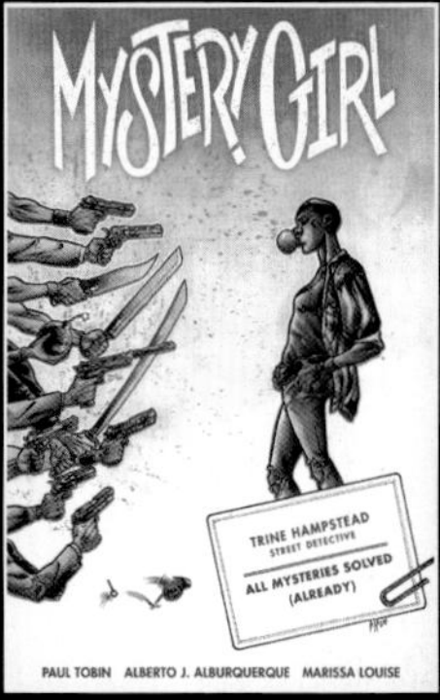
MYSTERY GIRL
TRINE HAMPSTEAD
STREET DETECTIVE
ALL MYSTERIES SOLVED
(ALREADY)
PAUL TOBIN ALBERTO J. ALBURQUERQUE MARISSA LOUISE

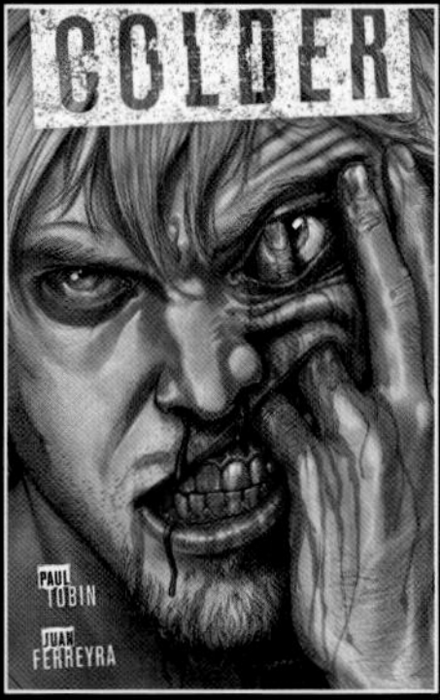
COLDER
PAUL TOBIN
JUAN FERREYRA

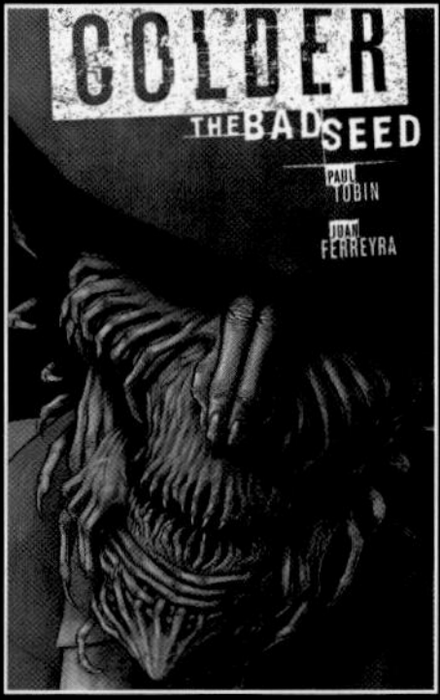
COLDER
THE BAD SEED
PAUL TOBIN
JUAN FERREYRA

ALSO FROM DARK HORSE BOOKS

DREAM LOGIC

Story and art by David Mack

Collecting the entire series of *Dream Logic* by David Mack, this hardcover volume includes original new stories, a gallery of artwork, sketches, a step-by-step art process with commentary on Mack's cover work, *Kabuki*, and never-before-seen extras.

ISBN 978-1-61655-678-5 | $34.99

THE NEW YORK FOUR

Story by Brian Wood, art by Ryan Kelly

Shy, literate Riley, overachieving but naive Lona, laid-back West Coaster Ren, and working-class girl Merissa claim newfound freedom living in the big city. But that freedom comes at a price: roommate drama, mysterious love interests, school troubles, and family conflicts. Welcome to adulthood!

ISBN 978-1-61655-605-1 | $19.99

THE ELTINGVILLE CLUB

Story and art by Evan Dorkin

Here is the ultimate word on the fugly side of fandom, collecting every *Eltingville* story from *Dork*, *House of Fun*, and *The Eltingville Club* #1–#2. Also features the Northwest Comix Collective alt-comics smackdown and an afterword about the 2002 Adult Swim animated pilot. Definitive, complete, and unashamed, this is fandom at its fan-dumbest!

ISBN 978-1-61655-415-6 | $19.99

LEAVING MEGALOPOLIS

Story by Gail Simone, art by Jim Calafiore

When the caped heroes of the world's safest city inexplicably turn into homicidal maniacs, the only rational thing to do is to get the hell out of town. If only it were that easy. A small group of terrified survivors make a desperate run for the city limits!

ISBN 978-1-61655-559-7 | $14.99

THE CREEP

Story by John Arcudi, art by Jonathan Case

A young boy puts a gun in his mouth and pulls the trigger. The police don't care—not about his death or the death of his best friend two months earlier. The dead boy's mom seeks help from an old flame that's employed as a detective. Will the detective's freakish appearance get in the way of uncovering the terrible secrets of these two teenagers?

ISBN 978-1-61655-061-5 | $19.99

BUFFY THE VAMPIRE SLAYER SEASON 10 VOLUME 1: NEW RULES

Story by Christos Gage, art by Rebekah Isaacs

From executive producer Joss Whedon! While slaying a hoard of zompires, Buffy and her pals are shocked to discover a new kind of vampire: harder to kill, able to transform and walk in the light of day—like Dracula! The rules of magic are literally being rewritten . . .

ISBN 978-1-61655-490-3 | $18.99

TOMB RAIDER VOLUME 1: SEASON OF THE WITCH

Story by Gail Simone, art by Nicolás Daniel Selma and Juan Gedeon

Lara and the other survivors of the *Endurance* are experiencing horrific visions after their ordeal in the lost kingdom of Yamatai. But the visions lead to a darker fate . . . Can Lara survive the calamities that await her as she struggles to piece this new mystery, and her life, back together?

ISBN 978-1-61655-491-0 | $19.99

MIND MGMT VOLUME 1

Story and art by Matt Kindt

A young journalist stumbles onto a big story—the top-secret Mind Management program. Her ensuing journey involves weaponized psychics, hypnotic advertising, talking dolphins, and seemingly immortal pursuers. But in a world where people can rewrite reality itself, can she trust anything she sees?

ISBN 978-1-59582-797-5 | $19.99

31901059545808